Black Studies and the Democratization of American Higher Education

Charles P. Henry

Black Studies and the Democratization of American Higher Education

Charles P. Henry
Department of African American Studies
University of California
Berkeley, California, USA

ISBN 978-3-319-81721-7 ISBN 978-3-319-35089-9 (eBook)
DOI 10.1007/978-3-319-35089-9

Softcover reprint of the hardcover 1st edition 2016

Printed on acid-free paper

This Palgrave Macmillan imprint is published by Springer Nature
The registered company is Springer International Publishing AG
The registered company address is: Gewerbestrasse 11, 6330 Cham, Switzerland

To Robert Chrisman and all of the students, faculty, and staff that made Black Studies possible.

Acknowledgments

Writing acknowledgments is inherently risky given the very real possibility that you might forget to mention someone—especially in a work that covers virtually you entire adult life. However, I would be remiss if I did not mention some of the individuals I have been privileged to know, who have had an impact on my work and on the development of Black Studies. They include Robert Chrisman, Harold Cruse, James Baldwin, Maulana Karenga, Darlene Clark Hine, Robert Allen, Dianne Pinderhughes, Ron Takaki, Carlos Munoz, William Nelson, Charlene Young, Delores Aldridge, William Little, Selase Williams, Molefi Asante, Abdul Alkalimat, Perry Hall, James Turner, Ray Winbush, Bertha Maxwell Roddy, Charles Jones, William Nichols, John Kirby, John Jackson, Francis Foster, Barbara Christian, St. Clair Drake, Clay Carson, Ron Walters, Joseph Russell, John Walter, Erskine Peters, Martin Kilson, Philip T.K. Daniel, James Turner, Carolyn Leonard, Edward Crosby, Rhett Jones, Earl Lewis, Jacqueline Wade, Lorenzo Morris, Lawrence Levine, William Banks, Veve Clark, Herbert Aptheker, David Goldberg, Michael Omi, Manning Marable, James Cone, William J. Wilson, Theodore Lowi, John Hope Franklin, Bertram Gross, Cathy Cohen, George Kent, Robert Blauner, Kenneth Clark, Reginald Jones, June Jordan, Richard Long, Sterling Brown, Ula Taylor, Percy Hintzen, Cecil Brown, Jacques Delpelchin, Roy Thomas, Margaret Wilkerson, Troy Duster, Hardy Frye, and Charles Long. Of course, they share none of the blame for any errors in my recollection and interpretation of events in this work.

Over a 40-year teaching career the glue that held my family together has been my wife, Loretta. To have been her partner for nearly 50 years is the single greatest blessing of my life.

Charles P. Henry
September 1, 2016

Contents

1 Nonnegotiable Demands: A Microstory 1

2 Black Intellectuals and Black Studies: A Macrostory 23

3 Institutionalizing Black Studies at the University of California 59

4 The National Council for Black Studies 95

5 The Black Scholar: Drum of the Black Studies Movement 121

6 Democratizing the Disciplines 149

7 Democratizing the National Identity 187

8 Postmodernism, Multiculturalism, and the Future of Black Studies 229

Bibliography 251

Index 263

List of Tables

Table 4.1 National Council for Black Studies Annual Meetings (Host Institutions and Coordinators) 101
Table 4.2 NCBS Presidents 104
Table 7.1 Major court decisions on school desegregation 191

CHAPTER 1

Nonnegotiable Demands: A Microstory

I thought the house would collapse. It was 1968 and James Brown's "Say It Loud—I'm Black and I'm Proud" was playing on the record player. The Black students at my holiday party were stamping their feet in time with the music. The whole house shook, and any minute I expected a knock on the door from the police telling me to end the party or worse.

My new bride, Loretta, and I married in the summer of 1968 between my junior and senior year at Denison University. We had trouble renting the house in the all-White village of Granville, Ohio. With help from the minister who married us, and a couple of members of his congregation in my nearby hometown of Newark, we were able to challenge the realtor and rent the house. Apparently, none of our neighbors called the police, and the party was a great success. The song "Say It Loud—I'm Black and I'm Proud" became a kind of anthem for my generation and is still used to start the "Black Graduation" ceremony each year at the University of California at Berkeley.

In many ways, 1968 was a year that defined a generation. Of course, the assassinations of Martin Luther King, Jr., and Robert Kennedy, along with the urban violence that followed, were the low points. But there was also global unrest with student protests in Mexico, France, and elsewhere. The ramping up of the war in Vietnam and the Tet offensive led to Lyndon Johnson's decision not to seek reelection and increased political instability culminating in the disastrous Democratic National Convention in 1968 in Chicago. Black power manifested itself in the form of the Black Panther

C.P. Henry, *Black Studies and the Democratization of American Higher Education*, DOI 10.1007/978-3-319-35089-9_1

Party on the one hand and the election of the first two Black big city mayors in Gary and Cleveland on the other hand.

Black power also manifested itself in the demand for Black Studies at San Francisco State University (SFSU), Cornell, Columbia, Berkeley, and scores of other campuses including Denison. In many ways, Denison was more typical than the better-known cases because it did not involve the police or threats of overt violence.[1] As Manning Marable states, there is a tendency to mythologize the origins of most Black Studies programs. He says that "[a]t many private liberal arts colleges and smaller state universities, modest African American interdisciplinary programs were frequently started without controversy or conflict."[2] I would add that student pressure was almost always the stimulus for change and that the tales of easy courses and faculty intimidation have also been greatly exaggerated.

Like many small college campuses throughout the Midwest, with a few notable exceptions such as Oberlin, Denison had been virtually all White until the mid-1960s. When I arrived on campus in the fall of 1965, I was the only Black male student and there were two Black female freshmen. I was commuting to school (which made it affordable) and had support from home, but the two Black women were isolated in all-White dorms in an all-White town with no public transportation.

Social life at Denison revolved around a dozen and a half fraternities and sororities. At least two of the fraternities had national charters prohibiting Black members—I am not sure about the sororities. During pledge week I went to all ten fraternity "rushes" to see if I would be barred at the door. Most were polite but in all cases but one, I was quickly placed with a group of potential rejects. The exception was the only non-Greek fraternity on campus, the American Commons Club (ACC). Started at Denison during World War II as an alternative to the Greeks, ACC grew to several other chapters before declining again in the 1960s. I joined along with the international students, theater majors, non-jocks, and geeks, who typically comprised the membership.[3] I did not live in the frat house but I ate lunch there, played on the intramural sports teams, and attended their social events.

For students interested in social activism the major organized activity revolved around the Denison Christian Association (DCA) (Dension was founded as a Baptist seminary). DCA students were involved in a variety of charity and tutoring programs in the local community and also connected to the National Student Association. By my junior year, I was chairing the DCA "race relations" committee, and our activities included going to

White churches in Columbus, Ohio, and then going home with parishioners to discuss race relations over Sunday dinner. Since most of the DCA students were White, the theory was that Whites should be educating other Whites on these issues. But by my junior year, the focus was shifting from "race relations" to "Black power."

A great example of the change was my class on "Race Relations." The course was taught by an older liberal sociologist and comprised about 50 White students and me. One of our texts was Milton Gordon's *Assimilation in American Life*, and a typical class involved the discussion of some current issue that ended with the professor asking me "what do Black/Negro people think about that Chuck" (everyone seemed to call me Chuck with no prompting from me). One day when the discussion got around to Black power, I said why not bring Stokely Carmichael to campus and ask him instead of me. Carmichael and Charles Hamilton had just published *Black Power*, and I spent a semester locating the funding and getting the commitment from the Student Nonviolent Coordinating Committee (SNCC). Unfortunately, after it had been announced in chapel and a few days before the actual event, Carmichael backed out.

Although there were minor incidents of one sort or another in other classes, the one that had the greatest impact on me was a course on "Recent African History." Given my high school education, all I knew about Africa came from shows like "Tarzan." I was excited about actually getting some detailed knowledge of the continent until in one of the first lectures the White professor—there were no Black faculty at Denison during my student days—announced that colonialism had been a good thing for Africa. To me this seemed intuitively wrong and, given what I was hearing in the news from African independence leaders, it seemed factually wrong. I did not know enough to challenge the professor in class but it spurred me to read up on the subject on my own. Eventually, I offered my own "recent African history" class as one of the first courses in the new, student-run experimental college. We explicitly and perhaps naively rejected asking for credit for the courses to prove we were in it for the knowledge alone. I also decided to do my senior thesis in political science on "African Socialism." My adviser's expertise was Eastern European politics but at least he let me work on my own.

Incidents like this had happened to the other Black students on campus, and by my junior year we numbered around 13 in a total student population of over 1800. As James Baldwin states in *Nobody Knows My Name*, "[t]he questions which one asks oneself begin to illuminate the world, and become one's key to the experience of others. One can only face in others what one can face in oneself. On this confrontation depends the measure of our wisdom and compassion."[4] We began to ask ourselves what kind of education we wanted and started to meet among ourselves and with sympathetic faculty contending that we needed a Black Studies or Black Culture course that would address many of these issues. In the spring of 1968, a faculty–student committee met several times to design an interdepartmental course, "Black Culture in America," and a White English professor, William Nichols, who had directed one Honors project in Afro-American literature, was chosen to coordinate the new course.

The course was offered in the fall of 1968 with several speakers from outside the college, including Richard Lugar, the then mayor of Indianapolis and an alumnus; Reverend John Frye, a Presbyterian minister who was working with the Blackstone Rangers on Chicago's south side; and Reverend Joseph Washington, a scholar on Black religion in America. The topics and the speakers were interesting enough that our Wednesday evening lectures often filled Fellows Auditorium. We discarded a plan to limit the class to 20 formally enrolled students when we saw the high quality of the written applications, and the enrollment reached 67, including all 13 of the Black students then on campus. Because the class was large, four members of the faculty agreed to volunteer as discussion leaders, and I became a teaching assistant. In addition, several members of the faculty gave lecturers. So the Black Culture course had a great deal going for it—intense student interest, resource people from outside the college, and enthusiastic faculty participation.

From the very beginning, however, the course was marked by disappointment, anger, suspicion, confusion, recrimination, and, finally, a student boycott. Neither students nor faculty were prepared for the conflict that the course generated, and it required some serious negotiations to hold the course together through the semester. We could rationally plan the course, but we had no way of anticipating the feelings it would generate. As Ralph Ellison says, there is "an area in which a man's feelings are more rational than his mind, and it is precisely in that area that his will is pulled in several directions at the same time." He continues that his problem was "that I always tried to go in everyone's way but my own. I have also been called one thing and then another while no one really wished to hear what I called myself. So after years of trying to adopt the opinions of others I finally rebelled. I am an *invisible man*."[5] Actually, the course did more than stay together; it introduced the college to a range of themes that were to become the core of Black Studies: the history of slavery, the crisis of the inner city, the development of jazz, Black theater and literature, economics of the ghetto, Black politics, and religion. If there was an embarrassing innocence in our attempt to cover such a range of material in one course, there was a refreshing humility on the part of most faculty. This field is crucially important many admitted, but we have not yet learned how to make the necessary connections, how to get beyond the limits of our own educations and see the invisible.

Through the Denison Experimental College we also tried to take our courses to the local community. With the local community action program (LEADS), we suggested six student-led courses: Black Culture, community action and organization, basic reading and writing for adults, elementary sewing, vocational typing, and diving and water safety instruction. Four target areas were selected, and course leaders were required to undergo sensitivity training and meet with community officials to familiarize themselves with resident attitudes. I stated that our courses could "bring campus knowledge into the community and community experience onto the campus."[6] We hoped to fully incorporate area residents as leaders in and outside the classes.

Beyond the courses, Black students at Denison began to organize. Influenced by what was happening on other campuses, we formed the Afro-American Lounge Steering Committee (AALSC) during the 1968–69 academic year. Our chief objective was to obtain campus space to meet, study, and organize. We were successful in getting some space in a dormitory that the university agreed to remodel and furnish. I distinctly remember being given the assignment—since I had a car—of buying the stereo system for our new lounge. It was a great day when we could officially bring the music of James Brown to campus! The next year the AALSC morphed into the Black Student Union (BSU).

In 1969–70, there was obviously no need to simulate racial conflict at Denison. The movement for Black Studies was at the center of a series of disagreements and decisions that seemed at the time to be cataclysmic. Whatever else the year meant for Denison, it established the mood within which the Black Studies program would try to develop in the next few years.

On December 19, 1969, the BSU presented the college with a set of demands, asking for a reply by January 9, 1970, in the form of total acceptance or total rejection (nonnegotiable). The demands were essentially the same ones being presented at predominantly White colleges all over the country, but the Denison demands were couched in unusually moderate terms. The students wanted increased recruitment of Black students, Black faculty, and Black administrators, and the establishment of an autonomous Afro-American Studies Department. The document from the BSU included numerical goals for recruitment.

Joel P. Smith, in his first year as Denison's president, responded to the demands in an open letter to the BSU on January 9, 1970. The letter combined the painstaking analysis of a legal brief with moral exhortation; it identified complexities and problems in the issues raised by the demands, affirmed Smith's personal commitment to high standards and "the tantalizing dream of an integrated community," and finally recommended the establishment of a special task force.

During January, members of the faculty made several attempts to get the faculty—which was then the chief legislative body on campus, a situation that would change in little more than a year—to endorse the demands. On January 26 the faculty voted to endorse the demands "with the intention of implementation." Two provisions in the faculty resolution provided some qualification: The first warned that "some specific points may be reformulated during the discussion which will be part of the process of implementation," and the second called for subsequent action by the faculty on particular major changes necessary to meet the demands. At a faculty meeting on February 9, the Chief Minister of the BSU, Henry Durand, tried to test the college's interpretation of the resolution by asking the President, the Chairman of the Board of Trustees, and a representative of the faculty to sign the following statement: "We accept the demands of the Black Student Union in full, without qualification." The president refused to sign the statement because it did not represent his interpretation of the resolution and the faculty voted to leave the interpretation of the resolution up to the Task Force. The resolution itself was strong enough, however, that a confrontation seemed avoidable until the Board of Trustees held a special meeting to discuss the BSU demands and the faculty response. After a one-day discussion, the Board on February 20 issued a statement characterizing the demands as "strident in tone and extreme in substance," reprimanding the faculty for being "more responsive to the emotions of the moment than to a careful analysis of the implications of all of the demands for the College as a whole," and outlining the difficulties in the way of implementing some of the BSU demands as well as the undesirability of implementing others.

The direct consequence of the statement by the Board of Trustees was a boycott of classes that initially involved 30 faculty members and approximately half the student body. To look back at the many written statements prepared by members of the Denison community during the weeks following the boycott is to be reminded that this was a time of extraordinary pain and self-examination. And the written record barely hints at the trauma of faculty resignations, rumors of impending violence, and broken and damaged friendships. How the college worked its way through this period, when, for a time, the administration met secretly off-campus and communication with the college-at-large took place through mimeographed releases and mass meetings is a story that will take a full chapter in some future Denison history. But by April 11, 1970, the Board of Trustees could issue a statement that seemed to acknowledge the legitimacy of the demands without, however, recognizing their existence. Three days later the BSU issued a statement, which interpreted the Board's statement of April 11 as "an unqualified commitment" to their demands. "We, therefore," the BSU statement continued, "are willing to strive together with the Faculty and Administration towards the implementation of the Black Student Union demands. During the process of implementation of the Black Student Union demands, we feel that all points of conflict will be resolved." On April 16 two days after the BSU's seemingly conciliatory response to the Board, President Smith and John E.F. Wood, Chairman of the Board, issued a statement which insisted that the Board's recommendations of April 11 did "not constitute acceptance of the demands previously submitted by the Black Student Union." Despite this apparently gratuitous call to renewed conflict, an important chapter in the history of Black Studies at Denison was over.

When one puts the student boycott of classes in 1970 in the context of our national traumas during the same period, Denison's efforts to resolve very difficult questions seem impressively rational. Questions regarding student involvement in personnel matters and student recruitment, the allocation of resources for increasing the number of Black students, faculty, and staff, and the appropriate form for a Black Studies program were tearing colleges apart all over the country.[7] Even the insensitivity of the Board of Trustees seems mild when one recalls the hysteria which greeted Black student demands elsewhere. The creation of an Alternative College by those who were boycotting demonstrated a continuing faith in the life of the mind that contrasted dramatically with destructive acts that drew publicity at some other colleges. And, in retrospect, the patience and maturity of the BSU leadership during those difficult months appear extraordinary.[8]

In entering the Ph.D. program in political science at the University of Chicago in the fall of 1969, I missed the student boycott of classes at Denison in 1970. Ironically, I also missed the Black student protests demanding Black Studies, Black housing, and increased Black student enrollment at the University of Chicago in spring 1968. The university had responded by creating an Ad Hoc Committee on African and African American Studies in the curriculum. James Bruce, an assistant professor in the undergraduate college, chaired the committee and convened a major meeting in June 1968. Invited participants from outside the university included historian Lerone Bennett, artist Jeff Donaldson, editor Hoyt Fuller, and poet Amiri Baraka as well as Chicago-trained sociologist Gerald McWhorter (later Abdul Alkalimat). According to Fabio Rojas, the meeting failed to produce a clear plan for the future because the only kinds of reform the participants would endorse—autonomous institutes and programs for the Black community—were incompatible with the university's goal of educating an elite group of students. No leadership emerged that could formulate an agenda and build a coalition that could encompass the demands of the students with the desires of the administration. By the time of my arrival, Stuart Tave, a dean at the university, had developed a proposal between that of Bruce and the administration as represented by Donald Levine, master of the college. Tave's proposal called for an institute that would supplement existing activities and bring in speakers who would serve as possible trial job talks leading to appointments. This incrementalist approach was accepted by the administration and shaped the development of Black Studies at Chicago for decades. One of the first speakers invited was literary scholar George Kent who was hired by the English department in 1970 and assumed the chair of the Committee on African and Black American Humanities by 1971.[9]

I took two courses in Black literature from Kent. But prior to Kent's arrival I enrolled in historian John Hope Franklin's course on Black history in fall 1969. It was the first course I had from a Black teacher in any grade from first grade to graduate school.[10] Of course, Franklin attracted a number of Black students who were not history majors to his courses. He had a devoted following of graduate students in history but was equally generous with his time with non-history graduate students. I was especially impressed with the time he took to read and comment on student papers including grammatical errors. I learned this attention to detail the hard way receiving a paper back covered with the marks of his red pen. Franklin, however, was not a supporter of Black Studies.

Franklin was representative of a generation of pre-Black Studies scholars who had conflicted views about the development of the field. This generation, which included many of the scholars Franklin worked with when he taught at Howard, saw the relevance of scholarship directed at solving the problems of their community. However, they also knew that scholarship in the area of "Negro studies" would never allow them to be fully recognized in their respective disciplines. To reach their full professional status they must prove their scholarship in areas outside Negro/ Black Studies. In short, to commit to Black Studies in the late 1960s and early 1970s was to commit "disciplinary suicide."

Franklin and a handful of other Black scholars were just beginning to be recognized for their work by the traditional disciplines. E. Franklin Frazier was president of the American Sociological Association in 1948; Ralph Bunche had been elected president of the American Political Science Association (APSA) in 1953; W. Montague Cobb became president of the American Association of Physical Anthropology in 1957; Kenneth Clark was president of the American Psychological Association in 1970; and Franklin was elected president of the Organization of American Historians in 1975 and the American Historical Association in 1979.[11] Their natural preference was to see these traditional disciplines reformed rather than to develop the new field of Black Studies.

Franklin was explicit in pointing out the burden placed on Black scholars who would prefer to focus on research not related to race.

> Imagine, if you can, what it meant to a competent Negro student of Greek literature, W. H. Crogman, to desert his chosen field and write a book entitled *The Progress of the Race*. Think of the frustration of the distinguished Negro physician C. V. Roman, who abandoned his medical research and practice, temporarily at least, to write *The Negro in American Civilization*. What must have been the feeling of the Negro student of English literature Benjamin Brawley, who forsook his field to write *The Negro Genius* and other works that underscored the intellectual powers of the Negro? How much poorer is the field of the biological sciences because an extremely able and well-trained Negro scientist, Julian Lewis, felt compelled to spend years of his productive life writing a book entitled *The Biology of the Negro*?[12]

Franklin asked how many scholars have been drawn away from the "standard branches of learning" to focus on "Negro studies" where they would be insulated from the attacks of White scholars.

Franklin, however, was in an even more complex position. He was a pioneer in the field of Black history and his textbook, "From Slavery to Freedom," was widely used in both history and Black Studies. Franklin's name often came up in discussions of who could lead the emerging Black Studies departments in schools like his alma mater of Harvard. Yet, far from leading such a program, Franklin kept his distance from the efforts to bring Black Studies to Chicago. As the most famous Black scholar on campus and one of the best-known in the country, he might have been expected to play a leading role at Chicago. Instead, Franklin kept his distance and in fact defended friends of his such as historian Daniel Boorstin who was under attack by student activists.[13] Franklin's autobiography totally ignores the struggle for Black Studies at Chicago. Franklin was not opposed to activism. He had been part of a protest against lynching while a student at Fisk University and was a founding member of the Black Academy of Arts and Letters established by the economist Robert Browne in 1969. However, he also believed in objectivity and in the separation of scholarship from activism. Black Studies to him blurred the line. As Nathan Huggins stated in his Ford Foundation report on Black Studies, "[t]his older generation of scholars tended also to be distrustful of the students' efforts to politicize the program."[14] With his leadership, rather than that of an assistant professor, the outcome for Black Studies at Chicago might have been different.

Part of the problem in developing Black Studies at Chicago as opposed to a college like Denison was the fact that two-thirds of the students at the University of Chicago were graduate students and only one-third undergraduates. Undergraduates were taught in the college division, often by junior faculty. Academic life revolved around the departments and departments revolved around the graduate program. Graduate students were more concerned about getting their degree and beginning a professional career than they were about the undergraduate curriculum. They were also more concerned about offending faculty members who might be the key to finding a teaching job than were undergraduate students.

As graduate students they were also no longer exempt from the draft. It was the height of the war in Vietnam and most men my age were dealing with their draft eligibility. I had participated in the first protest against any war in my hometown during my undergraduate years at Denison. I had also applied for conscious objector status but was rejected on the grounds that I did not oppose all wars. It was not long after my arrival in Chicago that I received greetings from the draft board ordering me to report the army center in downtown Chicago for a physical. I consulted some of the draft counselors readily available to students including pro bono attorneys. Since I had a serious injury to my foot as a nine-year old that had put me in the hospital for two weeks, it was suggested that I try for a medical deferment (1-H). They also said if I passed the physical I would have to refuse the oath or I would be inducted. Despite my giving the army doctors my extensive medical records, I passed the physical and reached the point of swearing in. I refused to take the oath and was photographed, fingerprinted, and sent home.

At that point it seemed I had two alternatives. One was to leave the country and I applied for a passport. The other was to simply refuse induction and go to prison. It was at that time my pro bono counsel called to say he had arranged a special medical examination for me through Senator Charles Percy's office. He added that nine out of ten people who took this special physical failed. I arrived for the special physical with the same medical documents I had before and went to the same induction center where I had passed the previous examination. This time I failed and was designated 4F! I felt sorry for a number of inductees who seemed in far worse shape than me but happy I could continue my education. It was a great lesson in how the system was being manipulated by those with the resources and connections (e.g., Bill Clinton and George W. Bush) to avoid the draft.

The draft and our careers were the dominant concerns of most male graduate students. By the time of my arrival I do not recall hearing any discussion among students about Black Studies. I had decided to take the maximum number of courses I could outside my major and those courses were either taught by a Black professor or were on Black subject matter. The short list included courses by Franklin, Kent, Roy Morrison, and Charles Long. My efforts to recruit Black faculty were directed at the political science department where I joined the handful of other Black students in asking the department chair to make special recruitment efforts. When told that there were very few Black political scientists of the caliber necessary to teach at Chicago, we pointed out that the handful of previous Black Ph.D.s produced by the department must "by definition" be of high caliber. One of those graduates, Charles Hamilton, had coauthored the classic *Black Power* with Stokely Carmichael in 1967.

My reasons for choosing to do my graduate work at Chicago were primarily my interest in political theory and the fact that with the help of my undergraduate adviser and Professor Lowi at Chicago, I was able to secure a full scholarship.[15] The first year of my graduate work was funded by a Ford Foundation grant (the first of several I would benefit from) and the next two years were supported by a National Institutes of Mental Health fellowship. After two courses with a leading political theorist, David Easton, I decided that political theory had little power to explain what was happening in the streets around me. I than began to focus more on public policy and Theodore Lowi, who had just written an influential critique of liberalism, became my adviser.

The "streets" provided another kind of political education. Once I got over the shock of living in a big city that was rigidly segregated and the Hyde Park community that was heavily patrolled by the police, I began to take advantage of my environment. It paid to be careful; Hyde Park police were not used to African American males with Afros running to class early in the morning. Shortly after my arrival the Chicago police working with the district attorney assassinated two Black Panther leaders, Fred Hampton and Mark Clark. I toured the scene of the murders, which the Panthers were showing to the world. A Black state senator, Richard Newhouse, was beginning to challenge the Daley machine, and I became a Newhouse volunteer. The Chicago Eight/Seven trial was unfolding in the Chicago district federal court, and I observed Judge Julius Hoffman overruling the objections of defense counsel before they could finish a sentence. On Saturdays my wife and I got a spiritual lift by attending Operation Breadbasket meetings led by Jesse Jackson. I did some work with Operation Breadbasket's political action committee. This work culminated in my attending the National Black Political Assembly convention in Gary in spring 1972.

By spring 1972, I had also decided I needed to get some teaching experience having obtained my M.A. degree the previous year. Primarily a graduate school, the University of Chicago did not use teaching assistants; therefore, there were no opportunities for graduate students to gain teaching experience under the supervision of an experienced instructor. Nor were we required to take a course in pedagogy as we require of our Ph.D. students in African American Studies at Berkeley. I was able to find a position teaching an introductory course in American political life at Malcolm X City College on the west side of Chicago. When I interviewed for the job, my interviewer stated that Malcolm X in its new, African themed building was at the forefront of "urban education." When I asked for a definition of urban education, I received no reply but still got the job.

Until May 1968, Malcolm X City College had been Crane City College. It had a predominantly Black student body surrounded by a virtually all Black community yet offered a traditional Eurocentric curriculum taught by a large number of White faculty. That May the student body led by its authorized representatives and influenced by the Black Panther Party issued a set of ten demands designed to make the school "intellectually and socially relevant to the community as a whole."[16] The demands included a new Black president, more Black instructors, upgrading existing Black workers, and more Black courses as well as more courses leading to transfer to four-year institutions. By the following year, the name had been changed to Malcolm X (system administrators first suggested Booker T. Washington as the new name), and Charles Hurst, an audiologist from Howard University, was hired as the first Black president in the City College system.[17] Hurst, a gifted speaker who wore African attire, was also an advocate of Black capitalism and supporter of President Nixon. Other University of Chicago students such as Stan Willis, who studied history with Franklin, and Robert Rhodes, who was a long-time political science graduate student, were also active at Malcolm X and other vanguard educational formations such as the Communiversity, the City for Inner-City Studies, and the DuSable Museum.[18] I had little contact with them since my course was at night and there was no common venue for interaction. I was trying to learn how to teach while keeping ahead of a class in which all the students were older than me. I can only hope that my performance did not permanently damage their desire to get an education.

Washington, D.C., was an exciting place to be in the early 1970s, especially if you were a student of politics. I had never been to D.C. before my move there from Chicago in the fall of 1972 to begin my year as an APSA Congressional Fellow while my wife went to work with an educational consulting firm. The Fellows program was a well-established one that sought to give young scholars and journalists an insiders' view of the legislative process. I had been inspired to apply after listening to the tales of one of my undergraduate professors who had been a fellow. Fellows spent half a year working for a member of the House of Representatives as a legislative assistant and the other half working with a Senator. In reading the accounts of previous Fellows, I decided that Hubert Humphrey's office provided one of the best experiences and applied there. I was eventually chosen as one of two Fellows on Humphrey's staff and began work just after Thanksgiving. Initially, I had been reluctant to apply to Humphrey for a position because of my opposition to the war in Vietnam. Humphrey was regarded as the politics of the past by many young people and had just returned to the Senate after his term as Vice President. He turned out to be a great person to work for, and I learned a great deal from him and his staff.

In the spring of 1973, I moved over to the House to work for the recently formed Congressional Black Caucus (CBC). The chair of the CBC was Representative Louis Stokes of Cleveland while the staff director was Augustus Adair, a political scientist from Morgan State University. Once again the experience was enlightening, especially my work in coordinating the first CBC legislative weekend in 1973. My contacts in the Senate assisted me in organizing a workshop featuring the Humphrey–Hawkins full employment bill in which both Humphrey and Congressman Augustus Hawkins participated. The CBC staff always referred to the bill as the Hawkins–Humphrey bill since the California Congressman had initiated the legislation. A weakened bill eventually passed as a tribute to Humphrey who died in 1978.

Although the CBC offered me a full-time staff position, I decided that I preferred the independence of a professor over the dependence of a Congressional staffer. Your identity and therefore your influence are totally linked to your member on the Hill. I did agree to work part time for the Caucus and began a search for a teaching position. After turning down one teaching position in California and having another withdrawn because of a budget freeze, I applied for an opening in political science at Howard University. Not only did Howard give me a chance to stay in D.C., it also provided me the first opportunity to work and study in a predominantly Black environment. An added bonus was the fact that Howard was one of the few historically Black universities with an extensive graduate program.

The 26-member political science department faculty at Howard was very diverse including professors from Greece, South Africa, Nigeria, the Philippines, the West Indies, and Yugoslavia. There was only one woman on the faculty and two of the African American faculty had been there since the time of Ralph Bunche. Fifty percent of the tenured faculty were White including the South African. I was one of four young African Americans/West Indians hired with the help of a Ford Foundation grant that enabled the department to reduce the normal teaching load from four courses per semester to three per semester. Ron Walters, a leader in the developing field of Black politics, was the chair of the department.

Drawing on my experience in Congress, I taught courses in the legislative process, American political parties and race and public policy.

However, I was particularly excited about developing courses in Black politics—an area that did not exist in my undergraduate and graduate years. I finished my dissertation on the civil rights movement in 1974 and immediately proceeded to teach graduate as well as undergraduate courses. All four of the new junior faculty were given significant administrative responsibilities—only much later in my career did I discover that junior faculty should be protected from heavy administrative duties. To make ends meet for the family my wife and I were starting, I taught summer school and picked up an additional honors course at the University of Maryland.[19]

By the spring of 1975, I realized that my administrative work, teaching load, and the lack of research support would make it nearly impossible to publish and gave me new respect for an earlier generation of Black scholars who rarely published. At that point my only publication was a conference paper on the CBC that had been part of the proceedings of the National Capital Area Political Science Association. My junior colleagues and I approached the dean about a raise in the spring or summer of 1975. He not so subtly informed us that we should look for positions elsewhere if we were not happy at Howard. As I began to look for a new job during the 1975–76 academic year, one of my former professors in political science at Denison contacted me about returning to my alma mater to teach. He was now provost and suggested I needed to come back to save the Black Studies program.

Since the student strike in 1970, the Black Studies program had struggled to take shape. During the first two years, under the direction of a Black psychologist on leave from Lincoln University, Carleton Trotman, there was an attempt to find the appropriate structure for a Black Studies program at Denison and to collect resources. Because Trotman's appointment occurred at a time when communication had broken down between the administration and the BSU, his office had little support from the latter. During this time individual departments established courses in Black Studies; some were one-time offerings and others, in the History, English, and Religion departments, were offered consistently. But there was not much progress in developing a coordinated, interdisciplinary program that could feed into many courses and diversify the academic program. Perhaps the chief accomplishment of those first two years was establishing contact with several Black scholars and intellectuals around the country, some of them had continued their relationship with the college. Most notable among these connections was the hiring of Naomi Garrett as a

Distinguished Visiting Professor with expertise in African and Caribbean literature.

When Arthur Zebbs, a Black minister, took over the Center for Black Studies in 1972, there was an active Black Studies Committee, and the academic program had begun to evolve. Although the Black Studies major, which was soon established, had been a secondary part of the program, its shape suggested what the committee saw as Black Studies. In addition to an introductory course on the nature of Black Studies and departmental courses, the major had included a required course in the literature of Africa or the West Indies, reflecting the committee's conviction that the African American experience could not be understood in isolation from the Black experience elsewhere in the world. The major attempted, in addition, to link the methods and subject matter of Black Studies with another, more traditional, area of study.

During Zebbs' four years as director, the Center for Black Studies found it necessary to attend to a number of matters outside the academic program. Denison had begun to increase the number of Black students, and the Center needed to provide counseling and other supportive services for students who often found the Denison environment a difficult one. Ironically, as these services began to be handled more adequately by the Office of Student Personnel, the number of Black freshmen recruited by the college began to fall off. Consequently, in 1974–75, the Black Studies Committee spent much of its time negotiating with the administration for a renewed commitment of resources to the recruitment of Black students. It was only in 1975–76, following the presentation of another set of demands from the BSU, that the administration and Trustees took the steps necessary to increase significantly Denison's recruitment of Black students. This pattern of dependence on student initiative seemed to be an inevitable part of the Black Studies program—or perhaps any other ethnic studies or women's studies program—because such programs lacked the power to compete with departments in the day-to-day governance of the institution.

When I returned to Denison in the fall of 1976 as director of Black Studies and assistant professor of political science, I immediately sought to develop allies for our program both on and off campus. It helped that I had the academic credentials that the previous director had lacked. Women's Studies had emerged at Denison during my absence and I, along with others, saw a natural link between the study and teaching of race and gender issues (now called intersectionality). When I proposed a general education requirement in Black Studies and/or Women's Studies to the Black Studies Committee, they were generally supportive but thought the chances it would be approved by the academic senate were slim. Their reasons included some past conflict with Women's Studies, general campus conservatism, and the lack of criteria for general education requirements. Despite these obstacles the Black Studies Committee, along with Women's Studies faculty, began to work toward the requirement.

Among the issues to be resolved were whether to broaden the Black Studies component to a more general Ethnic Studies (unfortunately, no other Ethnic Studies courses were currently offered), whether to require one large new course or have students choose from existing courses, and whether to make the requirement a one-semester or two-semester course load. There were no models we could look at and the effort took over a year of planning. We had general support from the administration and developed strong student support. In 1979, proposal 382, a Minority/Women's Studies General Education requirement was approved giving Denison one of the first such general education requirements in the country.

The year 1979 was also the year Black Studies underwent an external review headed by John Walter of Bowdoin College and Joseph Russell of Indiana University. I had met Walter and Russell in my work with the National Council for Black Studies (NCBS). Walter was on the NCBS board, and Russell was the organization's executive director. I believed an evaluation and recommendations from the disciplines only national professional organization would strengthen the legitimacy and recognition of our program both on campus and in the larger academic community. They raised a number of questions concerning our limited curriculum, lack of tenure for the Black Studies director, failure to develop a separate academic department, and general skepticism among Black students toward Black Studies that helped shape the discussion of Black Studies at Denison for the next decade.

My own immersion in Black Studies was greatly enhanced when I was invited to join the planning committee for the first annual meeting of the NCBS at Ohio State University in 1977. The invitation came from the Chair of the Black Studies Department at Ohio State, political scientist William Nelson,[20] who I had met years earlier at the annual meetings of the National Conference of Black Political Scientists (NCOBPS). One highlight of the conference was the appearance of poet Leon Damas, a cofounder of the philosophy of Negritude. With the help of Damas's old friend Naomi Garrett, Denison had brought him to campus during that period which enabled him to attend the NCBS conference. A year later Denison inaugurated the Damas Collection on Negritude housed at the Center for Black Studies.

As a result of my work on the NCBS planning committee I was asked to join the executive board of the NCBS and named the permanent chair of the annual student essay contest. I also helped organize two regional Black Studies groups. In November 1978, Denison hosted the first Great Lakes Colleges Association (GLCA) "Black Studies/Minority Studies Concerns" conference. The goal was to assess the status and role of Black Studies at small, predominantly White, private colleges and meet other GLCA faculty interested in Black Studies. Representatives from all GLCA colleges attended along with Joseph Russell from the NCBS. The keynote address was delivered by Robert Chrisman, the publisher of the *Black Scholar*, who noted November 1978 marked the tenth anniversary of the initial movement for Black Studies at San Francisco State University. I also joined a GLCA planning committee for a Workshop on Racism/Sexism. The workshop was hosted in April 1979 at Earlham College and featured Barbara Smith, then a Fellow at the Harvard's Du Bois Institute and coeditor of *Black Women's Studies*, and Florence Howe of the Feminist Press.

Another effort at building an infrastructure for Black Studies was the Ohio Consortium of Black Studies. The Ohio Consortium grew from both the top and bottom. From the top it became part of the NCBS's regional structure. From the bottom it grew from the merger of the Central Ohio Black Studies Consortium and the Northeastern Ohio Black Studies Consortium. Our first annual meeting was at Kent State University in May 1980, and I served as the Ohio Consortium's treasurer.

The Center for Black Studies at Denison was involved in efforts to divest university investments from South Africa, voter registration campaigns and efforts to work with the Licking County Inter-Cultural Center on community issues. A personal highlight of my time at Denison was my first trip to Africa coleading a group of students to the Second World Black Arts Festival (FESTAC) in Nigeria in 1977. But by 1980, I had to decide whether to commit fully to Black Studies and leave political science. I was awarded a National Endowment for the Humanities (NEH) postdoctoral fellowship to participate in a course on African American Folk Thought taught by Professor Richard Long at Atlanta University. But I also had an offer to join the faculty in African American Studies at the University of California at Berkeley. In the end, Berkeley agreed to wait a year so I could take the NEH fellowship before I headed west.[21]

Notes

1. During my senior year in high school, Tom Jones, a future leader of the Black Student Union (BSU) at Cornell, and I often walked home together. Tom was only at my high school his senior year and I did not know him well, but it was clear he was more sharply critical of Whites than I was. For example, he was the first person I knew to refer to Whites as "honkies." In any case, he went off to Cornell and I to Denison, and we both were caught up in the Black Studies movement. The iconic pictures of Tom and his fellow students with guns at Cornell created a slight problem for him later in life when he was nominated as a Cornell trustee. Now, as a very successful investment banker, Tom's views, at least publicly, had changed. Some older faculty remembered his role with the BSU and challenged his nomination. Apparently, he was successful in overcoming their objections and joined the board. See Denise K. Magner, "60s Dissident at Cornell Should Not Be a Trustee," *The Chronicle of Higher Education*, March 3, 1993.
2. Manning Marable, "Black Studies and the Racial Mountain," *Souls*, Summer 2000, p. 25.
3. During my senior year the American Commons Club decided to affiliate with the Greek fraternity Delta Chi. My best friend on campus and I tried to talk them into forming an alternative grouping such as a dining club; however, we were unsuccessful and withdrew from the fraternity.
4. James Baldwin, *Nobody Knows My Name*, in *Collected Essays*, (New York: Literary Classics of the United States, Inc., 1998), p. 136.
5. Ralph Ellison, *Invisible Man*, (New York: Modern Library, 1994).
6. "DU Experimental College To Aid In LEADS Courses," *Newark Advocate*, October 16, 1968, p. 2.
7. Of course, the best-known cases were Cornell, Columbia, and San Francisco State University. In each of these cases, the media attention focused on the tactics used by students and/or the administration rather than the major student demands of more Black faculty, increased Black enrollments, and Black Studies units. An exception was Antioch College, which received a great deal of attention over student demands for a separate Black dormitory and the subsequent resignation of Board of Trustees member Kenneth Clark.

8. Much of the material for this section is drawn from an unpublished paper by William Nichols and Charles Henry entitled "Black Studies at Denison." Additional material is available in the Denison Archives under the "Writing Our History" label in including correspondence between the college president and BSU leader and the "Time for Change" document issued by the students.
9. Fabio Rojas, *From Black Power to Black Studies*, (Baltimore: Johns Hopkins University Press, 2007), p. 110.
10. I had tried to change this for current students at my high school by voluntarily teaching a Black history segment in all the American history classes for a six-week period during my senior year in college. This required giving the same talk to several different sections a day and also kept me busy staying ahead of the students in terms of content. I gained new respect for high school teachers who did it every day. I also gained some practical political experience in convincing the board of education to let me offer the segments. The board promised to continue them after my graduation from Denison, but to my knowledge this did not happen.
11. Robert Fikes, Jr., "Black Presidents of Predominantly White Academic Associations," *Journal of Blacks in Higher Education*, No. 44, (Summer 2004), p. 108.
12. John Hope Franklin, "The Dilemma of the American Negro Scholar," in Herbert Hill (ed.), *Soon, One Morning*, (New York: Knopf, 1963), pp. 66–67.
13. John Hope Franklin, *Mirror to America*, (New York: Farrar, Straus and Giroux, 2005), pp. 244–245.
14. Nathan Huggins in *Inclusive Scholarship, A 25th Anniversary Retrospective of Ford Foundation Grant Making 1982–2007*, (New York: Ford Foundation, 2007), p. 45. This distrust included Huggins himself.
15. I was initially accepted for graduate school at the University of Chicago but received no financial aid. This was surprising given the fact that I had no assets and my family was in no position to help. My adviser at Denison, Roy Morey, contacted Professor Lowi at Chicago and pointed out that it was almost an insult to accept me but then deny financial aid. Lowi, who I had met when he served as an outside examiner for our senior oral examinations in political science at Denison, quickly intervened, and I received a full fellowship. I had financed my undergraduate education at Denison with

no help from the university. The first three years were covered by a small settlement as a result of a construction accident that injured my foot. A loan from the state covered my senior year tuition.

16. Martha Biondi, *The Black Revolution on Campus*, (Berkeley: University of California Press, 2012), p. 107.
17. According to Martha Biondi, the students' first choice for president was Barbara Lewis King who was the dean of community relations. However, the largely male leadership of the college chose Hurst who quickly "did Barbara in." Ibid., p. 108.
18. Ibid. p. 111.
19. Howard University established a Department of African American Studies in 1970 headed by political scientist Russell Adams. Despite Adams discipline, I had no contact with African American Studies at Howard and I am not aware of any links between political science and African American Studies at Howard during this period. I did teach an evening honors course on "Community Power Structure" at Maryland during the 1974–75 academic year that was sponsored, at least in part, by the Black Studies program at the University of Maryland.
20. Nelson and I were anxious to record some of the innovative developments in the new Black Studies units and proposed an edited book on the subject. We requested and received a number of papers for the book; however, our attempt to gain a contract from Ohio State University Press was unsuccessful and the project died.
21. When I accepted the position of director of the Center for Black Studies and assistant professor of political science at Denison (later I would also become an assistant dean of the college) it was with the understanding that I would come up for tenure in political science since programs such as Black Studies did not have tenure lines. However, as I moved toward tenure after my third year at Denison (and sixth year of teaching counting Howard), the political science department claimed that they were unaware that I was on a tenure track in their department despite the fact that the provost was a senior political scientist and former chair. I threatened legal action as a matter of principle but really had not intended to stay at Denison preferring a research university that would permit more time for publications. I had interviewed at Harvard during the 1978–79 academic year despite the fact that it had few faculty and even fewer majors. At the end of my interview, the chair,

Professor Eileen Southern, informally offered less salary than I was making at Denison and little to no chance for promotion to tenure from the junior ranks. I politely withdrew my interest in teaching at Harvard. The following year I applied for a position in the African American Studies Department at the University of California at Berkeley. During my interview I met with a junior female faculty member in political science. She told me the political science department had no interest in womens' politics or Black politics. I also met with Carlos Munoz, a pioneering Chicano political scientist teaching in the Ethnic Studies Department. Munoz also indicated that political science was hostile to my research interests. Therefore, when the dean asked if I was interested in a joint appointment, remembering my experience at Denison, I said no. As of this date, the political science department at Berkeley, almost alone among elite universities, has never had an African American political scientist on tenure track or tenured.

CHAPTER 2

Black Intellectuals and Black Studies: A Macrostory

In the years following World War II, when the term "integration" became popular, many people thought Blacks wanted to be just like Whites. White liberals believed Blacks were just like them on the inside, while conservative Whites thought Blacks wanted to be White but did not have the necessary attributes to accomplish the task. Thus, when the civil rights movement finally succeeded in breaking down the barriers of "Jim Crow," it came as a shock that Blacks were not satisfied. Langston Hughes perfectly captured the dilemma in his folk story about the "desegregated Negro."

> A Negro of Washington, D.C. could scarcely believe his eyes when he read in the newspapers that Jim Crow had been ended in the restaurants of his city. He was overjoyed. He had never expected to live to see the day. Since the miracle had happened, however, he decided to experience it for himself—at least once. But he would not act too hastily. The changeover was bound to take a little time. He decided to wait three weeks.
>
> Then one Sunday evening he put on his best clothes, caught a taxi and directed the driver to one of the most elegant restaurants he knew.
>
> He was greeted with a smile at the door and again inside, where the waiter gave him his choice of locations and placed a handsome menu in his hand. The Negro put on his glasses and began reading attentively. He perused the menu so long, in fact, that the waiter, still courtesy itself, came over and asked if he was ready to order.
>
> The Negro looked perplexed. "I don't see any chitterlings here," he said.
>
> "No, I'm afraid we don't have any chitterlings," the waiter agreed.

C.P. Henry, *Black Studies and the Democratization of American Higher Education*, DOI 10.1007/978-3-319-35089-9_2

Once more the customer scanned the menu. "How about turnip greens and ham hock?"

Puzzlement turned to frustration on the face of the desegregated Negro. "I'd like to order black-eyed peas and hog jowl."

"We don't have that either," the waiter told him sadly.

The Negro put his glasses back in their case, pushed his chair back and rose slowly. "You folks," he observed thoughtfully, "you folks just ain't ready for integration."[1]

My co-author, Lorenzo Morris, and I liked this folktale so much that we titled our first book, *The Chit'lin Controversy.* In a very direct way it emphasizes the complex nature of the process of integration. Remarking on the slow progress on integration in the early 1960s, Martin Luther King, Jr., said that Blacks and Whites had different definitions of integration. For the latter, it simply meant the removal of legal and social prohibitions. This action, King stated, was properly termed desegregation. It was eliminative and negative. True integration, on the other hand, was creative and positive. It welcomed Negroes into the total range of human activities. This is what Negroes sought, and it is the ultimate goal of our national community.[2]

The desegregated Negro in our story was not satisfied with the simple removal of the physical prohibition on eating at an elegant restaurant. The diner was not ashamed to ask for something he wanted and similar to Ralph Ellison's protagonist you could not humiliate him by confronting him with something he liked. "Not all of us, but so many," says Ellison, could be humiliated "[s]imply by walking up and shaking a set of chitterlings or a well-boiled hog maw at them during the clear light of day!"[3] He wanted something more inclusive. This customer wanted a menu that reflected his culinary tastes. In short, he wanted integration.

This story is a near perfect analogy to the struggle for Black Studies over its nearly 50-year existence. Blacks with educational aspirations fought first for the right to read and write, then for the right to attend the public school of their choice, and finally for the right to higher education. Once arriving in the ivory tower, however, Black students found a menu (curriculum) that ignored their history and assaulted their identity. Black Studies, then, was a demand for inclusion not exclusion.

While our story raises the question of curriculum or menu, it does not address the question of the ownership of the restaurant itself. Certainly, one could argue that the existence of historically Black colleges and universities (HBCUs) is evidence that African Americans have controlled the curriculum at such institutions. Yet one could also argue that these institutions were only marginally under the control of Blacks, and in any case, the curriculum largely mimicked those found in historically White colleges and universities (HWCUs).

While student protests on HBCU campuses in the 1920s led to a replacement of White college presidents with Black college presidents and some darkening of boards of trustees, the legacy of moral instruction and Eurocentric curricula remained. Writing from Howard in the 1930s, Ralph Bunche believed, "Negro scholars even more completely than white, are subject to the munificence of the controlling wealthy groups in the population. Negro institutions of higher learning, particularly, are the inevitable puppets of white philanthropy. Obviously, therefore, whatever reorganization and reorientation of 'Negro Education' is to be contemplated, must meet the full approval of these controlling interests. It is hardly to be expected that under such conditions 'Negro Education' could ever direct itself to really effective solutions for the problems of the masses of working-class Negroes..."[4] Black colleges, for example, as a part of moral instruction held on to the segregation of male and female dormitories long after most HWCUs had integrated them. Francile Wilson reports that for many years Howard University would not hire married women in faculty positions.[5] Many of the tenured professors at HBCUs were White. As late as 1973 when I arrived at Howard, for example, White professors were half of the tenured faculty in Howard's political science department. By contrast, there were only sixty Black professors teaching at White institutions in 1948.[6]

When he surveyed his fellow students at Lincoln University in the late 1920s, Langston Hughes found only a few objected to the absence of a Black history or literature course and two-thirds of 127 juniors and seniors did not want Black professors.[7] Reflecting on his education at Howard in the early 1960s, Stokely Carmichael (Kwame Toure) acknowledged the narrow line Howard administrators had to walk to secure Congressional appropriations every year. The result, however, was a "constraint translated into a series of attitudes, rules, and injunctions calculated to prevent any activity on the part of the students that was likely to offend 'powerful white folk'."[8]

While the students were constrained, academic apartheid permitted Howard to assemble the greatest group of Black scholars ever employed on one campus during the 1930s. And these scholars, shielded to some degree from White interference by Howard University president Mordecai

Johnson, brought a new level of analysis to the "Negro dilemma" and actively sought to upset the political, economic, and social status quo. In 1932, Bunche reported that of the 271 Howard faculty members (including Whites), 211 were Howard graduates. As late as 1936, more than 80 percent of all Black PhDs were employed by Howard, Atlanta, and Fisk Universities. By the late 1940s, government service and elite White universities began luring away many of Howard's most noted faculty members. These faculty included Bunche, Abram Harris, E. Franklin Frazier, Sterling Brown, Leo Hansbury, Kelly Miller, Charles Drew, Percy Julian, Charles Hamilton Houston, Charles Wesley, Rayford Logan, and Alain Locke.[9]

Aided by two new journals established at Howard—the *Journal of Negro History* and the *Journal of Negro Education*—young scholars broke from the paradigms they saw as holding back race advancement. Symbolic of their split with the previous generation of Black intellectuals was the confrontation between W.E.B. Du Bois and Harris, Frazier, and Bunche at the National Association for the Advancement of Colored People's (NAACP) Amenia meeting in August 1933. The three young Howard social scientists charged Du Bois and James Weldon Johnson with racial provincialism and urged the NAACP to join in solidarity with White labor to push economic reform legislation. They argued the older "race men" and the NAACP were ignoring the economic needs of the Black masses during the "Great Depression" while focusing on the middle-class needs of the Black business elite. The Howard radicals were appointed to a special committee to follow up the Amenia conference with specific recommendations, but the subsequent report of the committee was ultimately rejected. One consequence of this rejection was Bunche's joining with John Davis in 1935 as a co-founder of the National Negro Congress (NNC). At the founding conference in 1936 at Howard, communist leaders were able to join labor leaders, church leaders, and Black activists in a common front to address economic issues and the New Deal.[10] For the young radicals, only a united front with Whites could successfully challenge the exploitation of both Black and White workers. Yet the history of Blacks in education revealed that such an alliance was fraught with difficulty.

Prior to the Revolutionary War, school systems in both the North and South were private and decentralized (community control). At any point in the history of the United States, the decision of an African American to become an intellectual runs counter to common sense. In a country that proclaimed Blacks too ignorant for schooling and then ironically prohibited them from learning to read and write, intellectual success stories have been hard to find yet they exist.

Most Southern states during the antebellum period prohibited or strictly limited Black literacy. Where it was permitted it was solely to promote Christian obedience through Bible study. Even these limited exceptions were curtailed in the fear following Nat Turner's insurrection. Still exceptions existed such as the story of his education chronicled by Booker T. Washington in *Up From Slavery.*

Among free Blacks in the North, Jupiter Hammon and Phyllis Wheatley are the earliest examples demonstrating intellectual attainment through their published writing. Yet Thomas Jefferson refused to recognize Wheatley as a poet and believed that Black mathematician Benjamin Banneker had the help of a White friend in producing his Almanac. The author of the Declaration of Independence steadfastly refused to accept any fact contrary to his belief in Black intellectual inferiority.[11]

By the turn of the nineteenth century church groups in the North had formed public school societies to educate the poor. Soon a debate developed over whether to extend education to a working class rapidly expanding due to immigration. Reformers, such as Horace Mann in Massachusetts, in the 1840s and 1850s promoted universal education but did not want the working class to control it. State control over education, teacher certification, and a uniform curriculum evolved as methods of controlling the education of immigrants. Punctuality and respect for authority, traits required by industry, were inculcated into students. Moreover, costs were kept low through the feminization of the teaching staff.[12]

Free Blacks in the North and West attempted to educate themselves, sometimes with the aid of White allies. Yet White support did not provide a shield from hostile Whites. In the early 1830s, Arthur Tappan tried to found a school for Black boys in New Haven as he had in New York. Local opponents, including some from Yale, stopped the school and tore down Tappan's house. In Canterbury, Connecticut, when a girl of mixed descent was permitted to enroll in a school for young ladies, it was destroyed and the girl was forced to leave the state.[13]

Throughout the nineteenth century, African Americans formed their own religious, educational, and benevolent associations often called Free African societies. Black churches frequently served as schools as well as meeting places. The lines between sacred and secular functions were blurred as church space was virtually the only space in which Blacks could exercise a degree of independence and autonomy.[14]

A few Blacks were able to obtain a higher education with Alexander Twilight graduating with a BA from Middlebury College in 1823, and John Russwurm completing his studies at Bowdoin College in 1826. Lucy Stanton completed the "women's course" at Oberlin in 1850. Other Black students attended Harvard, Franklin, and Rutland Colleges. A total of 27 African Americans received bachelor's degrees prior to the Emancipation Proclamation.[15] In 1855 the Cincinnati Conference of the Methodist Episcopal Church established a Negro college, which was incorporated the following year as Wilberforce University. It was closed briefly at the beginning of the Civil War and then reopened under the auspices of the African Methodist Episcopal Church.[16]

Slavery largely isolated the South from these changes in education. With the coming of the Civil War, and specifically the Freedman's Bureau, things began to change. Over the five years of the Bureau's existence from 1865 to 1870, some $5 million was spent on 4239 schools, 9300 teachers, and 247,000 pupils. The freed slaves themselves contributed over $785,000 to the schools. While problems included White hostility, poor teachers, and a lack of funds, W.E.B. Du Bois considered its efforts in education the Bureau's greatest success.[17]

Teachers for the Bureau schools came from the North, were both Black and White, and often church based. They delivered a strong dose of moral instructions along with racial pride and a liberal arts curriculum. That is, they believed the ex-slaves were capable of learning the same content as their Northern White students. Although the schools were open to Whites as well as Blacks, the former slave masters believed the schools were for paupers. This same period produced the first wave of Black colleges. Howard University, for example, was established in 1868 and named after Freedman's Bureau head General Oliver Howard.[18]

The end of Reconstruction brought an end to equal school funding and a uniform curriculum. Education became part of a larger conflict between agriculture and industry in the South. The rise of populism led to a shift in funding from the state to the local level. Whites in the Black Belt directed funds disproportionately to White students and teachers—a pattern that lasted until the civil rights movement. In South Carolina in 1908–09, for example, the state spent over a million and a half dollars to educate 153,807 White pupils, but only $308,153 to educate 181,095 Black pupils. White male teachers earned $480 per year compared to $91 per year for Black male teachers. White female teachers earned $249, while their Black counterparts made $91 per year.[19] The justification for defunding Black education focused on the curriculum. Blacks, it was argued, had no need for a liberal arts education since they were meant to be agricultural workers, that is, sharecroppers. Vocational or industrial education cost less, and therefore less spending was justified.

Within the generation following the Civil War, over one hundred Black colleges and universities were established. Some were state-sponsored like Howard and Tuskegee, but most were church supported such as Morehouse and Fisk. By 1900, there were only 390 Black graduates from White colleges (128 from Oberlin alone) but 1941 graduates of HBCUs. Some 53 percent of these graduates entered teaching, while another 17 percent became preachers.[20] The obvious explanation for this overwhelming concentration of Black graduates in two areas was the availability of jobs. Segregated schools and segregated churches provided the primary occupations for Black professionals. Even then, one-third of Black public school teachers in fifteen Southern states in 1930 had not completed high school. Only 17 Blacks had doctorates by 1925, and 14 years, later the number stood at 109.[21] By 1943, 40 percent of the PhDs held by Blacks were in the social sciences, and of those, 53 percent were in the fields of history and sociology. Until the 1930s, Black colleges in the South were unaccredited, and only three Black Ph.D.s held positions at HWCUs in 1936.[22]

It was in this context that Booker T. Washington rose to unprecedented heights of influence in the Black community and on the national stage. In his famous Atlanta Exposition address of 1895, the founder of Tuskegee pleaded to an audience of Northern industrialists and Southern politicians to invest in the vocational training of Southern Blacks who would be a much more compliant and less political workforce than White immigrants who had been exposed to radical European ideologies. In exchange, Blacks would drop demands for social and political rights.[23]

The response was overwhelming as Northern foundations began to pump millions of dollars into Southern education. John D. Rockefeller established the General Education Board in 1902 that stimulated the formation of the Anna T. Jeanes Fund as well as the Phelps Stokes Fund and the Rosenwald rural-school program. By 1917, the latter fund had spent $40 million on rural schools. However, the enthusiasm Northern philanthropists generated for education also sparked new interest in Southern Whites who controlled the public school systems for both races.

Washington's coronation as the national leader of Negroes by White philanthropists did not go unchallenged. Although William Monroe

Trotter had been the most conspicuous challenger to the "Tuskegee machine," Washington's publication of his autobiography *Up From Slavery* prompted Du Bois to respond, first in a *Dial* magazine article and then again in his *The Souls of Black Folk*. In the chapter of *Souls* entitled "Of Mr. Booker T. Washington and others," Du Bois questioned everything from Washington's leadership credibility to his public acceptance of second-class citizenship in the struggle for political and social rights. But it is his attack on Washington's insistence on vocational education for all African Americans that produced a foundational debate. While the Wizard of Tuskegee argued that vocational education best served the needs of all Negroes (his own children excepted), Du Bois maintained that a "talented tenth" of Blacks should be able to maximize their potential to the fullest through a liberal arts education. After all man did not live by bread alone, said Du Bois, and more strategically Black leaders without a cosmopolitan education could scarcely negotiate with Whites who had such a worldly knowledge.[24]

This dichotomy between vocational education and liberal arts education has served to obscure two vital areas of agreement between these seminal figures. First, that Du Bois, like Washington, believed that vocational or practical education was essential to meeting the needs of most Blacks for a skilled job and economic advancement. It was fundamental to his educational philosophy that Black colleges should train their students for existing needs in the community but that these needs did not prohibit students from developing a broad and cultivated world perspective. Second, the needs of the community had to flow from members of the community itself and not from on high. Washington stated, "it is idiotic to proceed as though we were white or yellow, English or Russian. Here we stand. We are American Negroes."[25] Du Bois agreed with this sentiment stating, "for Black professors, it made no sense to assume that they were teaching white Americans when in front of them sat Black victims of the American caste system."[26] For Du Bois this perspective did not mean a rejection of universalism but rather a universalism approached from the study of the Black condition and its causes just as universalism in HWCUs came from the socioeconomic base of White America. This "Afrocentric" or Black Studies approach to the core curriculum was echoed by Carter Woodson who declared the disciplines of economics, history, and philosophy as conceived by White Americans were nothing more than rationales for the caste system in America.[27]

By the 1920s, Du Bois had won the battle over vocational v. liberal arts education. Two factors contributed to the victory. First, Washington's death in 1915 left a void in Black leadership that no single leader would fill until the rise of Martin Luther King, Jr., some 40 years later. Second, World War I dramatically expanded Black horizons. Rural Blacks moved to the big city where they were exposed to a new world of possibilities. Returning Black veterans, having fought for their country and having received a semblance of equal treatment in Europe, were no longer content with Washington's second-class citizenship. The shift in thinking is best symbolized by the Harlem Renaissance. Another shift, however, was occurring on Black college campuses.

Black students were rejecting the Tuskegee model of vocational education in favor of a mainstream liberal arts curriculum that would prepare them for full participation in American life. In the words of Raymond Wolters, the Black colleges of the 1920s promoted the mainstream middle-class culture. Black youths were taught that the patois of the lower class ghettoes and fields was not proper English, and many folkways were deprecated as the unworthy legacy of an oppressive past. The colleges did not preserve folk culture but instead disseminated middle-class standards. Black students of the 1920s, like the youths from other minority groups, were exposed to Anglo-Saxon norms and urged to become facsimile White Anglo Saxon Protestants (WASPs).[28] For the next 30 years Black college students were characterized by their desire for acculturation—a desire to be "in" not "out" of the mainstream. They wanted to disprove the views of Howard trustee Albert Bushnell Hart, the distinguished Harvard historian, who wrote, for example, "the theory that the Negro mind ceases to develop after adolescence perhaps has something in it."[29]

The Howard scholars of the 1930s who challenged the "race men" were not successful in sustaining a mass alliance of Blacks and Whites dedicated to reforming or replacing capitalism. By 1940, the National Negro Congress had been co-opted by the Communist Party and lost its base of support in the national Black community. On the right of the NNC, the New Deal had attracted Black voters to the Democratic Party and World War II brought about a shift in priorities toward victory abroad and victory at home. No intellectual, Black or White, was more profoundly affected by the changing environment than Bunche who became the principal Black scholar working on Gunnar Myrdal's *An American Dilemma*. My decision to write a biography of Bunche was, in part, motivated by a desire to understand his shift from the left of Du Bois prior to the War, to the center after the War. During the War, Bunche left Howard to join first the government's Office of Strategic Services (later CIA) and then after the War the United Nations. Bunche became a pillar of support for the NAACP and a welcome presence in civil rights marches. Although the movement away from integration and toward Black power initially puzzled him, he eventually supported "Blackism" and linked the movement ironically to the National Negro Congress.[30] When students did protest, as they did in the early civil rights sit-ins of the late 1950s and early 1960s, it was over segregation and discrimination in society-at-large and not with what they were studying in the classroom. It would take a change in the class composition of the relative flood of Black students onto both Black and White college campuses in the late 1960s to fully challenge the production of knowledge and its dissemination in the classroom—the menu.

What ownership of the restaurant really stands for is ownership of the means of knowledge production. And this more encompassing concept refers not just to universities but also to professional organizations, journals, libraries, and other sources of legitimation. Who decides what knowledge is and what content is worth studying?

The evolution of Black Studies is ultimately the story of the struggle for full inclusion in knowledge production and legitimation. It raises questions of value that are far more fundamental than sitting in a classroom or choosing a textbook. This work contends that the greatest success of the movement for Black Studies has been the creation of a critical community[31] of scholars primarily concerned about creating and legitimizing subject matter that had been invisible, ignored, or devalued. Unlike previous Black intellectuals who were usually isolated on Black campuses or in Black institutions, such as the church, the new critical community of Black Studies scholars is found in many of our nation's elite schools and influences a broad student body.

Black enrollment in higher education grew only incrementally in the 1930s and 1940s. Even with a boost in enrollment as a result of the GI bill, most of the growth was confined to Black colleges.[32] Ironically, the modern sit-in movement launched by Black students at North Carolina Agriculture & Technical College (an HBCU) in 1960 would help open the doors to historically White colleges. As a result of the civil rights movement and federal legislation, the numbers of Black students attending HWCUs rose 70 percent in 1965. Black students were about 4.5 percent or 200,000 of a total college population of 4.5 million. Still by 1969, a national survey revealed that White universities in the South had an average Black enrollment of only 1.76 percent, in the East 1.84 percent, in the Midwest 2.98 percent, and in the West 1.34 percent.[33]

Different kinds of demands emerged from college protests in the mid to late 1960s. Moreover, the emphasis was different on the campuses of HBCUs as opposed to HWCUs. Ironically, Black college campuses were calling for a "Black" university. By 1968, these conditions had resulted in a student rebellion culminating in the replacement of the university president at Howard and the convening of a "Towards a Black University" conference drawing some 2000 students to the DC campus in November 1968. Howard graduate Stokely Carmichael was joined by Maulana Karenga and Harold Cruse, as key speakers for the event.

In a special issue of the *Negro Digest* on the "Black University," Darwin Turner stated that "Negro educators—and I must include myself—have not conceived courses oriented to the Negro."[34] Stephen Henderson reflecting on the colonial experience said, "the single revolutionary concept that has emerged in recent years is that the black experience is not only relevant in such a search (for identity), it is fundamental and crucial."[35] In defining what Blackness meant in a university context Gerald McWorter (Abdul Alkalimat) contended that first it meant the African American community must be the focus; second it must consider limiting White participation; and finally, it must affirm an identity independent of modern nation states and linked to an emerging international identity.[36] A year earlier in the same journal, Charles Hamilton expressed the view that the Negro college was one of the very few legitimate places in this society where we can expect outspoken, militant protest to emerge. He believed the leaders of such protest should be faculty and administrators, not the students.[37]

The main surge in protest in the late 1960s came from Black students, not faculty or administrators, and it sprang from HWCUs not HBCUs. In 1964, there were 234,00 Blacks enrolled in college with over half in HBCUs. Six years later, the enrollment numbers had doubled, but only one-third were HBCUs. Even with this rapid increase, Black collegians were less than 6 percent of the nation's total college enrollment in 1969. Yet, this small percentage was extremely active participating in 57 percent of all campus protests in 1968–69.[38] These students demonstrated on more than 150 campuses during the 1967–68 academic year, 250 campuses the following academic year, and another 150 incidents were recorded in 1969–70. On one day alone, February 13, 1969, Black students disrupted classes in almost every area of the nation—the Midwest in Illinois and Wisconsin, the Northeast in New York, the Upper South in North Carolina, the Deep South in Mississippi, and the West Coast in the Bay Area.[39]

From 1965 to 1967 most Black student demands came through normal academic channels. However, by 1968 the tone and tactics shifted as students faced academic delay and rejection. More importantly, the size and class composition of the Black student body changed. The Higher Education Act of 1965 and increased student aid made it possible for a large number of first-generation Black students to attend college. A majority enrolled at HWCUs and many entered through remedial or special initiatives such as Equal Opportunity Programs. At San Francisco State University in 1968, for example, 80 percent of the students worked to pay their way through school and came from predominantly lower middle-class, poor, and working-class communities.[40] Surveys in 1968 and 1970 found that most Black students in college were women, grew up in cities, received little or no financial support from parents, majored in social science, were first-generation college students, expressed racial pride, blamed the system, and were interested in collective mobility.[41]

The change in the size and composition of incoming Black students, when combined with the assassination of King in April 1968, gave new urgency to Black demands. According to Ibram Rodgers, courses were more likely to be demanded by moderates from 1965 to spring 1968, while departments and programs were more likely to be demanded after the assassination as radicals gained control of many Black student unions (BSUs).[42]

Along with a changed curriculum, Black activists insisted on increased admission of Black students and the hiring of Black faculty. By 1970, the former demand had resulted in almost 1000 colleges adopting a more open admissions policy often accompanied by increased tutorial services and campus diversity training. In the most dramatic example of open admissions, some 35,000 freshmen entered the City University of New York (CUNY) campuses in 1970, an increase of 75 percent from the previous year. Ironically, the City College of New York, founded as an institution to serve the poor, had a total of only two Black college graduates by 1910.[43] Author Toni Cade, who mentored the students in CCNY's SEEK program, wrote that at least 90 percent of the several hundred rebellions on American college and high school campuses over the last six years were propelled by and revealed a gross dissatisfaction with the curriculum.[44]

Along with curriculum and admissions, the third non-negotiable demand was for more Black faculty. The relatively small number of African Americans with doctorates made this perhaps the most challenging demand for campuses to meet. Moreover, prominent figures in HBCUs such as Benjamin Mays and Vincent Harding criticized efforts of HWCUs to "steal" their faculty. For all of his criticism of Howard University, Carmichael fondly remembered that an "array of excellent scholars and a tradition of Black scholarship were also present as well as clear-eyed, dedicated teachers, many of them progressive."[45] He then cites many of them and adds that

> ...what was quite as important as actually taking their courses was their presence among us and what it represented. That they were there, and therefore their work and example existed for us. If you were bold, you could seek them out for conversation, but their example was so important—the example of consciously black intellectuals of the first order, who devoted their professional lives to properly studying the African Presence at a time when we were otherwise being ignored or disparaged by 'American scholarship'.[46]

It was precisely those examples the Black students at HWUCs were demanding.

Another set of demands was typically rejected by college administrators. These included admission quotas, separate admission or grading criteria, firing racist faculty, Black dormitories, a halt to building expansion in local communities, support for campus worker issues, Black holidays, divestment, financial autonomy for BSUs and student governments, or Black student control of anything, although students were added to some faculty recruitment committees for the first time.[47]

It is over control of the curriculum and those teaching the curriculum that the main battles were fought and that has had the most profound impact on higher education. That is, the battle over program versus departmental status for Black Studies was essentially a struggle for the power to legitimate knowledge.

It was not the Howard conference on the "Black University" in November 1968 that proved prophetic. Rather, it was the Yale conference in November 1967 on "Black Studies in the University" that would have a significant impact. Although both were organized by Black students and some of the key participants were the same, namely Cruse and Karenga, the settings and audience were different. While Howard was at the center of Black higher education, Yale represented the center of American higher education. The Yale audience was composed primarily of White liberal faculty, while Howard drew Black student leaders from across the country. Most importantly, McGeorge Bundy, president of the Ford Foundation and former White House advisor, was a prime participant at Yale but absent from the Howard gathering. Ford, under Bundy, would become the primary external funding source for Black Studies over the next 25 years. And Ford favored a model of development opposed by Cruse, Karenga, and many of the leading Black activists. Specifically, Ford promoted the "contributionist," "inclusionist," or "integrationist" approach to knowledge through programs controlled by traditional departments. The more radical approach pushed by scholars such as Nathan Hare and Gerald McWorter along with Cruse and Karenga demanded autonomous schools or at a minimum separate departments of Black Studies.

Cruse argued at Yale that the "integrationist ethic" had subverted and blocked America's underlying tendency toward what he called "democratic ethnic pluralism."[48] In addition, it had retarded the development of the Black bourgeoisie, which, in turn, affected the "intellectual class" in Black life. For Cruse, the demand for Black Studies fell under an ideology of "Black cultural nationalism." Karenga, the leading cultural nationalist of the period, agreed with Cruse and added that the university is not basically an educational institution but rather a political institution. McWorter contended that the university could be conceptualized as a manifestation of focused powers that have been used against the Black community rather than for them.[49]

Bundy and many of the White faculty present challenged the notion of a political university. He said, "there is a difference... between the political view of a set of historical events and the historical view of those events."[50] Bundy then went on to make a distinction between studying a subject because "of the subject's importance" and studying a subject "because of the importance of that act to you."[51] He termed the former action "real" and the latter action "unreal" but left unsaid who determined a subject's importance and that was at the heart of the discourse. In concluding the symposium, David Brion Davis, after a very thoughtful presentation of American mythology and nationalistic history, nonetheless insisted on maintaining the distinction between political ideology and education.[52]

For Bundy and many of the White liberal faculty at the Yale event, program status was the only way to ensure that Black Studies would have an educational thrust rather than a political thrust. In this view, they were joined by a number of well-known Black leaders and scholars. Bayard Rustin quickly published an edited work that was largely an attack on Black Studies. In it he argued that Black Studies could become a pretext for separatism, an escape from traditional disciplines to weak "soul courses" and a vehicle to promote political and ideological views.[53] Political scientist Martin Kilson, the first tenured African American faculty member at Harvard, lauded the patience and objectivity of earlier Black scholars in contrast to the Black Studies militants and recommended that any African American Studies major be required to fulfill a good part of the academic requirements in an established discipline.[54] Contributors Norman Hill and Andrew Brimmer were even more critical suggesting that Black students were afraid they could not meet White standards and were not likely to acquire the mental discipline and rigorous training they needed in Black Studies.[55] Perhaps the best defense of Black Studies in the book came from White historian C. Van Woodward who stated, "thoroughly Europa-centric in outlook, American whites subscribed completely to the myth that European culture, their culture, was so overwhelmingly superior that no other could survive under exposure to it."[56]

The Yale conference and the rise of Black Studies took place in an historical context marking the end of the civil rights movement and the emergence of identity politics. It was a time when the dominance of European culture was openly challenged. Equality was being demanded not because Blacks were just like (or could be like) Whites on the inside, but because they were humans and citizens.

Although the radicalization of Berkeley is almost always associated with the rise of the "free speech" movement in 1964, it was a group of alienated Black Berkeley students who—inspired by the students in the Student Nonviolent Coordinating Committee (SNCC)—began meeting in 1960 that planted the seeds that would blossom into the Black Studies demands at San Francisco State, Merritt College, University of California, Los Angeles (UCLA), and Berkeley later in the decade. A group calling itself the Afro-American Association and consisting of Donald Hopkins, Henry Ramsey, Donald Warden, Ortho Green, and others had a remarkable influence. Led by Warden, a Howard graduate and military veteran who preached from texts ranging from Du Bois to the ancient African kingdoms, the group at various times included Huey Newton, Bobby Seale, Ron Everett (Maulana Karenga), and students from San Francisco State University. The organization only lasted a few years as the active phase of the civil rights movement ended and some members joined the Revolutionary Action Movement (RAM) while Newton and Seale would go in a different direction than Karenga.[57]

Just days after Lyndon Johnson signed the Voting Rights Act, Watts, in the heart of Los Angeles, exploded in violence. The August 1965 rebellion essentially marked the end of the modern civil rights movement. The Voting Rights Act would be the last of four pieces of legislation passed dealing with civil and political rights including the 1957, 1960, and 1964 civil rights bills. Backlash to more legislation had already begun in California in 1964 when voters, through a state initiative, repealed the Rumford Fair Housing legislation passed by the state legislature. Given the new legal protections for civil and political rights now in place, Whites were asking, "what more does the Negro want"?[58]

Watts was also a wake-up call for the leadership of the civil rights movement. The movement's great protest campaigns in Montgomery, Birmingham, and Selma had all been in the South. While Northern Blacks applauded these courageous efforts to end overt discrimination, they did not see any progress in the more covert prejudice they faced every day at the hands of teachers, landlords, employers, and the police. Watts convinced Martin Luther King, Jr., to shift his focus to the North, over the objections of Rustin, where he confronted the issues of poor housing and poor schools in Chicago.

Finally, Watts represented a break with the leadership of the civil rights establishment and the emergence of new leaders imbued with a new psychology. When State Legislator Mervyn Dymally called for peace in Watts he was told to go back to the middle-class enclave of Baldwin Hills where he lived. Comedian/activist Dick Gregory was shot in the leg as he attempted to pacify militants in South Central Los Angeles.[59] As Carmichael would explain to King in the Meredith march a year later, he was more concerned about what Blacks thought of his new slogan "Black Power" than what Whites thought.[60]

While the Watts uprising was spontaneous, it inspired a host of new organizations and leaders who drew their inspiration more from Malcolm X than King. Malcolm spoke the language of Northern ghetto dwellers could relate to. Instead of King's moral appeals for "redemptive suffering," they responded to calls for self-defense and community control. A month after Watts, Los Angeles resident Karenga dropped out of the PhD program at UCLA and founded the cultural nationalist organization US (as opposed to them) in September 1965. After Watts, community college students Bobby Seale and Huey Newton began to discuss the need for a new kind of organization in Oakland to deal with the same issues uncovered in Los Angeles. The result was the founding of the Black Panther Party for Self Defense in October 1966. A similar pattern emerged after violence in Detroit in 1967. Emerging from that conflict was the Republic of New Africa led by Imari Obadele (Milton Henry), the League of Revolutionary Black Workers, and Albert Cleage's Shrine of the Black Madonna.

Of course, these urban rebellions also placed added pressure on Black college students everywhere to find answers to the problems facing the communities many of them came from. As a Cornell University graduate student, for example, Harry Edwards recalled that the reality and implications of Watts had utterly failed to penetrate the pastoral, ivory-tower milieu of Cornell and was treated as an apparition as distant as the war in Southeast Asia. He found it more and more difficult to relate his theory courses to his social and political concerns. "Some of my professors," Edwards said, "were not only unsympathetic to my 'nonacademic' concerns, they were hostile to the very idea of any attempt on my part to synthesize my political and social concerns with my scholarly interests."[61]

James Turner, a key figure in the development of Black Studies at Cornell and Northwestern, talked about the networking done at the Howard conference in 1968. As a representative of the Northwestern student leaders attending the conference, Turner met the delegation of students coming from Cornell. The Cornell students were looking for a director of Black Studies, and Turner was a graduate student at Northwestern. As a result of their meeting, Turner was invited to Cornell for an interview and eventually offered the position of director of Africana Studies. The contact with Turner occurred before the takeover of Willard Straight Hall at Cornell.[62]

Like many other early Black Studies activists, Turner saw Black Studies as fundamentally a nationalist project. He states,

> The people who were pushing for this, who were willing to talk about challenging the major white institution and creating a Black site and space that would be defined as a Black space and would be commanded and controlled by Black people, who would be in charge of their own self-determination, these were nationalist precepts.[63]

Turner contrasts this vision with the Marxist perspective that saw Black Studies as "false consciousness" and the integrationist perspective that believed assimilation was the way racism would be defeated. The Black Nationalist position, on the other hand, was that once Black people were able to control power and resources on their own behalf, they could then be in a position to negotiate with other groups. "For me," says Turner, "the notion of how to be a people not only *within* ourselves but *for* ourselves was the critical question. And to me that is still the critical question."[64]

The emergence of new organizations and new leadership reflected more than a willingness to embrace self-defense or even guerilla warfare. It represented a new racial pride that was both a product of the self-confidence gained through the civil rights protests and a reaction to the failure of the larger society to accept true integration rather than mere desegregation. It was a rejection of one-way assimilation and a plea for cultural pluralism. Black power called for a decentering of the White norm, but it was not clear what would replace it.

Black Studies was the branch of Black power that addressed education, especially higher education. Older Black leaders were skeptical, if not hostile, as we saw with Bayard Rustin. Roy Wilkens, head of the NAACP, agreed with increased Black enrollments and faculty but worried about separate Black dorms. King said we must no longer be ashamed of being Black and contrasted the many negative synonyms for Blackness in comparison to the positive synonyms for Whiteness in the English language. He believed there was a tendency to ignore the Negro's contribution to American life and to strip him of his personhood that was as old as the earliest history books and as contemporary as the morning's newspaper. "Psychological freedom," King said, "a firm sense of self-esteem, is the most powerful weapon against the long night of physical slavery."[65]

Yet for those who had struggled so long and hard for school desegregation, the acceptance of something called Black Studies was a difficult transition. Jimmy Garrett, a key leader of the student strike at SFSU, recalled speaking at a Freedom School in Greenville, Mississippi, in 1964:

> We had some real struggles with Bob Moses and his wife, Donna Moses who said we were teaching propaganda. Bob Moses denounced us at the SNCC conference in Greenville, the regional Mississippi conference on the Delta, as being infiltrators, teaching propaganda rather than history and so forth. His wife, Donna Moses, later became Dr. Marimba Ani, who studies under John Hendrik Clarke in the Africana Studies Program at Hunter College. Only after she had gone to Africa and came back when I met her in Atlanta around 1991 or 1992, right after she had written *Yurugu*, that she ran up to me screaming and hugged me and said something like you all were right…[66]

Civil rights leaders were not the only Blacks expressing mixed views about Black Studies.

Earlier generations of Black intellectuals had wrestled with some of the same issues confronting Black students in the 1960s. Philosopher Alain Locke, editor of *The New Negro* and the first Black Rhodes scholar, considered the "melting pot" idea to be another form of absolutism.

If Americans wished to solve their problems of community life, they needed to change their attitudes toward minorities, said Locke, "they should not try to change the minorities themselves."[67] He added that these differences are as real and hard as "facts" and should be accepted as unemotionally and objectively as we accept facts. For Locke the pluralism–relativism principle stated that the values of each cultural group were on the same footing and cultural reciprocity should replace cultural domination with cultural tolerance as the goal.[68]

E. Franklin Frazier, Locke's Howard colleague[69] and perhaps the best-known Black social scientist of his generation, worried that civil rights leaders would be seduced by assimilation and ignore the economic and social organization of American life. It was the responsibility of the Negro intellectual to provide a positive identity through history, literature, art, music, and drama. The aim of the sit-ins is assimilation, said Frazier, which is the failure of the Negro intellectual.[70] He understood that racism was sustained and reproduced in everyday life as much by the ideas of "objective" scholars as by the lynch mob. Frazier rejected the "moral neutrality" of the Chicago school of sociology and condemned Black intellectuals for not studying the Negro. His own efforts to formulate a set of values that would develop the notion of cultural self-determination for Black Americans were problematic. On the one hand, Frazier rejected Melville Herskovits's contention that forms of African music and language had survived the Middle Passage. On the other hand, he believed the authentic Black folk culture of the antebellum period had been destroyed by Black migration and urbanization of the twentieth century. Frazier attacked the Black bourgeoisie for mimicking the White middle class but left them with no viable alternative to build on.[71]

Historian John Hope Franklin, Frazier's most distinguished Howard student, took a view directly opposite from his mentor. He argued that as the respectability of Negro scholars working on Negro issues grew it defeated a basic principle of scholarship that with the proper skills and mental capacity, any person could engage in the study of any field. In sharp contrast to Frazier, Franklin condemned the field of Negro studies created by Du Bois, Woodson, Locke, Frazier, and others and stated "it is tragic indeed, and a commentary on the condition of American society, that these Negro scholars felt compelled [emphasis mine] to make the choice they did."[72] What prompted this compulsion is not clear as Franklin goes on to state that there were other Negro scholars who did not choose the road to Negro studies and thus entered "what may be termed the main stream of American scholarship."[73] It is clear, however, that Franklin believed the only way to become a legitimate or mainstream scholar was to study any subject other than the Negro—a position contradicted by his own work.

Surely as an historian Franklin realized that the popular negative conceptions of Reconstruction, in *Gone with the Wind* for example, had been largely shaped by highly subjective work of White historians. Historians William A. Dunning and John W. Burgess influenced the perception of a generation of American historians and politicians toward Black participation in politics through their work on Reconstruction. Joining their "objective" scientific research were the sociologists and psychologists in leading universities working to prove the innately inferior status of Negroes. G. Stanley Hall, the first PhD in psychology in the United States and the founder of the *American Journal of Psychology*, used his academic legitimacy in support of anti-Negro propaganda while he was president of Clark University and sought to take the problem of the Negro out of the hands of politicians and philanthropists and "place it where it belongs,—with economists, anthropologists, and sociologists."[74] Given these attacks, it is small wonder that the first generation of Black intellectuals felt "compelled" to join the racial discourse. For the 15-year period from 1932 to 1947, about 85 percent of the 2535 MA theses and 359 PhD dissertations on Negro subjects accepted by American universities were done by Blacks. Since Black professors and graduate students were grossly underrepresented in higher education, these figures are an indication of the relative neglect of the field in general.[75]

All of this discourse between Black intellectuals and their work in general was largely unknown to the Black college students of the 1960s until the publication of *The Crisis of the Negro Intellectual* by Harold Cruse in 1967.[76] Perhaps, they had heard of the "utopian" efforts of Marcus Garvey to return to Africa or the more sophisticated might have read Richard Wright's apologetic nationalism: "I would like to explain that the Black Nationalism that we, American Negroes, practiced in America, and which we were forced to practice, was a reluctant nationalism, a proud defensive one."[77] Cruse made no such apologies. Surprisingly, Cruse was not a college graduate and held no academic post at the time of the book's publication. Yet his highly personal account of Black intellectual history would become the most influential work of its kind since Gunnar Myrdal's *An American Dilemma* a generation earlier.

Cruse had the good fortune to publish his work at a time when the new wave of Black college students was questioning the menu they were being offered at newly accessible HWCUs. Many were first-generation college students who were looking for answers to the social and political turmoil characteristic of the late 1960s. They were not finding those answers in the classroom.

Reading Cruse was a revelation to me and other college students in several respects. A significant number of these students had never had a Black teacher and knew no Black intellectuals. Their high school history books had jumped from slavery to Booker T. Washington—often with a side reference to George Washington Carver—to current events. There was no context, no background knowledge to place current events in an historical perspective that made sense. Cruse's Harlem revealed a previously hidden world of art, culture, and intellectual striving. Often, the first objection White faculty had to Black Studies was that there was nothing to study. Now, the response quickly rose what about Du Bois, Richard Wright, Ralph Ellison, Loraine Hansberry, and others.

For those that argued Black students should be grateful that the college gates previously closed to them were now opening, Cruse provided a response. He contended the unequal power relationship between White liberals and Black intellectuals prevented a critical discourse on Black liberation that went beyond a narrowly defined liberalism. The integrationist paradigm of White liberals and their Black counterparts, such as James Baldwin, undercut Black intellectual development and the creation of an indigenous theory of revolution. In fact, Black political history for Cruse was a dichotomy of integration versus nationalism, not liberalism versus conservatism. Liberalism's focus on the individual and his/her moral dilemma obscured the proper focus on group power. The timidity of White intellectuals was a matter of historical record as witnessed by the statements of Reinhold Niebuhr and William Faulkner questioning the wisdom of the Supreme Court's *Brown* decision in pushing the South to desegregate too fast.[78]

Historically, the only group of Whites to forcefully support integration had been the Communist Party, and Cruse singled it out for special attention. Once again the history of Black involvement with the American Communist Party (CPUSA) was unknown to many Black college students in the 1960s. Paul Robeson, who supported the Party, was a name known to the parents of the students, but he had been effectively isolated and silenced by the US government in the postwar period as had Du Bois.[79] Cruse, who had personal experience with the CPUSA, was especially critical of the role played by intellectuals in the Party. White scholars, like Du Bois's close friend Herbert Aptheker, became the Party authorities on Black issues. In addition, said Cruse, the Party discouraged the promotion and development of ethnic/racial nationalism but permitted the support of Zionism.[80] In short, Cruse's critique of the CPUSA in particular and the White left in general made Black students suspicious of an alliance with White radical students. This attitude would manifest itself in the division that developed between cultural nationalists who opposed such alliances and revolutionary nationalists who were willing to work with radical Whites.

What Cruse offered in place of the "integrationist paradigm" or a worker's utopia was his own brand of cultural nationalism. Arguing that White Americans were just as insecure about their cultural identity as African Americans, he targeted culture rather than economics or politics as the weak link in American society. While the American Creed proclaimed the rights of the individual, Cruse said group power determined the fate of each individual. There were three main power groups according to Cruse—Protestants, Catholics, and Jews—and none of them wanted to integrate with the others. Only one subgroup, intellectuals and artists, stood above the reality of ethnic separatism. "Thus," he says, "*it is only through a cultural analysis of the Negro approach to group 'politics' that the errors, weaknesses and goal failure can cogently be analyzed and positively worked out.*"[81] And it was only an elite (talented tenth), the Negro intellectual, who had the perspective to perform this role.

A sure sign of the book's influence were the many critiques it generated. Writing two years after Cruse in his *Black Awakening in Capitalist America*, Robert Allen contended that Cruse failed to show the centrality of the cultural apparatus to any revolution and that he overemphasized the power of intellectuals. American capitalism, said Allen, was fully capable of allowing cultural pluralism without any change to the political and economic structure of the country. In addition, a focus on Black elites and a Black middle-class support system for Black creative arts only exacerbated intraracial discord. Thus, Cruse was promoting a reformist cultural pluralism, not a real revolution.[82]

Over the years since its publication, *The Crisis of the Negro Intellectual*'s case studies of key historical events in African American intellectual development and its highly polemical attacks on Black intellectuals ruined by inter-racialism have all come under attack. In a recent edited reconsideration of Cruse, Jerry Watts summarized a number of them. Cruse omits the crucial role the Black church and Black music have played culturally. He does not believe Black intellectuals should disagree with each other and assumed racial uniformity. Female Black intellectuals were marginalized, while the centrality of Harlem was privileged. Finally, Cruse separated African Americans from Africa and its diaspora with the exception of an attack on West Indian intellectuals in the United States.[83]

All of these criticisms are to some extent true and help explain many of the issues Black Studies has confronted over its nearly 50 years. Afrocentrism, Black feminism, and African diasporic studies may, in one sense, be seen as ways of filling the gaps in the Cruse analysis. Yet Cruse's conceptual challenge to what he called the "integrationist paradigm" and what would later be termed "Eurocentrism" proved a guiding principle in the development of Black Studies. As Perry Hall has stated, "the political struggles over structure, departmental control, tenure, academic credit and other tools of academic legitimacy actually had a strong epistemological basis."[84]

Under the program model promoted by the Ford Foundation, Black Studies would complement traditional disciplines in approaching the Black subject through an objective, morally neutral, and detached methodology. The Black subject would be assimilated into a mainstream curriculum in which the White, male, heterosexual subject was the norm. Under the department or separate school model favored by Karenga, McWorter, Turner, and many BSUs, Black Studies scholars would have the autonomy to commit their scholarship to the improvement of the Black community, however defined. In short, they would have the space to become a critical community dedicated to a culturally pluralistic pursuit of knowledge in all its forms.

This epistemological challenge to traditional disciplines has been both the most profound contribution of Black Studies to the Academy and its greatest source of resistance. From the beginning of racial discourse/struggle in what became the United States, the boundaries of that discourse were determined by Whites. That is, claims as to what was truthful or factual were legitimated by White sources.

For virtually the entire antebellum period, both abolitionists and defenders of slavery cited the Bible as the primary authority for their views. Black preachers and their followers identified with Exodus and the escape of the Hebrew slaves from Egypt while slave masters quoted Genesis and the story of Noah and his son Ham as justification for Black bondage. The important question of whether a Christian could be held in bondage was resolved early in Virginia colony. In deciding that they could, slave masters were free to use the Bible as a means of pacification rather than liberation. Black Christianity, however, was characterized by a prophetic tradition calling for liberation.[85] Virtually, all of the slave narratives were immersed in religious references and often attested as "truthful" by upstanding White witnesses. Of course, the most popular slave narrative of the nineteenth century was the fictional *Uncle Tom's Cabin* in which the White author, Harriett Beecher Stowe, gave Uncle Tom Christ-like qualities.

A year before the Civil War, Charles Darwin published his *Origin of the Species*. This work, along with his *Descent of Man*, would serve as the catalyst for shifting the foundation of racial discourse from religion to science. And with this shift the authority for "truth" moved from emotional belief to cold, hard, objective fact. Thus, American apartheid or "Jim Crow" could now claim to be based on biological difference and a racial hierarchy resting on evolution. Black leaders of the late nineteenth and early twentieth centuries, such as Edward Blyden, Alexander Crummel, W.E.B. Du Bois, and Booker T. Washington, generally accepted the notion of biological difference among the races but challenged the hierarchy put forth by Social Darwinists. They preferred to see the races as having unique characteristics that complemented rather than competed with each other. Sociologist Robert Park would call the Negro the "woman of the races," and the intellectuals of the philosophy of Negritude praised those (Africans) who never invented anything.[86]

By the 1930s, the work of anthropologist Franz Boas and his students Margaret Mead and Ruth Benedict began to undercut biological concepts of race and replace them with cultural relativism. But it was Swedish economist Gunnar Myrdal, not Boas, who produced the next authoritative text to guide racial discourse. His publication of *An American Dilemma* in 1944 had the virtue of collaboration with a host of Black researchers and a reception in a new post-World War II environment. His hypothesis that the gap between the philosophy of the "American Creed" and the reality of American segregation created a "moral dilemma" among White Americans was widely embraced by both Black and White intellectuals and prompted a whole new area of research into the psychological effects of segregation culminating in Kenneth Clark's "doll test" research cited by the Supreme Court's *Brown* decision in 1954. Myrdal's work was eagerly read in college classrooms by students like the young Martin Luther King, Jr., and a series of psychological studies including the *Mark of Oppression* and the *Nature of Prejudice* shaped racial discourse and research. Although Myrdal broke with previous sociological theories, Stanford Lyman contended that he does not break the paradigm: "*An American Dilemma* contains a massive critique of the entire corpus of classical and Chicago School sociology, and includes an attack on American Marxism as having the same 'do-nothing' or 'laissez-faire' orientation as the sociological theories of Sumner an Park, it ultimately committed the same kind or errors in the name of a mechanistic, value-conscious sociology."[87] Favoring a political economy approach, Myrdal's principle Black collaborator, Ralph Bunche, disagreed with his moral dilemma approach, and Blacks were left with little agency other than to behave more like Whites—as Myrdal encouraged—and wait for individual Whites to confront their prejudice.[88] In fact, Myrdal suggests that the process might be speeded up if the Black population were divided into two strata and that the "higher" stratum—that is, the educated and better-off Negroes—be enfranchised immediately, while the "lower" stratum—the poor and less educated—be granted the vote only gradually and in increments.[89]

King had read Myrdal as a college student, and his assassination was seen by many Blacks as the end of racial discourse based on moral appeals. Younger Blacks, in particular, believed that Black power, not moral reasoning, was central to Black progress. Black power opened the door for an identity politics that would come to include Brown power, Red power, Women's power, Gay power, and a host of other identity groups. No central leader emerged to lead these initiatives similar to King's influence over the civil rights movement. Instead Black power emerged in a variety of settings with a host of leaders including business, the professions, politics, and education. And there was no central text that shaped the parameters of racial discourse.

Black Studies, then, emerged as a manifestation of Black power on many college campuses with a diverse set of leaders. It did not stop with the simple challenge of desegregating college admissions and the traditional disciplines. At its most radical, it challenged the epistemological foundations of knowledge. It asked how do we know what we know and who does this knowledge benefit?

Several typologies have been produced to describe how Black intellectuals attempted to answer these questions. Responding to the decline in Black Studies units in the mid-1970s, Robert Allen described three schools of thought. The first school envisioned Black Studies as a purely academic field emphasizing research on his Black history and illuminating the contributions of African Americans to American society. A second school of thought, influenced by Harold Cruse, saw Black Studies as an expression of cultural nationalism that critiqued the "integrationist ethic" and challenged the dominant Anglo-Saxon culture. A third viewpoint best expressed by Nathan Hare believed Black Studies could be a vehicle for social change. From his perspective, Black Studies had to be used to break down the walls separating Black intellectuals from the Black community. A decline in Black college enrollment, along with administrative attacks on radical or independent Black Studies units, says Allen, accounts for their decline. In response, Black scholars must define their field and clarify their relationship to Ethnic Studies. Additionally, they need to standardize and develop Black Studies curriculum and professionalize the field.[90] While Allen leans toward Hare's perspective, he agrees with cultural nationalists such as Karenga that the university is a political institution, and the immediate challenge was the construction of a militant Black institution inside a conservative White institution that was for all practical purposes hostile to the former's existence.

Manning Marable writing over 25 years after Allen sees three Black intellectual traditions reflected in Black Studies. A "descriptive tradition" might describe an academic approach that sought to uncover and contribute Black content to traditional disciplines. A tradition focused on "corrective" research could be linked to an ideological perspective that decentered the White norm and created a Black psychology or a Black economics, for example. A third tradition is prescriptive or what Marable called "transformative" as it went beyond the assumption of racism at the ideological level to argue that it had become an integral factor in the construction of the US political economy and social class hierarchy. This intellectual project, said Marable, must go beyond the "racial mountain" if it wanted to effect change in the larger society.[91]

While Allen and Marable examined Black Studies units, another way of viewing the same struggle was through curriculum. James Banks delineated four possible levels of integration of "ethnic content" (multiculturalism):

a contributions approach (academic or descriptive), a new theories and concepts approach (ideological or corrective), a transformative approach (radical), and an empowerment/social action approach (instrumental or prescriptive).[92]

Martin Kilson, the early Black Studies skeptic, emphasized Black public intellectual traditions rather than administrative units. His four Black public intellectual categories include: pragmatic activists (instrumental), ethno-activists (ideological), Black conservatives who would oppose all forms of Black Studies, and establishmentarians (academic).[93]

Whether the focus was personalities, content, or administrative units, it is clear that racial discourse is no longer determined by White authorities who set the parameters of the debate. However, Black Studies is not totally defined internally either. In an insightful article, Mario Small has described the three constituencies a Black Studies unit must appeal to—the campus, the profession, and the wider community (public). He does this by examining the evolution of two models of Black Studies development at Harvard and Temple. These two schools have had strong leaders with departments that represent opposite ends along a continuum of possible organization.[94]

Representing the academic approach Harvard's Black Studies department has a faculty made up almost entirely of joint appointments with traditional departments. Its "dream team" of Henry Louis Gates, Cornell West, and William J. Wilson achieved their academic reputations in traditional disciplines well before their arrival at Harvard.[95] Thus, Harvard's credibility in the wider academic community comes from its grounding in traditional disciplines and through its major research projects conducted through the W.E.B. Du Bois Institute. Moreover, Gates has built an elite following as a public intellectual through regular contributions to the *New York Times* and *Atlantic Monthly*, several Public Broadcasting System (PBS) television series, a professional journal, and several nonacademic books intended for a general audience.[96]

In contrast to this very broad interdisciplinary approach, Molefi Asante at Temple has constructed a department much more narrowly defined by Afrocentrism. Most all of Temple's Black Studies faculty are appointed solely in the department, and Asante has been associated with Black Studies since its earliest days, first at UCLA and then Temple. Temple implemented the first PhD program in Black Studies (Harvard's came much later) and Asante sought legitimacy with scholars in the National Council for Black Studies and the African Heritage Studies Association not traditional professional organizations. Like Gates, Asante has a public presence, but it is concentrated among public school teachers and community activists. Asante has published over two dozen books and edited the *Journal of Black Studies* for over 40 years.[97]

Within this continuum of development from a very broad to a very concise conception of Black Studies rest the vast majority of Black Studies units. The University of California at Berkeley (UCB), for example, has pioneered in developing a focus on the African Diaspora in its graduate program. Other units have emphasized African American history, Black feminism, and cultural studies. Given that tenured faculty have a good deal of autonomy, most Black Studies units house faculty of diverse viewpoints and various levels of activism either on or off campus. There is a great deal of tolerance for both ideological and methodological diversity. While the older generation of Black Studies scholars was trained in traditional disciplines, the newer generation has benefited from graduate training in multidisciplinary areas. Other differences between the pre-Black Studies scholars and post-Black Studies scholars include a shift from an early focus on history and social science to cultural studies. The number of Black female faculty members has increased substantially. Unfortunately, the growing academic credibility of Black Studies has come at the expense of less significant community involvement. In addition, the development of graduate programs has been limited almost entirely to HWCUs. The creation of these graduate programs, which represent the ability to reproduce this critical community, would not have been possible without the institutionalization and professionalization of Black Studies.

Notes

1. Langston Hughes and Arna Bontemps, (eds.), *The Book of Negro Folklore* (New York: Dodd, Mead and Co., 1958), p. 508.
2. Martin Luther King, Jr., in James M. Washington, (ed.), *A Testament of Hope* (San Francisco: Harper & Row, 1986), p. 118.
3. Ralph Ellison, *Invisible Man* (New York: Modern Library, 1994), p. 258.
4. Ralph J. Bunche, "Education in Black and White," *Journal of Negro Education* 5 (July 1936) p. 356.
5. Francille Rusan Wilson, *The Segregated Scholars* (Charlottesville, Virginia: University of Virginia, 2006), p. 192.
6. Ibram H. Rodgers, *The Black Campus* Movement (New York: Palgrave Macmillan 2012), p. 25. Following his receipt of the

Nobel Peace Prize in 1950, Ralph Bunche received numerous teaching offers from elite HWCUs including Harvard, Berkeley, and the University of Chicago. He briefly accepted the Harvard offer but could not bring himself to resign from the United Nations. See Charles P. Henry, *Ralph Bunche* (New York: New York University Press, 1999), p. 171.

7. Rodgers, p. 20.
8. Stokely Carmichael, *Ready For Revolution* (New York: Scribner, 2003), pp. 116–117.
9. By the time I arrived at Howard in fall 1973, there were still two former students of Bunche teaching in the political science department—Vincent Browne and Robert Martin. Martin had also served as a research assistant for Alain Locke. Unfortunately, due to the lack of a faculty club or forum for interdepartmental socializing, I never met Merze Tate who was teaching in the history department and was the first Black woman to receive a doctorate in political science.
10. For a detailed discussion of the Howard School of Thought see Henry, also Holloway. Robert Vitalis in "Black Order, White Power" recovers the history of Howard scholar's work in international relations. He states, The first black professors of international thought all taught at Howard University, starting with Alain Locke in the 1910s and ending with Merze Tate, who taught from 1942 to 1977, the first black woman to receive a PhD in international relations and one of the first American woman to attend Alfred Zimmern's School of International Studies in Geneva. The Howard school thinkers stand out for their early and relentless critiques of the supposed truths of racial science and of the role racism played in sustaining imperialism. They stand out as well for the connections they forged—unique among their generation of professors—to the theoreticians of liberation and the future leaders of Africa and the island nations of the Caribbean. These might be thought of as the critical counter-networks to the ones dedicated to upgrading the institutions of colonial rule that the white professors forged with the so-called Geneva Institutions in the era of the League of Nations. Dissidents within IR today owe it to themselves to wrestle with these scholars, their era, and ideas. The self-identified postcolonial theorists are the descendants of the

Howard School and need to know more about their mongrel roots.

11. Ronald Takaki, *A Different Mirror* (New York: Back Bay Books, 2008), pp. 65–67.
12. Martin Carnoy, *Education as Cultural Imperialism* (New York: McKay, 1974), pp. 234–238.
13. Nell Irvin Painter, *Creating Black Americans* (New York: Oxford University Press, 2007), p. 79.
14. Ibid.
15. Ibram H. Rodgers, *Op. Cit.*, pp. 9–13.
16. John Hope Franklin, *From Slavery To Freedom* (New York: Knopf, 1967), p. 231.
17. The official name of the Freedman's Bureau was Bureau of Refugees, Freedman, and Abandoned Lands. See Henry Allen Bullock, *A History of Negro Education In The South* (New York: Praeger, 1970), Chapter 1. See also W.E.B. Du Bois, *The Souls of Black Folk* (New York: Penguin, 1989).
18. Bullock, *Op. Cit.*, pp. 219, 285.
19. Painter, *Op. Cit.*, p. 166.
20. William M. Banks, *Black Intellectuals* (New York: Norton, 1996), p. 44. By 1898 there were 252 Black women with college degrees and their number increased rapidly after 1900. However, the majority were enrolled in certificate-granting normal school departments rather than regular bachelor's degree programs. See Francille Rusan Wilson, *Op. Cit.*, p. 103.
21. Ibid. p. 93.
22. Michael R. Winston, "Through the Back Door," *Daedalus,* Summer 1971, pp. 694–695.
23. Louis R. Harlan, *Booker T. Washington: The Making of a Black Leader 1856–1901* (New York: Oxford University Press, 1972).
24. David Levering Lewis, *W.E.B. Du Bois: Biography of a Race 1868–1919* (New York: Holt, 1993), pp. 287–288.
25. Allen B. Ballard, *The Education of Black Folk* (New York: Harper & Row, 1973), p. 20.
26. Ibid. p. 21.
27. Ibid. p. 21.
28. Raymond Wolters, *The New Negro on Campus* (Princeton: Princeton University Press, 1975), p. 342.
29. Winston, p. 686. Hart voted against a Black president for Howard.

30. Charles P. Henry, (ed.), *Ralph Bunche: Selected Speeches and Writings* (Ann Arbor: University of Michigan Press, 1995), pp. 297–304.
31. Thomas Rochon defines critical community as a self-aware, mutually interacting group who have developed a sensitivity to some problem, an analysis of the sources of the problem, and a prescription for what should be done about the problem. They are different than epistemic communities in that they are critical, offer new perspectives, and do not have ties to established political institutions. Thomas R. Rochon, *Culture Moves* (Princeton: Princeton University Press, 1998), pp. 22–25.
32. See Ira Katznelson, *When Affirmative Action Was White* (New York: Norton, 2005), Chap. 5.
33. Martha Biondi, *The Black Revolution on Campus* (Berkeley: University of California Press, 2012) p. 17.
34. Darwin T. Turner, "The Black University: A Practical Approach," in *Negro Digest*, March 1968, p. 19.
35. Stephen E. Henderson, "The Black University: Towards Its Realization," in *Negro Digest*, March 1968, p. 23.
36. Gerald A. McWorter, "Struggle, Ideology and the Black University," *Negro Digest*, March 1968, p. 8.
37. Charles V. Hamilton, "The Place of the Black College in the Human Rights Struggle," *Negro Digest*, September 1967, p. 8.
38. Lea Redmond and Charles P. Henry, "The Roots of Black Studies," in James L. Conyers, Jr., (ed.), *Afrocentric Traditions* (New Brunswick, NJ: Transaction, 2005), p. 168. See also Ballard p. 65. The bulk of the remaining college protests were over the war in Vietnam.
39. Rodgers, pp. 2, 123.
40. Noliwe M. Rooks, *White Money/Black Power* (Boston: Beacon, 2006), p. 36.
41. Rodgers, p. 85.
42. Ibid., p. 114.
43. Ballard, *Op. Cit.*, p. 52.
44. Biondi, *Op. Cit.*, pp. 126, 134.
45. Carmichael, *Op. Cit.*, p. 127.
46. Ibid., p. 129. See Henry, *Ralph Bunche*, Chap. 4 and Jonathan Scott Holloway, *Confronting the Veil* (Chapel Hill, NC: University of North Carolina Press, 2002) on Black scholars at Howard.

47. Rodgers, p. 120.
48. Harold Cruse in Armstead L. Robinson, et al., (eds.), *Black Studies in the University* (New Haven: Yale University Press, 1969), p. 4.
49. Maulana Karenga in Robinson, p. 37, and Gerald McWorter in Robinson, p. 56.
50. McGeorge Bundy in Robinson, p. 173.
51. Ibid.
52. David Brion Davis in Robinson, p. 219. In part as a result of the Black Studies movement, the political origins of the university have become more manifest. See, for example, Gray Brechin's *Imperial San Francisco* (Berkeley: University of California Press, 1999) on the political history of Stanford and the University of California.
53. Bayard Rustin, et al., *Black Studies: Myths & Realities* (New York: A. Philip Randolph Educational Fund, September, 1969), pp. 6–7.
54. Martin Kilson, Ibid. p. 11.
55. Andrew Brimmer, Ibid. p. 41, Hill, p. 44.
56. C. Vann Woodward, Ibid. p. 20.
57. Peniel E. Joseph, "Black Studies, Student Activism, and the Black Power Movement," *Journal of African American History*, Vol. 88, No. 2, (Spring, 2003), p. 188. See also Murch.
58. Newsweek cover. At Howard University's commencement in June 1965, President Johnson delivered one of the most remarkable speeches on race of any American president. On the one hand, he called for equality of results and not just opportunity, while on the other hand he cited the failure of Negro family life. See Taylor Branch, *At Canaan's Edge* (New York: Simon & Schuster, 2006), pp. 232–234.
59. Charles P. Henry, "An Event-Oriented Approach to the Civil Rights Movement," (University of Chicago: PhD dissertation, 1974).
60. Taylor Branch, *At Canaan's Edge*, p. 489. Carmichael and other members of SNCC who worked with the Mississippi Freedom Democratic Party (MFDP) at the 1964 Democratic National Convention had been seriously disillusioned with the moral approach to politics when many of their liberal friends reluctantly supported President Johnson's refusal to seat the MFDP delegates offering a token compromise instead. They vowed to pursue Black power as a result. See Taylor Branch, *Pillar of Fire* (New York:

Simon & Schuster, 1998), pp. 468–476 and Carmichael, pp. 437–438.

61. Harry Edwards, *The Struggle That Must Be* (New York: Macmillan, 1980), p. 148.
62. Jonathan B. Fenderson and Candace Katungi, "Committed to Institution Building," *Journal of African American Studies*, (2012), Vol. 16, p. 128. The struggle over Black Studies at Cornell was life-changing experience for a number of scholars who were there. Not only were Edwards and Turner present but also Alan Bloom, Thomas Sowell, and Theodore Lowi. The latter three saw it as a very negative experience that changed their view of liberal education. See Bloom's *The Closing of the American Mind*, Sowell's *Black Education: Myths and Tragedies*, and Lowi's *The Politics of Disorder.*
63. Ibid., p. 155.
64. Ibid., p. 155.
65. Martin Luther King, Jr., in Washington, pp. 245–246.
66. Joyce A. Joyce, *Black Studies as Human Studies* (Albany, NY: State University of New York Press, 2005), p. 145.
67. Alain Locke in Johnny Washington, *Alain Locke and Philosophy* (Westport, CT: Greenwood, 1986), p. 45.
68. Ibid. p. 46. See Will Kymlicka, *Multicultural Citizenship* (New York: Oxford University Press, 1995) for a more recent discussion.
69. See Andrew M. Platt, *E. Franklin Frazier Reconsidered* (New Brunswick, NJ: Rutgers University Press, 1991), p. 66. Platt reports that 80 percent of all Black PhDs were employed at Howard, Atlanta, or Fisk in 1936.
70. E. Franklin Frazier in Joyce A. Ladner, (ed.), *The Death of White Sociology* (New York: Vintage, 1973), pp. 63–65.
71. Platt, pp. 163, 167, 128. Of course, Frazier's work becomes the foundation for the "culture of pathology" model of Black life. Frazier condemns Black intellectuals for not recognizing the "mark of oppression" on the Negroes' condition and suggests that the reason for the oversight is the intellectuals' own unconscious victimization of by these experiences. See E. Franklin Frazier, "The Failure of the Negro Intellectual" in Ladner, p. 58.
72. John Hope Franklin, "The Dilemma of the American Negro Scholar," in Herbert Hill, (ed.) *Soon, One Morning* (New York:

Knopf, 1963), p. 70. Franklin does not mention the White scholars who served as gatekeepers controlling the flow of research funds in the area of "Negro research." The most notorious case involved the Carnegie Foundation's funding of the project that became *An American Dilemma*. Social scientists Melville Herskovits and Donald Young recommended Gunnar Myrdal rather than any of the Black scholars who had made proposals of such a study for years. See Henry, *Ralph Bunche*, pp. 91–92.

73. Franklin, p. 70.
74. G. Stanley Hall quoted in Winston, p. 685.
75. Winston, *Op. Cit.*, p. 701.
76. While I believe I am correct in assuming most college students were not aware of Cruse's earlier work, it should be noted that his 1962 article, "Revolutionary Nationalism and the Afro American," in *Studies on the Left* did influence militant students in the early 1960s. For example, two Ohio-based college students, Donald Freeman and Max Stanford, who formed the Reform Action Movement (later the Revolutionary Action Movement), were in part inspired by Cruse's essay. See Joseph, *Op. Cit.*, p. 188.
77. Richard Wright quoted in Peniel E. Joseph, "Dashikis and Democracy," *Journal of African American History,* Vol. 88, No. 2., p. 184. I distinctly remember reading David Cronin's *Black Moses*, the only published biography of Garvey. It portrayed Garvey as a slightly corrupt dreamer detached from reality.
78. Carol Polsgrove, *Divided Minds* (New York: Norton, 2001), pp. 43–44.
79. See Mary Dudziak, *Cold War Civil Rights* (Princeton, Princeton University Press, 2000) and Penny Von Eschen, *Race Against Empire* (Ithaca, NY: Cornell University Press, 1997).
80. Cruse pp. 147–170.
81. Ibid. p. 14. Cruse was greatly influenced by the work of sociologists C. Wright Mills and his work *The Power Elite* as well as Milton Gordon and his work *Assimilation in American Life.*
82. Allen, pp. 171–182. Stokely Carmichael and Charles V. Hamiltons' *Black Power* has also been criticized for using revolutionary rhetoric to hide what is essentially ethnic group model of reformist politics.
83. Jerry Watts, (ed.), *Harold Cruse's The Crisis of the Negro Intellectual Reconsidered* (New York: Routledge, 2004), pp. 301–311.

84. Perry A. Hall, *In the Vineyard* (Knoxville, TN: University of Tennessee Press, 1999), p. 34.
85. See Gayraud S. Wilmore, *Black Religion and Black Radicalism* (Maryknoll, NY: Orbis Books, 1986); Winthrop D. Jordon, *White Over Black* (New York: Norton, 1968); Leon A. Higginbotham, *In the Matter of Color* (New York: Oxford University Press, 1978), and David Brion Davis, *Inhuman Bondage* (New York: Oxford University Press, 2006).
86. See Scott L. Malcomson, *One Drop of* Blood (New York: Farrar Straus Giroux, 2000); Banton, Wilson Jeremiah Moses, *The Golden Age of Black Nationalism, 1850–1925* (New York: Oxford University Press, 1978); Lee D. Baker, *From Savage to Negro* (Berkeley: University of California Press, 1998); and Charles Mills, *Blackness Visible* (Ithaca, NY: Cornell University Press, 1998).
87. Stanford M. Lyman, "Race Relations as Social Process," in Herbert Hill and James E. Jones, (eds.), *Race in America* (Madison: University of Wisconsin Press, 1993), p. 388.
88. See Walter Jackson, *Gunnar Myrdal and America's Conscience* (Chapel Hill, University of North Carolina Press, 1990) and David W. Southern, *Gunnar Myrdal and Black-White Relations* (Baton Rouge, LA: Louisiana State University Press, 1987).
89. Lyman, p. 391.
90. Robert L. Allen, "Politics of the Attack on Black Studies," *Black Scholar*, Vol. 6, No. 1, September 1974, pp. 2–7.
91. Manning Marable, "Black Studies and the Racial Mountain," *Souls*, Summer 2000, pp. 17–36.
92. James Banks in James B. Stewart, *Flight in Search of Vision* (Trenton, NJ: Africa World Press, 2004), pp. 294–297.
93. Martin Kilson, "Thinking About Black Intellectuals," forthcoming, p. 57.
94. Mario L. Small, "Department Conditions and the Emergence of New Disciplines," *Theory and Society*, Vol. 28, No. 5, October 1999, pp. 659–708.
95. See, for example, Claudia Kalb and Mark Starr, "Up From Mediocrity," *Newsweek*, February 19, 1996, p. 64.
96. Ibid.
97. Ibid.

CHAPTER 3

Institutionalizing Black Studies at the University of California

In September 1984, Berkeley historian and Ethnic Studies professor Ron Takaki led a successful effort to create the first comparative Ethnic Studies Ph.D. program in the United States. The African American Studies (AAS) department joined the Ethnic Studies department in supporting the Ethnic Studies Graduate Group, and I served as chair of the executive committee overseeing the program. Graduate students entering the program were required to study two of the four minority groups (African American, Asian American, Chicano/a, and Native American) as they matriculated. While several African American students completed the program, most of the inquiries received by the AAS department indicated a strong student interest in pursuing a doctorate solely in AAS. Of course, this was around the time that Temple University under the leadership of Molefi Asante had succeeded in establishing the nation's first doctorate in Black Studies. That Berkeley's first doctorate in the field was in Ethnic Studies while Temple's was in AAS was a reflection of the units' histories and locations. Berkeley's African American and Ethnic Studies departments were products of the Third World Liberation Front (TWLF), which comprised student activists of color. Temple's department was established primarily through the actions of Black student activists. Consequently, Berkeley has had a pioneering Ethnic Studies department while Temple does not have an Ethnic Studies department or program, but has a pioneering AAS department.

In announcing the doctoral program, Takaki, the principal architect and graduate adviser for the program, said three years ago he was not certain

C.P. Henry, *Black Studies and the Democratization of American Higher Education*, DOI 10.1007/978-3-319-35089-9_3

the university would view ethnic studies "as a valid academic subject suitable for a graduate study."[1] However, he was delighted that the university speedily approved the program, and eight students were accepted in the first class. One of the new students who received her undergraduate degree from Brown University noted that it was difficult to study Asian American history at Brown, and students had to put their own classes together. She said: "In the Ivy League there's a hole in ethnic studies. Part of it is geographical: the percentage of Asians in Massachusetts or Rhode Island is a lot smaller than here. Nowhere is there a concentrated Third World focus."[2] Another Ivy Leaguer stated at Berkeley that "we have a whole Native American studies program…you know how many courses in Native American Studies we have at Harvard? Two."[3]

The histories of these two pioneering graduate programs emphasize the importance of geographical location and demographic composition in influencing the development of AAS and more broadly Ethnic Studies. These factors, as well as funding, played a crucial rule in the evolution of Black Studies. After all, the student demands were uniformly the same; however, the shape that Black Studies took on college campuses varied significantly.

Two recent books have helped revive the debate over the influence of external funding—specifically from the Ford Foundation—in the historic development of Black Studies. Noliwe M. Rooks in *White Money/ Black Power* contends that Ford's decision to fund Black Studies units with an "integrationist" or racial cooperation philosophy over "militant" or Black Nationalist oriented units was decisive in determining the direction of key Black Studies units. Specifically, in 1969, under the direction of Ford president McGeorge Bundy and with the advice of economist Sir Arthur Lewis, Ford chose to promote a Yale model of Black Studies that resulted in programs drawing their faculty from traditional disciplines rather than autonomous departments in control of their own full-time equivalent (FTE) faculty. From 1968 to 1972, Ford invested some ten million dollars in support of two dozen programs at elite institutions that adopted the Yale model of an interdisciplinary program. Later, Ford would invest another ten million dollars in support of graduate programs in Black Studies again at elite schools.[4]

Fabio Rojas in *From Black Power to Black Studies* challenges Rooks's position on the determinative influence of Ford funding. He argues that Ford Foundation funding was too episodic and inconsistent to have an impact across an entire discipline. In fact, from 1970 to 1980, Ford made no grants to Black Studies units. In total, says Rojas, Ford made grants to about 14 percent or 1 in 7 of approximately 120 Black Studies degree programs. The determinative factor for survival for Rojas is whether Black Studies programs "resonated with the culture of higher education," not whether they received or were influenced by Ford funding. "Other forms of black studies—such as inner-city studies or nationalist Black Studies—failed," says Rojas, "because they were incompatible with the beliefs of what constituted legitimate teaching and research."[5]

An example of the tricky terrain Black Studies had to negotiate between structure, location, ideology, and autonomy can be seen in the rise and demise of the Institute for the Black World (IBW) in Atlanta. Originally called the Du Bois Institute and housed in Du Bois's old home at the edge of the Atlanta University (AU) campus, the IBW was a Black Studies–oriented research institute (Black think tank) that sought support from both AU and the King Center. However, IBW's attempt to influence the development of Black Studies at AU quickly soured when student protesters for a "Black University" at AU detained Morehouse Board members Martin Luther King, Sr. and Benjamin Mays and involved two IBW staff members. In addition, the published work of Harding and others at the Institute promoting a "Black University" led AU officials to distance themselves from the IBW. The Ford Foundation rewarded this action by awarding a $315,000 grant to the AU Center (a five-college consortium) to establish a graduate program under the direction of AU literary scholar Richard Long.[6]

Harding, who had a personal relationship with the King family, believed the King Center would provide a more independent source of funding and support for the IBW than the university. However, as the IBW sought to expand its activities and funding for both the IBW and the Center proved to be less than expected, relations between the two began to deteriorate. Perhaps even more important than the structural relationship was the ideological division between the two entities. Although Harding had defined the Institute's ideology as one of "pragmatic nationalism," the King Center board members saw themselves as protecting King's legacy of integration and nonviolence. The conflict came to a head when the IBW invited Stokely Carmichael to speak in Atlanta shortly after his return from a 14-month residence in Africa. When King Center officials sought to limit the IBW's autonomy, believing that it tarnished King's legacy, the IBW was forced to sever the relationship.[7] The IBW experience demonstrated the difficulty that Black Studies–oriented research organizations had in obtaining support from entities off campus and how difficult it was to achieve autonomy on campus.

Of course, both Rooks and Rojas could be right. Ford promoted the Yale model and that model of an interdisciplinary program rather than a department might be the acceptable form of institutionalization in the culture of higher education. To test this proposition, this work offers a case study of the development of three Black Studies units in the same university system—the University of California. This has the advantage of comparing units that draw primarily on the same student demographic of high school seniors from the state of California who are UC-eligible (top 12 percent). Moreover, two of the three units examined received significant Ford Foundation funding. The three units are the Center for African American Studies (CAAS) at the University of California, Los Angeles (UCLA); the Center for Black Studies (CBS) and the Department of Black Studies at University of California, Santa Barbara (UCSB); and the Department of African American Studies at the UC B.

In analyzing these three units conceptually, two studies are particularly useful. Ama Mazama in “Interdisciplinary, Transdisciplinary, or Unidisciplinary?” contends that new disciplines face two contradictory requirements. In the first place they must differentiate themselves from existing fields. That is, they must identify and demarcate a space or turf in the academic world. For example, anthropology and sociology have engaged in such boundary disputes for decades sometimes finding themselves in the same department and sometimes resulting in separate departments. Political science has historically debated whether its proper focus should be the study of formal governing structures or whether the more inclusive perspective of political behavior and psychology should be incorporated. In fact, some prominent institutions—Harvard and the University of Virginia, for example—still have departments of government rather than political science. This kind of boundary work has generally been more determined by methodology or theory than by subject matter. However, says Mazama, Black Studies is still under attack, in part because it is differentiated by the subject matter of race rather than method.[8]

The contradiction emerges because while new disciplines must differentiate themselves, they must not be so different that they fail to conform to both formal and informal academic norms. They must be legitimized within the academy. They, in turn, may legitimize or credential their graduates. This interplay of differentiation and conformity is the delicate tightrope all new disciplines face.

Perhaps the most controversial study of its kind was Harvard scholar Nathan Huggins's report on the status of Black Studies in 1982. Coming roughly a decade after the peak of Black Studies creation and funded by Ford, the study focused on six campuses and was widely viewed as an evaluation of the field itself. In the report, Huggins privileges the interdisciplinary program model and the research center because both seemed "best suited to ensure the legitimization of the field through the production of new knowledge and by maintaining contact and relationships with established disciplines."[9] He believed the integration and transformation of traditional disciplines, not the creation of a new discipline, was the fundamental goal of Black Studies.

This fundamental goal would appear to be immune to local influence or context. In discussing student demands in the late 1960s Huggins states that "the remedies they seized were 'in the air' rather than derived from specific needs in particular circumstances. I am persuaded in this by the near-uniformity of the demands nationally and by the adamantly collective character of the protest; there was little if any individual refinement or qualification." These concerns were summarized by Huggins as (1) the political need for turf and a place, (2) the psychological need for identity, and (3) the academic need for recognition.[10]

How those demands were implemented on each campus was significantly different. As Sociologist Mario Small has noted, the local institutional arena is the first site of contestation.[11] Moreover, the initial demands were almost always for a Department of Black Studies contrary to Huggins's stated preference. This chapter suggests that Huggins overemphasized the need for legitimacy to the exclusion of place and identity needs. And it is in these latter two categories that Black Studies innovation (differentiation) has emerged.

Black Studies at UCB

Ron Takaki asking me to chair the first Ethnic Studies Graduate Group was no accident nor was it based on any outstanding knowledge of Ethnic Studies on my part. Takaki was aware that in the more than a decade history of Ethnic Studies and AAS at Berkeley, the two departments had engaged in few, if any, joint undertakings despite the rhetoric around the TWLF a decade and a half earlier. Moreover, without the support of the AAS department the administration was likely to play off the two departments against each other perhaps claiming that they could not fund two separate graduate programs and that therefore they would not fund any. It was good strategy then for the AAS department to support in a visible way the creation of an Ethnic Studies doctorate. In return, Ethnic Studies agreed to support our demand for a doctorate program at some point in the future.

The unity behind the Ethnic Studies Graduate Group was a major step toward healing a breach that occurred when AAS decided to enter the College of Letters and Science in 1974 and abandon the idea of a Third World College. When I arrived on campus in 1981 it was clear that there was still some latent animosity around our department's decision, especially among older students. In addition, the fact that our department was in a different college than Ethnic Studies, which reported directly to the Vice-Chancellor, made it difficult to offer joint courses. Carlos Munoz in Chicano Studies and I, for example, proposed a joint course on social movements. However, when we discovered all the administrative hurdles we would have to overcome, we abandoned the project. We did, however, write a joint article on Black and Chicano political coalitions,[12] which we later discovered was the first coauthored work to come from the two departments.

That Takaki was surprised by the university's relatively rapid approval of the Ph.D. proposal is a testament to the status both departments had achieved by the time of my arrival. At one level it is confirmation of Rojas's assertion that the elimination of the most radical elements of the Black Studies movement had to be purged for Black Studies units to gain legitimacy. On another level, the fact that the Ethnic Studies and AAS faculties would now administer their own doctoral programs—reproduce themselves—was assurance that both units had achieved an important permanence. At the outset, none of these developments could have been predicted.

Black Studies at Cal might be said to have formally begun with a course entitled "Social Analysis 139X" offered in the fall quarter of 1968. Although the course was initiated by students, it was cosponsored by four faculty—Edward Sampson, Janas Langer, Jan Dizard, and Troy Duster—the focal point of attention was a guest lecturer, Black Panther leader Eldridge Cleaver. Duster, the only Black faculty sponsor, recalled that they were "trying to be a wedge for institutional change." Calling their action "institutional insurgency" he said, "[h]ere was the regional head – actually, the national head of the Black Panther Party, who had a voice about current political issues, which I thought needed to be heard, and the campus was one of the places where it could happen."[13] Governor Reagan and Cleaver publicly traded insults and F.B.I. director J. Edgar Hoover transcribed one of Cleaver's speeches attacking Reagan and had it anonymously mailed to school officials, clergymen, alumni associations, and Rotarians.[14] The university administration and the Board of Regents questioned both Cleaver's academic credentials and the amount of time he would be lecturing (half the course). As students began to enroll in the new course, they quickly instituted a new rule stipulating that an Instructor could only have one guest lecturer per semester. Students responded by occupying and vandalizing a campus building for 16 hours. In the end, Cleaver delivered six lectures.[15]

The controversy over the course served to build support for the creation of a Black Studies department within an autonomous Third World College because it illustrated the intrusion of both the administration and regents in academic affairs. Rev. A. Cecil Williams at the California Negro Leadership Conference said, "it's a very sad day for the State of California when politics and politicians deem it necessary to infringe on the rights of the academic community."[16] The University's response to the "Cleaver course" seemed to underscore student demands for power over decision-making. This was the key demand in the efforts to institutionalize Black Studies at Cal.

In the wake of the assassination of Martin Luther King, Jr., in April 1968, the Afro-American Student Union (AASU) at the UCB submitted a "proposal for establishing a Black Studies program." After an opening statement detailing their alienation from the university and the irrelevance of a university education to the communities Black students come from, the proposal insists on a radical reform of education.

> It is important to note here that our proposal is not a product of reaction. We are well beyond reaction. We are addressing ourselves to a basic change of attitude. This change is primarily a product of self-discovery. A kind of self-discovery that has snatched our minds from the rank of a historically insignificant, persecuted, minority and placed us among the world's majority populace which is crying from one end of the earth to the other that "we are." We are decided that we alone can define ourselves, that we are beautiful despite the white negative concept of us, that we have a history, an art, and a culture that no race or nation can stamp out our "souls" no matter the intensity of this foolish effort.

> We must therefore ask with unrelenting insistence that our future education be radically reformed. We demand a program of "BLACK STUDIES," a program which will be of, by, and for black people. We demand that we be educated realistically; and that no form of education which attempts to lie to us, or otherwise mis-educate us will be accepted.[17]

The proposal then calls for the appointment of a Black Studies Coordinator who will report directly to the Chancellor. The primary goal of the Coordinator will be "establishing a Department of Afro-American Studies." Students had used Nathan Hare's document "A Conceptual Proposal for Black Studies" to help frame their call for an autonomous department.[18] Community outreach was also a significant part of the proposal that included provisions for experimental course development and course offerings available through Berkeley's university extension program.

The AASU submitted its proposal to Berkeley Chancellor Roger Heyns in April 1968, and Social Welfare professor Andrew Billingsly was named "Assistant Chancellor of Academic Affairs" with the charge of helping the AASU revise the proposal for review by the Academic Senate. In addition, the College of Letters and Science responded to student pressure by introducing five new Black Studies courses for the fall 1969 curriculum. By November 1969, Billingsley and the AASU in consultation with the Chancellor had agreed on a proposal outlining a four-year, degree-granting autonomous Department of Afro-American Studies that then went to the relevant committees of the Academic Senate for approval.

Berkeley's Black faculty, administrators, and graduate students supported the AASU proposal. However, some White faculty members with expertise on Africa or African Americans did not. They were insulted that they had not been consulted during the drafting of the AASU/Billingsley proposal and questioned the wisdom of establishing a Black Studies department. Historian Raymond Kent argued that the AASU did not speak for all Black students and that the failure to consult with relevant faculty was an assault on academic freedom. Fellow historian Kenneth Stampp agreed with Kent adding that the AASU did not "speak for Black intellectuals, the majority of black students, or the black community at large." Stampp recommended creating a "Center for the Study of Black History and Culture" headed by a distinguished Black scholar such as a Kenneth Clark or a John Hope Franklin (both of whom opposed Black Studies departments). Moreover, every member of the Center would have a [traditional] departmental affiliation rather than "building a ghetto on campus." Historian L. Perry Curtis called "Black" or "Afro-American Studies" semantically untenable because it blurred "all distinctions between African and American Negro cultures" violating "almost all canons of intellectual inquiry in an academic setting." Another faculty opponent, Woodrow Borah, believed that a Black Studies "group" composed of scholars of "recognized excellence" in "ordinary fields" would provide "one fairly effective check on the normal rootlessness of interdisciplinary programs and their tendency to confuse public policy with objective assessment and research." Concerning social upward mobility Borah concluded that "the needs of our society for people majoring in Black Studies will be limited to teachers, professional agitators, and certain specialized workers in social welfare."[19]

Given significant faculty opposition and the vocal resistance of segments of the tax-paying public, it is perhaps remarkable that the Executive Committee of the College of Letters and Science and the Committee on Educational Policy (CEP) approved the general concept of Afro-American or Black Studies in its November 5, 1968, report. The CEP was also aware that what happened at Berkeley would be closely watched and influence outcome on other campuses across the nation. The CEP could not agree, however, on the specific structure Black Studies should take.

Commenting on the student proposal the committee declared that

> [s]ome of the declared aims of Black Studies apparently resist such assimilation, perhaps decisively. We must squarely face the fact that some of the goals of Black Studies appear to be not only alien to but aggressively in conflict with basic principles of the University's current ideas and principles. The main conflict arises from the present opposition between the social and cultural needs Black Studies are intended to fulfill, and our current academic ideals of objectivity and free inquiry.[20]

In short, the committee believed the desire of Black Studies to strengthen Black students' self-esteem and sense of identity ran counter to academic objectivity citing Black reaction to the Moynihan report and William Styron's portrayal of Nat Turner as examples.

While the CEP recognized that a department would provide the "permanence and prestige necessary to recruit a first-rate permanent faculty on a national basis" and also have the ability to attract joint appointments with existing departments, it wanted some guarantee that such a unit would not limit its course material to that solely produced by Blacks or use courses to foster "aggressive black militancy and racism."[21] Duster framed the conflict as between Black students who wanted "community-based scholarship" and the university who wanted scholars with a track record of publications. Very few Black scholars met their criteria.[22] Consequently, on January 15, 1969, the Executive Committee of the College of Letters and Science unanimously approved a program in Afro-American Studies leading to the Bachelor of Arts (B.A.) to begin in September 1969. AASU members were outraged that a department had been rejected in favor of a program. In response, Dean of the College, Walter Knight, overruled the Executive Committee's decision and recommended a Black Studies department with two stipulations. First, there would be a six "man" implementing committee composed of a mandatory quota of three White members and no students. Second, the department would not be able to admit freshman students. The implementing committee excluded the AASU from its formal deliberations, and the Executive Committee eventually eliminated several key elements of the original proposal including community outreach and fieldwork, autonomy, and student input. The AASU and the TWLF rejected these changes, and a student strike was launched on January 22, 1969.[23]

California governor Ronald Reagan immediately responded to the strike by mobilizing the California National Guard. Meeting with the troops in Berkeley, he framed the strike as a struggle between primitives and the defenders of civilization.

> We are faced with the most evil enemy mankind has known in his long climb from the swamp to the stars. You are gathered here to further the kinds of plans that we have started and to make sure that the process in the six-thousand-year history of man, of pushing the jungle back, creating a clearing where men can live in peace and go about their business with some measure of safety for themselves and for their family. You are on the firing line for that at the local and at the international level. I commend you for it, and again pledge you the all out support that we can give you in achieving your purpose. Because of late the jungle has been creeping in again a little closer to our boundaries, the boundaries of those clearings that man has created over these centuries and these thousands of years. And so I wish you Godspeed and great success.[24]

George Napper, who worked for Billingsley at the time, insisted that while the administration's reaction to the proposal was a factor in calling for a strike, the most compelling reason was the strike that had begun at San Francisco State University some three months earlier. Napper states that "[t]he platform of the leadership at San Francisco brought into question the 'blackness' of the leadership of the black students at Berkeley. The production of an effective resistance tactic (work stoppage) for the ostensible purpose of acquiring a Black Studies Department was a convenient way to end all doubts on the questions of 'blackness' at Berkeley."[25] Thus, the strike reflected a long rivalry between Black students at the two universities in which Berkeley students were seen as "house Niggers" and San Francisco State students were labeled "field niggers."

The TWLF expanded the AASU demands to include the implementation of a Third World College. They believed the existing academic structures were designed to exclude new knowledge:

> [M]inority groups are no longer concerned simply about having more of their people as students or faculty members for the sake of conforming to some integrationist ethic, or to have more courses on issues and problems of their people to appease those who want to offer a wider variety of courses. While these are worthy and desirable goals on their own merits, the big issue before us is the particular way in which some substantial portion of these elements of concern can be brought together as an academic enterprise deliberately designed to focus on solving problems that have victimized Third World people, Third World communities in a way unencumbered by obstacles of tradition too characteristic of our educational institutions. While resistance to addressing these problems has certainly come from postures taken by influential members of the faculty, the main problem is historical and basically a structural one. That is, the existing colleges, department, schools and research institutes were conceived at another time in history to meet other needs. Thus there is a built-in resistance by design and inertia that mitigates against the incorporation of new perspectives, new content and the ability for the University to re-gear itself to come to grips with the problems of the times in a manner commensurate with its potential.[26]

It contended that the proposal was born of three primary factors. First, the systematic exclusion of minority groups from participation in higher education comparable to their distribution in the population. Second, the exclusion of minority group members from faculty and staff positions. Third, the exclusion of the cultural experience of minority groups from the academic and scholarly materials used in the university as teaching materials.[27]

Having dealt with the rationale the proposal then addresses mission. It rejects integration for integration's sake. That is, it rejects the notion that simply having more minority members on campus or information on minorities attached to more courses as adequate. "While these are worthy and desirable goals on their own merits," the proposal believes "the big issue before us is the particular way in which some substantial portion of these elements of concern can be brought together as an academic enterprise deliberately designed to focus on solving problems that have victimized Third World people, Third World communities in a way unencumbered by obstacles of tradition too characteristic of our educational institutions."[28] The authors of the proposal contend that the history and structure of the existing university create[] a "built-in resistance" to new perspectives, new content, and significant reform. In short, they would agree with Friere, Illich, Bourdieu, Passeron and others [that] "an educational institution's main role is to re-create the status order or class structure that already characterizes society."[29]

Envisioned within a College of Third World Studies or Ethnic Studies are four departments: Afro-American Studies, Chicano Studies, Asian Studies, and Native American Studies. In addition, this new college would house a new Institute on Race and Community Relations, which they said had already been approved, and Third World College extension programs. Within the Institute each of the four groups would have a center addressing the needs of their particular Third World community. Thus, the research conducted in each center would also involve a high level of community participation.

While it was not impossible for campus administrators to envision a separate college of Ethnic Studies, it was likely that demands around admission policy and community involvement were not acceptable. The proposal calls for equal participation of students and community leaders at all levels of the decision-making apparatus. Moreover, it states, "admission to the Third World College will be based primarily on their potential to learn as determined by the Third World College."[30] The curriculum and major requirements laid out in the proposal as well as the request for a specialized library are similar to what in fact was implemented. However, the university was unwilling to give up power over admissions or the decision-making process.

The proposal recognizes the difficulty of implementing its plan immediately and suggests an *interim* structure in which a Department of Third World Studies would be created and report directly to the Chancellor's Office until such time as a college structure was established. After an intense struggle of two months, the university agreed to institutionalize an Ethnic Studies department, and Troy Duster accepted the position as Chair of the Chancellor's advisory committee for the department in July 1969. By October, however, Duster had resigned his position saying the committee lacked the authority to implement goals. He wrote: "My strong impression during last year's fight over both Social Analysis 139X and the TWLF Strike is that the [Academic] Senate inner circle" unfortunately is "far less willing than the Senate at large to experiment."[31] He believed that Ethnic Studies is a "new educational development" and the climate in which it grows is important. Duster, while supportive of Black Studies, did not want to lead the department. He believed that "you needed people who were not already trained in a certain way of thinking. You needed to have an oppositional framework for those who were going to take these positions of leadership."[32]

In fact, this *interim* structure in the form of a Department of Ethnic Studies organized in 1970 became the permanent structure. Another shock occurred in 1972 when new Chancellor Albert Bowker dismissed Afro-American Studies coordinator Ron Lewis and replaced him with Educational Psychologist William Banks, a two-year member of the Afro-American Studies program. Banks had been fired by Lewis but, as the only ladder rank faculty member in the department, successfully appealed the lack of due process. The Chancellor cited Lewis's "failure to attract permanent full-time faculty and build a sound academic program" as the reasons for dismissal.[33] Bowker's action, however, violated the TWLF 1969 agreement that the Chancellor would seek participation by faculty, student, and community members before making such decisions. In addition, San Francisco Assemblyman, Willie Brown, and Berkeley Mayor Warren Widener and others protested Bowker's "plantation style" action. Widener suggested that Banks and Bowker were planning to move the program into the College of Letters and Science, which the administration quickly denied.[34] Black students launched a boycott of Banks and the Afro-American Studies program causing its enrollment to drop from 421 in fall 1971 to 93 in fall 1972.

Ironically, Banks had demanded that the university not cut Black Studies funding for five years and was given multiple faculty positions (FTE) as a condition of accepting the position of chair. Thus, Banks's demands guaranteed the survival of the unit at the very time students were abandoning it. Of course, part of the problem was student alliances with existing faculty. Banks had demanded that all the faculty and staff be fired and then agreed to rehire two faculty—Roy Thomas and Mohammed Hassan. This was possible because all of the faculty were lecturers with one-year appointments rather than tenure track faculty. Ron Lewis had been a supervisor of field work in the School of Social Welfare before his appointment as AAS coordinator, and no one in the program had a Ph.D. The conflict was heightened when a copy of Banks's agreement with the administration was leaked by a staff member. Banks used this period of intense conflict to hire a new group of highly credentialed permanent faculty including Reginald Jones (Ph.D., Ohio State), Henry Jackson (Ph.D., NYU), Albert Raboteau (Ph.D., Stanford), Aguibou Yansane (Ph.D., Yale), and Barbara Christian (Ph.D., Columbia and the university's first ladder rank Black woman). Christian was initially hired by the English department but moved her position to the AAS department after a year. Banks believed the department would succeed or fail on the research of its faculty rather than any grand design.

One transfer to the AAS department that did not occur was that of sociologist Harry Edwards. Edwards, as a result of his role in organizing a Black power protest at the Mexico City Olympic games and as a founder of the area of the sociology of sports, was perhaps the best-known Black professor at Berkeley. Nonetheless, as he recounts in his autobiography *The Struggle That Must Be*, he was encountering a great deal of difficulty in his relationship with the Sociology department at Berkeley. Consequently, when Edwards was approached in April 1974 by some students and faculty who were part of a search committee in the AAS department, he said he would be interested in transferring to the department. Shortly after he was told he was the department's choice for a tenured position, however, by September no offer had been received. When Edwards finally confronted the department he was told that there would not be a promotion to tenure and an office would not be immediately available. Then on October 12, 1974, the provost requested a meeting with him. "At the meeting," says Edwards, "he informed me that 'it would not be in the interest of your career at UC Berkeley to attempt to transfer to Afro-American studies… because a person of your prestige and academic achievement should not associate himself with a department like that.…Maybe in sixty years Afro-American Studies will be academically as creditable as, say P.E. or sociology'."[35] Of course, Edwards was astonished that he had been recruited by the department precisely because of his strong academic and teaching record, and the provost was telling him "that due to the very fact that I could meet these needs in that department, he would advise against my affiliation with it."[36] Edwards concluded that the administration did not want him in the AAS department because it would be the most difficult place from which to dislodge him. He went on to successfully fight a very public campaign to receive tenure in sociology.

Jones gives Banks credit for reforming the curriculum. "A lot of the courses had strange names," states Jones. "They were sort of like, the department was treated like a pork barrel where friends, people were brought in, literally off the street, teaching courses that didn't have any substance."[37] According to Jones, the chancellor at Berkeley helped recruit him from the University of California at Riverside saying they needed a Black scholar to counter the negative attention Berkeley was getting for having Arthur Jensen on its faculty.[38]

In fact, in 1974 Banks led the program into the Division of Social Science in the College of Letters and Science as the Department of Afro-American Studies (changed to African American Studies in 1991). This action had been recommended by the "Collins Report" that was the external periodic review that every academic unit receives at Berkeley. The other three programs decided to remain within the Department of Ethnic Studies reporting to the Chancellor's Office and continued to press for a College of Ethnic Studies until 2005 when the department also joined the Division of Social Science. These decisions were subject to intense debate within and between the four units throughout this period, and many saw the action as undermining any hopes of achieving a Third World College. Harold Cruse's *The Crisis of the Negro Intellectual* had influenced him the most, said Banks, because he was willing to criticize the Black movement. Following that independent spirit, Banks stated that ideally he would like to see a separate ethnic studies college but in the interim a place within the division was preferable to the department's current "limbo status."

According to Banks, his support of the Third World College concept was always less than wholehearted for two basic reasons. First, although there was a great deal of rhetoric around the TWLF, the reality was different. Each program had different needs and Banks found it difficult to form links to Ethnic Studies. He says, for example, that although Asian American Studies had the same fight over hiring community activists over scholars when Takaki was hired, they had different course needs. The early Asian American Studies curriculum had a disproportionate number of reading and composition courses when compared to AAS.[39]

The second reason for Banks's hesitation was his belief that the best course of action for the unit was to build a department equal to any other at Berkeley rather than act as a service center for the community. "What can a college sophomore offer the Black residents of East Oakland that will solve their problems" was the way Banks put it. The Nation of Islam had a presence on campus and the Berkeley Black Caucus often had committee meetings to discuss Black Studies at Berkeley. Banks did attend the meetings and developed some support among community activists.[40] The department was active in working with prison programs; however, its community imprint was slight compared to initial demands for Black Studies.

These two issues—entering Letters and Science and focusing on research and teaching over community activism—consumed most of the discourse around the unit in its early years. There were smaller conflicts around the hiring of a White professor, Gregg Thomson, to teach "Black Psychology" and the limited offerings on Africa. However, Thomson quickly proved his competence and most AAS faculty recognized the limited resources of the department in comparison to the great needs to cover Africa-related courses.

The success in creating an Ethnic Studies Graduate Group spurred activity to establish an AAS doctorate program. Although the department had talked about such a program for years, the idea lacked momentum. When I served as acting chair in 1987–88, I met with the graduate dean to ask what the formal requirements were. He said he had no idea since no such programs had been proposed during his tenure as dean. Fortunately, someone in his office with longer tenure did know and we finally had a list of the hurdles we faced.

During the 1989 academic year, AAS faculty and students engaged in a series of meetings and retreats aimed at laying out the mission and curriculum of the proposed program. It was decided that the program should reflect the research interests of the core faculty, which included significant expertise on the African Diaspora, especially the Caribbean, and already offered in a number of undergraduate courses. The student body was also changing. There was a significant increase in students from Africa and the Caribbean with an interest in the diaspora. African American students would be severely impacted by the prohibition of affirmative action at the University of California enacted first by the regents and then by the electorate in California in 1996. Moreover, the transnational focus reflected a desire to get back to the global interests of such scholars as Du Bois, Robeson, and Bunche as well as relate to the new work coming from scholars outside the United States. Planning for this ambitious proposal was greatly assisted by funding from the Ford Foundation. In

1989, AAS Chair Margaret Wilkerson was successful in approaching the Ford Foundation for the first of three major grants directed toward the graduate program, and Percy Hintzen was largely responsible for drafting the proposal. Ironically, as the department moved more toward a focus on the African Diaspora, it changed its name from Afro-American Studies to African American Studies in 1991.

The first grant proposal entitled "African Diaspora Studies, Multiculturalism, and Identity Construction: The Development of a Comprehensive Multidisciplinary Framework" had two primary components. The first involved the development of critical methodologies and analytical frameworks for AAS, particularly from an African Diasporian perspective. Central to this development was a series of forums, visiting lectureships, and conferences. The second component of the project involved the building and strengthening of networks within and without the university, as well as the allocation of support for scholarly resources on campus, technological, and otherwise. For example, AAS established a formal relationship with the British journal *Social Identities* and developed links to the University of Namibia, the University of Warwick, the University of the West Indies, the University of Western Ontario, and the University of Zimbabwe. From 1991 through 2000, Ford gave $685,000 to AAS at Berkeley.

On Du Bois's birthday in 1992, the AAS department formally submitted its Ph.D. proposal. After four years of struggle to overcome bureaucratic and financial obstacles, the proposal was approved in spring 1996 and the department welcomed its first graduate cohort of 14 students in fall 1997. The Ph.D. program was the third in the nation and the first to emphasize the African Diaspora.

Two other departmental milestones—the establishment of an American Cultures requirement and the hosting of the annual meeting of the National Council for Black Studies—are discussed in subsequent chapters.

In conclusion, Berkeley students did not get the College of Ethnic or Third World Studies that were a part of their original demands; however, reasonably stable and effective departments of Ethnic Studies and AAS did emerge. That AAS never underwent a crisis in which the very sustainability of the department such as those at Temple and Harvard experienced can be attributed in part to the outstanding leadership of several key faculty members who had campus-wide credibility. Banks built some early support among key faculty outside the department, and Barbara Christian, Margaret Wilkerson, and Reginald Jones provided strong leadership on campus and were respected scholars in their own fields. Moreover, Christian had originally been hired by the English department, and Wilkerson and Jones had joint appointments. Wilkerson cites the department's gender balance as contributing to its strength, and the role gender issues have had in the curriculum.[41] Later, during a period of the untimely deaths of Christian, Albert Johnson, and June Jordan, Professor Percy Hintzen provided stable leadership.

Ironically, the failure of the campus to meet the demand for a research center might have saved AAS from some of the tension and conflict created at UCLA and UCSB. The Department of African American Studies was the primary location for conferences, lecture series, public programs, the academic program, and research related to AAS. Only with another Ethnic Studies student protest in 2000 did the campus finally fund what became the Center for Race and Gender. Since its establishment both AAS and Ethnic Studies have been central to its administration.[42]

Black Studies at UCLA

The UCLA became the site of the most tragic eruption of those forces attempting to control Black Studies. Like many other campuses, UCLA had a program—the High Potential Program—designed to provide opportunities for Los Angeles area African American and Latino students with less than customary entrance requirements to gain access to higher education. During the 1968–69 school year, members from both US and the Black Panther Party (BPP) were taking preparatory and regular courses on the UCLA campus as members of the program. US was a leading cultural nationalist organization founded after the Watts uprising and led by Maulana Karenga who had B.A. and M.A. degrees in political science from UCLA.[43] The BPP was led by Huey Newton and Bobby Seale and both had been involved in promoting Black Studies as students at Merritt Community College in Oakland. The Panthers considered themselves revolutionary nationalists and were seeking to establish chapters in Southern California that US claimed as its "turf."

Complicating the problem was the fact that the ideological differences between the two organizations were exacerbated by differences in gang affiliations. Just as the Nation of Islam had found prisons fertile recruiting grounds, so too did the Panthers and US. For example, Alprentice ("Bunchy") Carter, a founder of the local L.A. Panthers, was with the Slauson gang, went to Soledad, became a Muslim, met BPP leader

Eldridge Cleaver, and joined the Panthers.[44] Huggins was also a student in the "High Potential Program."

By late 1968, the US–Panther rivalry had moved into the UCLA Black Student Union (BSU). The selection of the director of the forthcoming Black Studies program emerged as a particularly contentious issue as both groups sought to institutionalize their influence. The committee to select a director was composed of two members of the BSU Executive Committee, and representatives of the Chancellor's Office, the BSU community advisory board, and the faculty steering committee. US was seen as having the upper hand since Karenga and his associate Walter Bremond, executive director of the Black Congress, were members of the university community advisory committee on Black Studies. Earlier the community advisory board had set up a meeting with the Chancellor to promote Charles Thomas, a psychologist and the education director of the Watts Health Center, as its candidate for the position without getting adequate student input or representation. In fact, members of the BSU said they felt intimidated by US members at which point the Panthers offered to protect the students.[45] The BPP argued that Karenga had breached the students' right to self-determination and joined the BSU in setting up its own committee on Black Studies with Panther members John Huggins and Elaine Brown as members.[46]

A January 17, 1969, meeting in Campbell Hall convened to resolve these differences turned tragic just after the meeting adjourned. According to Bruce Tyler, Carter and Huggins were shot dead as they attempted to defend Elaine Brown who had been insulted and slapped. Eyewitnesses said the two Panthers were involved in a struggle with US member Harold Jones-Tawala who had been arguing with Brown. In response, Claude Hubert-Gaidi shot Carter and Huggins. Before he fell dead, Huggins apparently fired and wounded Larry Watani-Stiner. Shortly afterward, George Ali-Stiner and his brother Larry Watani-Stiner and Donald Hawkings-Stodi surrendered to the police after warrants were issued for their arrest. They were subsequently tried and convicted for conspiracy to commit murder and two counts of second-degree murder but the shooter, Hubert-Gaidi, and Jones-Tawala were never found.[47]

A number of historical accounts as well as the views of the Los Angeles district attorney and the official Panther position promote the theory that the murders were the result of a planned conspiracy by Karenga working with the government. However, this theory has a number of holes in it. First, Geronimo Pratt, who was Carter's head of security at the time, insisted that it was a spontaneous shoot-out. He stated the altercation with Huggins, Carter, and Tawala "caused one of the Panthers to pull out a gun, and which subsequently caused US members to pull out their guns to defend themselves."[48]

Second, according to Darthard Perry, a one-time Military Intelligence specialist who had infiltrated the BPP's Los Angeles chapter for the FBI, Claude Hubert and George and Larry Stiner were all FBI operatives who had infiltrated Karenga's organization and were instructed to assassinate Huggins and Carter. This account was confirmed by another FBI agent, M. Wesley Swearington, in 1995.[49] Finally, Karenga himself on hearing the news seemed distraught according to Amiri Baraka who was with Karenga in Harlem when he received the news. Komozi Woodard suggests Karenga was overcome with a "monstrous sense of dread" realizing that chaos would result and in the end the event precipitated the decline of both organizations.[50] The violence would also have long-lasting effects on the institutionalization of Black Studies at UCLA.

Robert Singleton, an acting assistant professor in the School of Business, agreed to serve as the interim or founding director for only a year because he wanted to return to his dissertation and finish his Ph.D. Before he took over he consulted with both Karenga and the Panthers to gain their consent and avoid any further conflict. Singleton had known Karenga when they were both undergraduates in the early 1960s at UCLA. He also had some connection with the Panthers that allayed their suspicions of him.[51]

The shooting had a chilling effect on the faculty and administration and took away some of the student momentum for the Black Studies. A faculty committee composed of Thomas Vreeland, Paul Bullock, June Moore, and Douglass Glasgow drafted the center proposal. However, the initial proposal had been put together by the education committee of the BSU during the spring of 1967. Virgil Roberts chaired the committee that included Art Frazier, Tim Ricks, and Michael Dawson. When they were writing the proposal the group received funds to travel to New York City to consult with Harold Cruse about creating a Center for the Study of Black Institutions. Although Roberts says that Cruse greatly influenced their thinking, it is not clear whether their initial proposal for a center rather than a department was his or their own creation. Roberts states:

> We thought the center might eventually become more than a department. The reason we didn't propose a department...we were really thinking about the center as being a vehicle to bring faculty to UCLA, and we really wanted

> them to be placed in departments throughout the university, as opposed to being isolated in a department that you could then cut off.[52]

Roberts also stated that by having an American cultures institute that would include all ethnic studies centers it would be more feasible politically. It is not clear from the interview with Roberts whether the education committee's proposal for a center rather than a department was responsible for their being officially excommunicated from the BSU. Roberts says: "there was a meeting (summer 1968) in which the BSU members said they felt that we were selling out to white folks and they were going to kill all of us."[53] Despite these threats, Roberts and his group worked closely with Singleton to implement the center proposal.

The UCLA Center for African American Studies (CAAS) was established as an Organized Research Unit (ORU) in 1969. The Center has as its mission the development of AAS through its five primary branches: research, academic programs, library, special projects, and publications. Given its status as an ORU, its formal function is to provide a supportive infrastructure for interdisciplinary research *complementary* to the academic goals of departments of instruction and research. The functions of an ORU are to facilitate research and research collaborations; disseminate research results through research conferences, meetings, and other activities; strengthen graduate and undergraduate education by providing students with training opportunities and access to facilities; seek extramural research funds; and carry out university and public service programs related to the ORU's research expertise. Such ORUs normally have a 15-year life span after which they are subject to administrative review and renewal. The Center for African American Studies and the other Ethnic Studies ORUs (Asian American, American Indian, and Chicano Studies) coordinate their activities through the Institute of American Cultures (established in 1972) and report directly to the Vice-Chancellor for Academic Affairs.

The ORU status of AAS and other Ethnic Studies at UCLA is neither due to any particular concept of intellectual or curriculum development nor due to the lack of core faculty in the relevant areas of interest. According to Robert Singleton, the structure of AAS is not the result of faculty opposition to departmental status for AAS but rather the Chancellor's preference for a center. ORUs as administrative creations do not require external approval, departments do. Consequently, the structure of CAAS is a product of political opposition not academic creativity.

Singleton reports that he was in favor of a department in 1969, but the chancellor's office had already convinced the students that a better choice was an "Organized Research Unit" (a Center or Institute), which he could launch without state-level approval. Governor Ronald Reagan was on the Board Regents and, Vice-Chancellor C.Z. Wilson claims, stood ready to decapitate anything that required approval at that level. The students were shell-shocked by the violence that seemed to accompany their every turn, so they agreed to a Center as a path of least resistance. For the short run, they were probably right. In the long run, I felt the department was a better choice. I went along with the Center idea, but only begrudgingly, said Singleton.[54]

A liberal history professor named Dr. Jere King moved an Academic Senate proposal for a department but could not get the votes needed. King's proposal was tied-in to an effort to keep all Ethnic Study Centers in Campbell Hall. The Chancellor's office had plans to move them to Royce Hall. The plan to move them from Campbell Hall served to solidify the four-student ethnic groups into a unified effort to keep the Centers where Bunchy Carter and John Huggins were killed. The unification of the four-student groups helped the four center directors make further demands. Unfortunately, says Singleton, we did not demand departments at that time, because we were not aware of Jere King's proposal. Had we known, we probably would have confronted the Regents openly and won many more demands, including Jere's department proposal.

There are also interdisciplinary degree programs (IDPs) that overlap and interact with the ORUs, but they report to a different administrative structure. The IDP known as the Afro-American Studies Program directs an undergraduate major with a required concentration in anthropology, economics, English, history, philosophy, political science, psychology, or sociology and a master's program in the same disciplines with the exception of economics. Some students elect to double major in the undergraduate program, combining Afro-American Studies with another field. The Afro-American Studies IDP reports to the Dean of Social Sciences, while CAAS reports to the Vice-Chancellor adding to the bureaucratic complexity.

This complex structure creates some problems for both units. Although CAAS has six FTEs, the decisions on who will fill the FTE are made by departments not by CAAS. Since departments control the FTE of their own faculty teaching in CAAS and CAAS's own FTE, the tendency of faculty is to identify more with the department than CAAS. Evidence of this is the difficulty CAAS has had in attracting faculty who will administer their research grants through CAAS rather than the department. There appear to be several reasons for this. One is departmental pressure to keep grants within the department. Another is faculty preference to associate themselves with established disciplines. However, a third and more telling reason is the inability of CAAS to provide much in the way of grant writing expertise and administration.

The inefficiency of CAAS in this regard is due to the extraordinary demands placed on it as an ORU. The initial proposal called for some ten programs, but Singleton found out later that most depended on him finding funds outside the university to implement them. In reality it attempts to perform many of the functions of a department including lecture series, conferences, community programs, a library that serves as a home for many African American students, and finally assisting the IDP in supporting the undergraduate and graduate teaching program. Given the small staff of CAAS this leaves little time for its main mission of knowledge creation and publication.

Perhaps the most visible manifestation of the administrative burdens born of the CAAS/IDP structure was the inability of the campus to fill the position of director for several years. Following Singleton's initial year, he was replaced by three codirectors—Douglass Glasgow, Henry McGee, and Reginald Alleyne, while a new search was launched. The chair of the search committee, Arthur Smith, Jr. (later Molefi Asante), ultimately took over as the director. However, Smith only stayed for two years before he moved to Temple University having been denied tenure at UCLA. Anthropologist Claudia Mitchell-Kernan, who served as director for thirteen years and was later Vice-Chancellor of the Graduate School, was quoted as saying the role of director of Afro-American Studies is "psychologically more difficult than being Vice-Chancellor."[55]

Faculty members Belinda Tucker and Eugene Grigsby each served a term as director of the Center before English professor Richard Yaborough assumed the directorship on an acting basis in 1996. After several failed searches, Sociologist Darnell Hunt was named permanent director in 2001. The lack of a permanent director probably accounts for the inactivity of the CAAS faculty advisory board over a period of years.

A second consequence of the CAAS/IDP structure is the tenuous connection between teaching and research. While those who teach in IDP are dedicated to their students, some faculty and staff report a sense of disconnection or even marginalization from the overall research and programming aspects of CAAS. This might be expected since those who are conducting research through the auspices of CAAS are not necessarily teaching in the IDP.

Related to this disconnection between the units is the lack of an explicit and coherent programmatic logic around which the undergraduate program is structured. While the offerings are rich and varied, they lack any particular organization rationale. Singleton states that "because as a center we could not really offer courses, what we wanted to do—and we never really did this—was to be able to simply request the funding for the courses other departments did not want to do, but that the faculty wanted to do."[56]

This is less of a problem for the graduate-level M.A. program.

It would be a mistake to assume that CAAS has not been productive over its forty-year existence. It has an impressive list of publications and has sponsored several important conferences. Two Ford Foundation grants—one for $312,000 in 1988 and another for $250,000 in 1999—have been instrumental in its success. However, these grants were for the Center and benefited primarily faculty and graduate work in interdisciplinary research rather than the undergraduate curriculum. For example, Ford-underwritten graduate student workshops on funding, research, and cross-cultural studies assisted graduate students in ways that had typically eluded them in their home departments.

Ultimately, the university-designed structure of an overarching institute, which houses similarly structured Ethnic Studies centers, could not be sustained. Asian American Studies, Chicano/a Studies, and AAS have now all achieved departmental status. Both Roberts and Singleton, two individuals central to the Center's creation, did not believe that "it has lived up to the vision of what we thought it could be and how it would operate."[57] Perhaps now, as a department, it can fulfill its initial goals and promise.

Black Studies at UC Santa Barbara

Like the AAS units at Berkeley and UCLA, Black Studies at Santa Barbara was the product of student protest. On October 14, 1968, 20 members of the BSU on the Santa Barbara campus seized control of the computer center in North Hall. Their demands included the development of a College of Black Studies with Black instructors, a graduate program in Afro-American Studies, Black Studies center, a library, an equal opportunity program, more Black staff and administrators, and a commission to investigate campus racism. The occupation ended nine and a half hours later when campus administrators promised to address the BSU concerns. Although the police were called to the scene, they took no action and the students received "suspended sentences" for their action.

The off-campus reaction was much less peaceful as Californians wrote to Chancellor Vernon Cheadle demanding more severe disciplinary measures. There was an overwhelmingly negative public reaction to the student demands with letter writers bemoaning the takeover of college campuses by "black savages," communists, and left-wing socialists. One member of the State legislature requested the names of the students involved in order to check the circumstances under which they were admitted while another legislator complained that student strikes were jeopardizing passage of a badly needed bond issue for higher education that fall.[58] Most of the backlash was directed at the students' methods rather than the content of their demands, which were given little attention.

Conflicts emerged on campus as well, particularly around who would implement any response. At UCSB discord quickly developed between Black students and the newly appointed chair of the Black Studies department. During the summer of 1969, a committee composed of Black students, faculty, and administrators met to recruit faculty and prepare a curriculum that might be offered in the fall quarter. The committee also included an advisory board for the department that included two community representatives as well as students, faculty, and administrators. Sethard Fisher, a newly appointed associate professor of sociology, was named as chair of the new department.

Less than a month after the fall semester began, student advisory board members and the BSU were demanding Fisher's removal. They charged him with a failure to work "in a cooperative spirit" and warned that the whole program was in danger of failing. Five faculty joined the chorus calling for resignation by submitting a petition charging the chair with "severely undermining the morale of both students and faculty connected with the department."[59] In an "open letter" Fisher defended himself stating that he disagreed with those demanding that the advisory board, staff, faculty, and teaching assistants only be Black. Moreover, he believed the advisory board was seeking too much influence in the department and cautioned that the department should neither become a political pork barrel nor breed anti-intellectualism.

Both the Chancellor and the Dean of the College of Letters and Science concluded that despite Fisher's hard work there was a real leadership issue.

Chancellor Cheadle created a Faculty Committee of Inquiry to sort out the various complaints against the chair and recommend solutions that would assure the vitality of the program. No Afro-American faculty was asked to join because, according to Cheadle, he was strongly advised that none would serve.

After a lengthy hearing on October 29, the Committee of Inquiry recommended that Fisher resign and his position be assumed by a three-man executive committee that had his support. The Chancellor agreed with the findings and Fisher resigned. The "Interim Trusteeship" assumed control on the condition that the students approve their appointment. Unfortunately, by the end of the year two of the three members had resigned.

At the root of the problem was a violation of autonomy and self-determination that had been fundamental to the struggle for Black Studies. The BSU called anything beyond the dismissal of Fisher unacceptable. They resented the recommendations of the all-White Committee of Inquiry appointed by the Chancellor and a trusteeship that placed decision-making for the department in the hands of outsiders. Some Black faculty challenged the Chancellor's assertion that no Black faculty would have volunteered to serve on the Inquiry Committee and prior to his decision they had proposed that UCSB's Black community elect members of the advisory board and executive committee once Fisher resigned. Their advice was ignored.

Given the instability around the Department of Black Studies it is not surprising that the CBS also had leadership problems. The Center had eight directors in its first eight years. This lack of leadership was undoubtedly one of the reasons CBS lost its status as an official ORU in 1975. It was not until the administration of noted theologian Charles Long from 1991 to 1996 that the Center received seed funding from the central administration. Even then, CBS leadership was unstable following Long's departure with two directors and three acting directors until 2004.

Given this instability and the lack of major grants similar to the Ford funding received by UCLA and Berkeley, the Center's ability to produce Black Studies research has been extremely limited. Perhaps CBS is best known nationally for its predoctoral dissertation fellows program. Since 1975, over 65 scholars from a wide variety of disciplines have benefited from the opportunity to advance their graduate training at Santa Barbara. The UCSB fellowship has been an important stepping stone in their careers, and many of them have made significant contributions to the field of Black Studies broadly defined. Several have gone on to hold positions at UCSB itself. However, this most successful of all the Center's programs has now been transferred to the Department of Black Studies. While this enables the fellows to better integrate their teaching experience on campus, it deprives the Center of its flagship program.

Now the Center's main functions appear to be the coordination of conferences such as the "Celebrating 30 Years of Ethnic Studies Research" conference in 2000, the "Legacy of Slavery" conference in 2001, and the "AfroGeeks" conference in 2004. In addition, the Center produces a number of public lectures of wide interest each academic year like the "food for thought" series. CBS also sponsors a visiting scholars/researchers program and publishes a journal—the *Journal of Haitian Studies.*

The publication of the *Journal of Haitian Studies* is a product of the research and teaching interests of the Center's then director Claudine Michel. Anthropologist Michel has made CBS one of the best-known centers for research on Haiti. However, the Haiti focus is also a sign of the Center's weakness. The research emphasis seems to shift which each new director and the Center has had many directors. Moreover, given the instability at the top, the role of the Center's faculty advisory board is constantly in flux. Each new director has to adjust to the advisory board and vice versa. In this context, the advisory board has been unusually active in comparison to other ORUs. Currently, the Center is headed by Asian American Studies professor Diane Fujina while Black Studies professor George Lipsitz serves as chair of the advisory board. Coincidently, Lipsitz is also editor of a new Center journal *Kalfou: A Journal of Comparative and Relational Ethnic Studies.*

With minimal staff, the Center is unable to offer effective grant-writing resources to campus faculty or effective grant administration. It has seldom pursued funding external to campus. Therefore, its initial mission of assisting faculty in pursuing and disseminating research has been frustrated. In fact, the Center for New Racial Studies established in 2003, directed by Sociologist Howard Winant and housed in the Institute for Social, Behavioral, and Economic Research, is likely to fulfill the goal that was originally envisioned for CBS.

The Department of Black Studies, unlike the Center, seems to be enjoying a resurgence. Initially with approximately ten FTEs, the department dropped to about half that number around 2004. At one point, central administration had to appoint a chair from outside the department. According to some faculty, the focus of the department has been teaching given the research mission of the Center. Yet without the department's involvement in helping to shape the research mission of the Center, both have faltered. In the last few years, however, the department has made several strategic hires and is now stronger than ever. Whether it can or wants to revive the research mission of CBS remains to be seen.

As the Ford Foundation study *Inclusive Scholarship* states the research center or institute has

> long been a means to encourage and support advanced scholarship in the social sciences and to a lesser degree, in the humanities. While some are unattached to a university, most major universities have been eager to house such centers because they are a source of prestige and serve as inducements to the best and most productive scholars, who, by means of the institute, can pursue advanced studies among colleagues of kindred interests and talents while sheltered to some extent from teaching obligations.[60]

As we have seen, Huggins privileges the AAS program and research center over the department because of his concern that the new field be linked to traditional departments to gain legitimacy. He believed the Institute of the Black World in Atlanta represented a successful model for the research center. Yet once the IBW severed its ties with the King Center and Ford reduced and then ended its funding, the IBW could not survive. The more common model is a center or institute attached to a major university. In 1968–69, the Ford Foundation funded the Urban Center at Columbia University. Ford reports that when the funds ran out in 1977 the center was allowed to expire having achieved nothing of an academic or scholarly character and having involved few of the university's faculty.[61]

Ford also funded research centers in Black Studies at Harvard, the University of Virginia, and UCLA. They report, however, that none has succeeded in establishing itself as an attractive and useful instrument to develop serious scholarship in the field. The report's authors posit several reasons: "(1) there are too few high-quality scholars in the field to support several competing centers; (2) ideology has tended to dominate some, weakening their appeal to some of the best scholars; (3) lack of capital funding has forced them all to rely on funds generated year by year on the generosity of a host institution."[62] They add that many such institutes rely on faculty-generated grants administered through the center; however, such external funding is generally scarce for Afro-American topics. Black Studies, for example, does not have a major source of government funds comparable to the National Science Foundation or the National Endowment for the Humanities.

Evidence from the University of California both supports and challenges these assumptions. The report cites no evidence of a lack of "high" quality scholars in the field. In fact, it mentions a number of well-known scholars at UCLA and the IBW who engage in research in the field. However, lacking a home department in AAS at UCLA these scholars chose to funnel their research grants through their home department rather than the understaffed and overburdened CAAS. At the IBW, the "Black power" ideology was what attracted Vincent Harding, William Strickland, Howard Dodson, Lerone Bennett, St. Clair Drake, and Sylvia Wynter to the institute. However, the IBW found it extremely difficult to find grants despite its stellar group of scholars. The experience of the University of California does support the assumption that a lack of capital funding has forced the centers at UCLA and UCSB to rely on year-to-year funding rather than build an endowment.

The more fundamental problem with the research center, however, is that it was asked to be far more than a producer of new knowledge. Center faculty and staff were asked to produce community programs, lecture series, libraries, and even help coordinate instruction. There was little expertise or time available to pursue research grants or administer them. While the CAAS structure was a product of political necessity at UCLA that no longer appears to be the case. At Santa Barbara, the Black Studies Center was originally envisioned as a complement to the Department of Black Studies. For some time the situation seemed the worst of both worlds. The research center was underfunded and attracted few scholars while the department seemed to concentrate on teaching producing little research. Berkeley appears to have faired the best. Its departmental structure permitted a few joint appointments, which helped with campus contacts. But it was also able to attract and help develop a group of respected scholars who were content with sole appointments in AAS.

To return to Huggins's initial demands during Black Studies' formative period both the Center model and the Yale model failed to produce the legitimization the Harvard scholar sought. With Ford funding and Harvard's reputation, the Du Bois Center on the Cambridge campus is perhaps the most successful of all Black Studies research centers attracting a wide array of talented scholars. Yet the Department of AAS has eclipsed the Center in its reputation and attraction to academic stars. The other research centers aided by Ford have largely failed at new knowledge production as acknowledged by Ford itself.

Huggins's belief that the interdisciplinary program provided the best path to academic legitimacy has also been challenged by our study and by subsequent Ford reports. The program at UCLA struggled to coordinate courses every year and lacked a coherent academic core. The departments of Black Studies/AAS at UCSB and UCB are able to offer required courses on a regular basis with their own faculty. In fact, the Yale model itself was not able to sustain its program status and the program at Yale became a department in 2000. All the leading Black Studies units in the nation, from Temple to Harvard, are departments.

Although Huggins proclaims "from an academic point of view, the 'program' approach has been the most successful," he does acknowledge that the great weakness of the program model "is its dependence for survival on the continued support and goodwill of others in the university."[63] Yet his quest for academic legitimacy led him to prefer the program over the department and to trust those very forces that had historically excluded African American students and scholars from the university. In doing so, Huggins downplays the other two demands of Black Studies advocates—the need for a place and the search for identity.

Without attention to these two demands the search for legitimacy occurs in a vacuum. The need for a place is essentially a demand for oppositional space. It was also initially a demand for inclusion of students who had not met traditional college admissions criteria. If one is only concerned with reforming traditional disciplines, as Huggins seems to be, then this demand is less important although it is unlikely that traditional disciplines will tenure scholars who seriously challenge orthodoxy. Of course, the initial demand at places such as Berkeley and San Francisco State was for autonomous schools of Ethnic Studies. While this happened to some extent at San Francisco State, it was not successful at Berkeley. Yet the establishment of a department with its own FTE permitted the development of the second great advantage of having your own space—the development of a graduate program. All units at research universities without Ph.D. programs are at a severe disadvantage. Graduate students not only provide intellectual stimulation in the classroom but, just as importantly, do the most tedious work in archives, labs, and survey research centers. Introductory and methods courses are often taught by graduate students freeing faculty to pursue their research and research-related courses.

Rojas contends that the university is one of the most difficult institutions to change in modern society. University practices are developed to facilitate research and teaching by autonomous scholars and any flagrant violation of these rules and disregard for the culture motivating them encourage investors, donors, patrons, and the state to withdraw their support.[64] Thus, it is not surprising that there was fierce resistance to bringing students or community members into the decision-making process. Black Studies has been no more successful in its community work than Schools of Education or Social Welfare. While the seeming abandonment of community work by Black Studies has been labeled by some as evidence of the cooptation of the original mission, others saw it as a gradual recognition of what Black Studies could do best. At Berkeley, Bil Banks justified the shift toward pedagogy and away from direct action as recognition "that the primary focus of the activity must be the intellectual growth of the student, not service to the community."[65] He believed that a corps of solidly trained and motivated college graduates would be of invaluable service to communities and societies at large. Barbara Christian saw this change as Black scholars increasingly realized that "ideas were weapons as much as community activity."[66]

However, the decentralization of the university also allows for the possibility of creating oppositional space. This decentralization works against the integration of traditional departments because these units are much like states in a federal system—they have state rights. But if you are successful in establishing your own space/state you also have rights. The most important right is duplicating yourself through the credentialing of Black Studies professionals. This legitimizing function has turned out to be the most important function of the departmental structure. As the number of graduate programs grows, the field will legitimize itself. As graduate students these nascent professionals free up and assist their professors to pursue new knowledge, and as faculty themselves they create new knowledge that further legitimizes the field. Of course the goal here is the establishment of a new field not the reform of a traditional discipline.

The second demand of Black Studies pioneers for relevant research relates to identity. Although courses meeting this demand have often been labeled as feel good courses, such labels could easily be applied to many of the courses that glorify Western civilization. As mentioned earlier, my first course on Africa as an undergraduate, for example, was taught from the perspective that colonization was good for Africa. While it is true that this view did not make me feel good, it is often not acknowledged that such views made those students descended from colonizing countries feel better about themselves and their ancestors. What is missing from this "feel good" critique of Black Studies is the notion of "oppositional consciousness." According to Jane

Mansbridge and Aldon Morris, "members of a group that others have traditionally treated as subordinate or deviant have an oppositional consciousness when they claim their previously subordinate identity as a positive identification, identify injustices done to their group, demand changes in the polity, economy, or society to rectify those injustices, and see other members of their group as sharing an interest in rectifying those injustices."[67] The "integrationist" model promoted by Huggins and Ford ignores if not suppresses this consciousness.

The importance of this search for identity cannot be overstated. It is responsible for the two most significant substantive developments in the field since its founding—the rise of Afrocentrism and the emergence of Black Women's Studies. While this is not the place to examine the circumstances under which they developed in the 1980s, it can be said the Afrocentrism helped spur the rise of Black Women's Studies. And while they are usually placed in opposition, they are both dominated by culturalism. According to Sunidata Keita Cha-Jua, they "both reject the European Enlightenment, repudiate posivitism [sic], share a belief in cultural relativism, and are preoccupied with discourse and issues of representation and identity."[68] In short, they emerge in oppositional spaces that focus on the identity and representation of Blacks. Historically, interdisciplinary programs and centers have provided no such space. The Yale model promoted by Huggins subtly or perhaps not so subtly shifts the emphasis from Black identity to the benefits diversity brings to White students.

This latter point is supported by Darlene Clark Hine's Ford Foundation report on Black Studies. She states that Black Studies now enjoys widespread administrative support on campuses not so much for its research as for its ability to attract dwindling numbers of Black students and faculty. That is, institutional expediency is a major motivation for external support of Black Studies. Yet Black Studies' more fundamental achievement as Noliwe Rooks argues is as a successful example of social justice, a means of multiracial democratic reform, (and) a harbinger of widespread institutional and cultural change in relation to race, integration, and desegregation at the postsecondary level.[69]

Notes

1. Edie Lau, "Ethnic Studies now gives doctorates," *The Daily Californian*, September 21, 1984, p. 3.
2. Ibid.

3. Ibid.
4. Noliwe M. Rooks, *White Money/Black Power*, (Boston: Beacon, 2006), pp. 77–78.
5. Fabio Rojas, *From Black Power to Black Studies*, (Baltimore: Johns Hopkins University Press, 2007), p. 13, 139.
6. Derrick E. White, "An Independent Approach to Black Studies," *Journal of African American Studies*, (2012), Volume 16, p. 76.
7. Ibid., p. 80. White distinguishes IBW's pragmatic nationalism from the cultural nationalism of Maulana Karenga, Amiri Baraka, and others and from the revolutionary nationalism of the Black Panthers. The former promotes a distinct aesthetic, sense of values, and communal ethos, while the latter is ideologically rigid. IBW had associates who reflected all of these schools of thought (p. 74).
8. Ama Mazama, "Interdisciplinary, Transdisciplinary, or Unidisciplinary?" in Molefi Kete Asante and Maulana Karenga, eds., *The Handbook of Black Studies*, (Thousand Oaks, CA: Sage, 2006), p. 4, 7.
9. Nathan Huggins in *Inclusive Scholarship: Developing Black Studies in the United States*, (New York: Ford Foundation, 2007), p. 5.
10. Ibid. pp. 4, 39.
11. Mario Small, "Departmental Conditions and the Emergence of New Disciplines," *Theory and Society*, 28: 659-7-7, 1999.
12. Charles P. Henry and Carlos Munoz, "The Rainbow Coalition in Four Big Cities," *PS: Political Science & Politics*, Summer 1986.
13. Troy Duster: An Oral History, ROHO, Bancroft Library, University of California, Berkeley, 2010, p. 92. Interview conducted by Nadine Wilmot in 2005.
14. Seth Rosenfeld, Subversives, (New York: Picador, 2012), p. 425.
15. Ula Taylor, "African American Studies at the University of California at Berkeley: A Historical Narrative," in Ronald Williams II, ed., *Forty and Counting*, (Berkeley: Department of African American Studies, 2010), p. 257.
16. Ibid.
17. Proposal for Establishing a Black Studies Program, Submitted to University of California by the Afro-American Student Union, Spring 1968, p. 3.
18. Taylor, Op. Cit., p. 257.
19. Karen Karlette Miller, "Black Studies in California Higher Education, 1965–1980," (University of California at Santa Barbara: unpublished Ph.D. dissertation, 1986), pp. 27–32.

20. Ibid. p. 48.
21. Ibid. p. 51.
22. Duster, Op. Cit., p. 92.
23. Taylor, Op. Cit., p. 258.
24. Rosenfeld, Op. Cit., p. 439.
25. George Napper, *Blacker Than Thou*, (Grand Rapids, MI: Eerdmans Publishing, 1973), p. 56.
26. Proposal for a Third World College, Winter 1969, pp. 4–5.
27. Proposal for a Third World College, Winter 1969, p. 4.
28. Ibid. pp. 4–5.
29. Quoted in Rojas, Op. Cit., p. xi.
30. Ibid. p. 10.
31. Taylor, Op. Cit., p. 259.
32. Duster, Op. Cit., p. 92.
33. Miller, Op. Cit., p. 100.
34. Ibid. p. 260.
35. Harry Edwards, *The Struggle That Must Be*, (New York: Macmillan, 1980), p. 288.
36. Ibid.
37. Reginald Jones: An Oral History, ROHO, Bancroft Library, University of California, Berkeley, 2010, p. 55.
38. Ibid., p. 54.
39. William Banks; An Oral History, ROHO, Bancroft Library, University of California, Berkeley, 2010, pp. 135–136.
40. Ibid. p. 161.
41. "Spring 2000 Departmental Retreat," Department of African American Studies, University of California at Berkeley, March 10, 2000, p. 83.
42. I (AAS) chaired the drafting committee for the Center for Race and Gender while Percy Hintzen (AAS) has served as acting director. Evelyn Glenn, professor of Ethnic Studies, has served as the director of the Center since its inception.
43. I first heard Karenga speak at the national convention of the Congress of Racial Equality in Columbus, Ohio, in 1968. He was on a platform with Muhammad Ali and Floyd Mckissick (CORE's new president) and "out talked" both of them. Most impressive for students like me was Karenga's ability to answer general questions with very specific answers. For example, when asked what constituted Black culture Karenga would deliver a number of specific

points. This was in great contrast to the confused answers students often received in the classroom. I would later get to know Karenga much better when I moved to California.

44. Gerald Horne, *Fire This Time: The Watts Uprising and the 1960s*, (New York: Da Capo Press, 1997), p. 197.
45. Virgil P. Roberts oral history interview conducted August 26, 1996, (UCLA-CAAS, BANC MSS 2002/134c), p. 42.
46. Scott Brown, *Fighting for US: Maulana Karenga, the US Organization, and Black Cultural Nationalism*, (New York: New York University Press, 2003), pp. 95–96.
47. Bruce Tyler, "Black Radicalism in Southern California, 1950–1982," (University of California at Los Angeles, unpublished Ph.D. dissertation, 1983), p. 358; Brown, p. 96.
48. Brown, p. 96.
49. Ward Churchill, "To Disrupt, Discredit and Destroy" in Kathleen Cleaver and George Katsiaficas, eds., *Liberation, Imagination, and the Black Panther Party*, (New York: Routledge, 2001), p. 93.
50. Komozi Woodard, *A nation within a nation: Amiri Baraka (Leroi Jones) & Black Power Politics*, (Chapel Hill, University of North Carolina Press, 1999) p. 120.
51. Robert Singleton interview conducted in 1999 (UCLA-CAAS, BANC MSS 2002/273C), pp. 168–171.
52. Roberts, Op. Cit., p. 81.
53. Ibid. p. 42.
54. Singleton, Op. Cit., pp. 208–9.
55. *Inclusive Scholarship*, Op. Cit., p. 202.
56. Singleton, Op Cit., p. 204.
57. Roberts, Op Cit., p. 99.
58. Miller, Op. Cit., p. 30.
59. Ibid. p. 93.
60. *Inclusive Scholarship*, Op. Cit., p. 58.
61. Ibid. p. 58.
62. Ibid. p. 61.
63. Ibid. p. 52.
64. Rojas, Op. Cit., p. 211.
65. Miller, Op. Cit., p. 139.
66. Ibid.

67. Jane Mansbridge and Aldon Morris, eds., *Oppositional Consciousness: The Subjective Roots of Social Protest*, (Chicago: University of Chicago Press, 2001), p. 1.
68. Sundiata Keita Cha-Jau, “Black Studies in the new millennium,” *Souls*, 2:3, Summer 2000, p. 46.
69. Rooks, Op. Cit., p. 8.

CHAPTER 4

The National Council for Black Studies

The first international meeting and 17th annual meeting of the National Council for Black Studies (NCBS) opened in the new Chinese-constructed national theater of Ghana in the summer of 1993. As president of the NCBS, I introduced our keynote speaker, the Minister of Education for Ghana. He gave an excellent presentation on the ties that bind African Americans with Africa and the plans for education in Ghana. Imagine my surprise when backstage after the talk he asked me for help in introducing "Afrocentric education" to Ghana! I asked him to repeat himself to make sure I heard him correctly. Yes, he explained, Ghana's universities still sent their final examinations to England for grading, and the campus bookstore at Legon was filled with British classics. Once I had recovered from the shock, I suggested he consult with some of the Afrocentric scholars present at the conference who had also served as consultants for school districts. The experience demonstrated that as poorly resourced and crisis-oriented as the NCBS was, we had nearly 20 years of experience in developing an alternative to the traditional curriculum taught not only in the United States but throughout the world.

Like many scholars charged with developing a Black Studies program, Bertha L. Maxwell, a professor in the School of Education at the University of North Carolina at Charlotte (UNCC) and a former administrator in the Charlotte-Mecklenburg School System, was faced with the question of academic legitimacy. Black students at UNCC led by Ben Chavis and others had generated the impetus for Black Studies during protests in 1969. Four years later the program was ready to be awarded degree-granting status by

C.P. Henry, *Black Studies and the Democratization of American Higher Education*, DOI 10.1007/978-3-319-35089-9_4

the university's governing board. As Mario Small demonstrates in his article "Departmental Conditions and the Emergence of New Disciplines," the endorsement of a program by an external accrediting agency is often a crucial factor in gaining approval.[1] Unfortunately, Maxwell discovered that such a validating body for Black Studies did not exist.[2]

Seeing the need for such an organization, Maxwell called for a conference in the spring of 1975 whose objective would be the formation of a national organization to evaluate and accredit Black Studies programs. While the announcement for the conference called it a "National Conference for the Southeastern United States," Maxwell consulted Nathan Hare of the *Black Scholar*, James Turner at Cornell, Ewart Guinier at Harvard, and Curtiss Porter at the University of Pittsburgh among others. Nick Aaron Ford, author of *Black Studies: Threat or Challenge?*, was the keynote speaker. Although attendance was far below expectations, the participants agreed on three challenges facing the new field: (1) ways and means must be identified by which they can be evaluated, (2) support was needed in identifying and describing models that were functioning in diverse institutions, and (3) support was needed in identifying and describing a communication network that would allow dissemination of information about these programs.[3] The group agreed to a follow-up meeting to form the NCBS.

This meeting was held from July 16 to 18, 1975, at the Educational Testing Service (ETS) in Princeton, New Jersey, and hosted by William U. Harris and Joseph H. Williams of ETS. Those attending included Carlos Brossard of Raleigh, North Carolina; William Pitts and William King of the University of Colorado at Boulder; Valerie Edmunson of Fayetteville State University; Andres Taylor of the University of the District of Columbia; Ron McMullen of Wesleyan University; Andrew Goodrich of the University of Maryland at College Park; Leonard Jeffries of the City University of New York; and Maxwell. Another group, meeting over several sessions with the founders, included Howard Taylor of Princeton University as well as Williams, Harris, and Pat Taylor of ETS.[4]

The ETS meeting put in place a plan to implement both a state model and a regional model of development. At a follow-up meeting held during the annual meeting of the Association for the Study of Afro-American Life and History (ASAALH) in Atlanta in October 1975, Joseph Russell of Indiana University, soon to become NCBS executive director, joined the group and plans were made for a November meeting in Boulder. In Boulder, Herman Hudson, Vice-Chancellor for Afro-American Affairs at

Indiana University, offered to host a constitutional convention for the NCBS and to host the national office.

On April 13, 1976, the constitutional convention began, and an executive board chaired by Maxwell with William King as vice-chair was created. "Academic Excellence and Social Responsibility" was adopted as the motto for the new group. At its first executive board meeting in July 1976 at ETS, the group began to plan for its first annual conference to be held at Ohio State University in February 1977 with William Nelson, Director of Black Studies, as host.

The founders of the NCBS envisioned a state and regional structure that would support the national office and vice versa. Much like Carter G. Woodson's ASAALH it was believed state and regional structures would provide more access for community members and nonacademics to be involved in Black Studies. Woodson's ASAALH represented a significant break with the original organization of Black intelligentsia, the American Negro Academy founded in 1897. Martin Kilson believed that this pioneering organization—established by Alexander Crummel and including the most educated Black scholars of the period—was forced to close in 1928 because it lacked the support of the Black masses. He attributes its failure to the organization's "high-knowledge mode of Black intelligentsia formation—a mode of solo-intellectual formation utilized by the mainstream White (WASP) intelligentsia" that removed them from Black popular society realities.[5] While Du Bois was eventually able to break with this elitist mode, it was Woodson who organized Black intellectuals more broadly. Maxwell was a former school teacher, principal, and school superintendent who saw the NCBS as a resource and clearinghouse for K-12 as well as institutions of higher education. Therefore, the organization's constitution designated 11 regions with large states having the option of joining a region or forming a separate state organization of the NCBS. A local area such as the San Francisco Bay Area might also become a part of the NCBS. There were regional, state, and at-large representatives on the executive board. A person could join the organization as an individual member or as a member of a group with organizational or institutional membership such as a church, college, high school, or professional society.[6]

As a result of this federal structure the annual meetings of the NCBS took on a more local flavor of the host city rather than the typical meetings of academic groups. Maxwell, unlike Woodson, did not attempt to dominate the organization, which permitted leadership to flow from a number of sources. Ironically, though the origins of the NCBS like the ASAALH were in the South, the early strength of the NCBS was in the Midwest. Moreover, it revolved primarily around large public universities rather than historically Black colleges and universities (HBCUs) or private elite schools. However, it was not the NCBS but rather the African Heritage Studies Association (AHSA) that would be the first collective voice of professional academic to promote "Afrocentric" education.

As Black power led to the formation of autonomous or semiautonomous Black controlled groups in every sphere of social and political life from church associations to Congress, Black intellectuals were no exception. Among the first of these organizations was the African Heritage Study Association (AHSA), which grew from the discontent of Black members of the African Studies Association (ASA) that had been established in 1957. Although the formation of Black caucuses and/or independent Black organizations would occur in all the traditional social science and humanities disciplines in the late 1960s and early 1970s, the conflict within ASA had particular relevance. First, the formation of the ASA was relatively recent as compared to the traditional disciplines. Moreover, its scope reached across disciplines to focus on a region rather than a single discipline. Second, a majority of its 2000 members, including the leadership positions, were composed of Whites. Third, although the organization claimed to want to protect its "scholarly objectivity" from the political currents of the time, ASA worked closed with government agencies and benefited from increased government attention to the continent. Finally, the subject matter of the scholars of the ASA dealt directly with the identity of a people currently engaged in a freedom struggle both in the United States and in Africa.

At the annual meeting of the ASA in Los Angeles in 1968, a Black caucus was convened by Dr. P. Chike Onuwauchi, an anthropologist from Fisk University. Believing the ASA needed to participate in conferences in Africa and engage the Black community in the United States as well, the Black caucus charged that too few Africans and African Americans were included in ASAs work. The organization responded by convening a Committee on Afro-American Issues that was to report to the 1969 annual meeting in Montreal. In the meantime, a group of scholars formed a separate organization, the AHSA, in the spring of 1969, although as John Henrik Clarke stated, it was not the original intent of the Black caucus to leave the ASA.

When the 12th annual meeting cohosted by the Canadian African Studies Association convened in October of 1969 with over 3000 participants,

Black delegates made a number of demands including equal membership of Blacks on the board of directors and adoption of a pan-Africanist or Afrocentric perspective on African scholarship. As Clarke explained, "This perspective defines that all black people are African people and rejects the division of African peoples by geographical locations based on colonialist spheres of influence."[7] These demands and others calling for material support for the liberation movements in southern Africa were ultimately defeated. As a result, many Black Africanists left the ASA and joined the AHSA, which elected Clarke as its first president at its June 1969 annual meeting. ASHAs purpose was put forward as the "reconstruction of African history and cultural studies along *Afrocentric* lines while affecting an intellectual union among black scholars the world over."[8]

By way of contrast, the NCBS had none of the interracial tension of the AHSA founding, and its members were clearly committed to activist politics. The most visible leaders during this developmental phase were Joseph Russell, the executive director, and Herman Hudson, the National Advisory Chairperson, both from Indiana University. Their ability to leverage the resources of their university to support the national office of the NCBS meant that the locus of action was in Bloomington, not Charlotte, which was represented by Maxwell as chairperson and Beverly Ford as secretary. Of the ten regional coordinators in 1977, eight were from public state universities, one was from a community college, and one was from a private university. Only one regional representative was from the South (Kentucky). There were five at-large representatives with three coming from public state universities. None of the members of the executive committee, regional coordinators, or representatives at-large were from an HBCU.[9]

The desire to develop a regional structure sprang from the discipline's commitment to maintain contact with local Black communities. This objective was apparent at the regional caucuses meeting held at the third annual NCBS convention in Sacramento in March 1979. In his report on the regional caucuses the vice-chairperson, William Nelson, summarized the meeting. He said "[i]t is quite evident that a number of our most active members are concerned about the development of NCBS from the bottom-up as well as the top down."[10] He urged the holding of regional conferences that would further develop the regional structures and recruit new members. "Let us not forget that we are both <u>of</u> and <u>in</u> the community, whether we recognize it or not," said Nelson, "[o]ur programs did not spring from white demands for Black Studies; our fundamental goal ought to be to serve Black people wherever they are." Urging that Black Studies be defined as a process extending beyond the artificial boundaries of college campuses, he added that "[a]s we mobilize to serve our campus constituents, we must mobilize to serve our community constituents as well."[11]

Nelson practiced what he preached as he played a major role in the formation of the Ohio Consortium of Black Studies (OCBS) a year later. Holding its first annual conference at Kent State University, OCBS was composed of individuals representing 15 different institutions in the state with membership open to anyone or any group related to Black Studies. The Consortium explained its objective as an "attempt (1) to relate to the experiences, needs, and aspirations of Black people in the community; (2) to assist in developing solutions to community problems; and (3) to generate interaction and cooperation between Black Studies programs and community organizations."[12]

The first annual meeting of the NCBS was hosted by Nelson at Ohio State University, another strong leader from the Midwest. Nelson, a political scientist, was successful not only in obtaining support for the NCBS but also in recruiting one of the largest Black Studies faculties in the country. Ohio State was also notable for its community-based Black Studies extension center, and a panel on Black Studies and the Black community was included in the program. Participants in the annual meeting included Harold Cruse, James Turner, Tony Brown, Lerone Bennet, Jr., and Leon Damas. An NCBS tradition launched at this conference was the student essay contest for both graduate and undergraduate students. Nelson, who I had known as a fellow political scientist in the National Conference of Black Political Scientists, invited me to serve on the planning committee for the first annual meeting. As a result of my activity, I was asked to take over administration of the student essay contest and did so for a number of years and also asked to join the NCBS board of directors. In addition, I served as treasurer of the short-lived OCBS.

Like the national office, NCBS annual meetings generally reflect the ability of the host (usually the chair or director of a Black Studies unit) to leverage resources from their university to sponsor the annual meeting, albeit on a temporary rather than permanent basis. Often this is done with the support of other local academic institutions and a few community partners. Sponsorship would usually involve the use of campus meeting facilities. More recently, the annual meetings have been held at large hotels with their own meeting facilities. The national office assists the local host committee in dealing with the hotel and coordinating logistics and registration (Table 4.1).

Table 4.1 National Council for Black Studies Annual Meetings (Host Institutions and Coordinators)

1975	University of North Carolina at Charlotte (Bertha Maxwell) (Organizational Meeting)
1976	Indiana University (Herman Hudson) (Founding Meeting)
1977	Ohio State University (William Nelson) (First Annual Meeting)
1978	University of Massachusetts at Amherst (John Bracey)
1979	California State University at Sacramento (Otis Scott)
1980	University of Wisconsin at Milwaukee (Winston Van Horne)
1981	City College of University of New York (Leonard Jeffries)
1982	University of Illinois at Chicago (Gerald McWorter aka Abdul Alkalimat)
1983	University of California at Berkeley (Charles Henry)
1984	University of North Carolina (Bertha Maxwell)
1985	Cornell University (James Turner)
1986	Boston (New England Regional Conference)
1987	Ohio State University (William Nelson)
1988	Philadelphia (Molefi Asante, James Stewart, Jacqui Wade)
1989	Tennessee State University (Andrew Jackson)
1990	California State University at Northridge (Selase Williams)
1991	Georgia State University (Charles Jones)
1992	St. Louis University (Barbara Woods)
1993	University of Ghana at Legon (Selase Williams/William Little)
1994	University of Guyana (Percy Hintzen)
1995	University of California at Berkeley (Percy Hintzen)
1996	Gallaudet University
1997	South Africa
1998	Loyola Marymount University (John Davis)
1999	St. Louis University (summit meeting replaced conference)
2000	Georgia State University (Charles Jones)
2001	University of North Carolina at Charlotte
2002	San Diego State University (Shirley Weber)
2003	Georgia State University (Charles Jones)
2004	Georgia State University (Charles Jones)
2005	New Orleans (Al Colon)
2006	University of Houston (James Conyers)
2007	San Diego State University (Shirley Weber)
2008	Georgia State University (Charles Jones)
2009	Georgia State University (Charles Jones)
2010	Dillard University (Al Colon)
2011	University of Cincinnati (Terry Kershaw)
2012	Georgia State University (Charles Jones)
2013	Indiana State University
2014	Miami, Florida
2015	Los Angeles
2016	University of North Carolina at Charlotte

It was 1989 before an HBCU, Tennessee State University, hosted the annual meeting. Loyola Marymount University became the first private school host in 1998.

The absence of HBCUs from NCBS leadership will not come as a surprise to anyone familiar with Carter Woodson's *The Miseducation of the Negro* or E. Franklin Frazier's *Black Bourgeoisie*. One early national survey of Black Studies programs indicated that the South was the region of the country with the fewest Black Studies units.[13] Another early survey noted, "some of the most distinguished black colleges have one or more departments with more white than black teachers."[14] A more recent study suggests that the disproportionate dependency of HBCUs on federal loan programs might account for their caution in launching Black Studies programs.[15]

Yet it would be a mistake to discount the role of HBCUs in Black Studies development. Some have argued that the prevalence of the Black experience in most courses taught at HBCUs made separate Black Studies units redundant. Indeed, there is some evidence to support this position. Nick Aaron Ford has compiled a list of courses concerned with the Black experience taught at HBCUs between 1921 and 1972.[16] The list would certainly compare favorably to a list drawn from predominantly White universities during the same time period. Moreover, it is clear that Black students at HBCUs would not feel the isolation and alienation that led such students at predominantly White schools to demand cultural centers and Black-themed residential units.

But it is equally manifest that Black students on HBCU campuses were not satisfied with the curriculum being offered. It was the Howard University Student Association that convened a conference on "The Black University" in November 1968. This conference, like the Yale conference a year earlier, featured some of the major figures promoting Black Studies. However, as Ford points out, "[t]he fact that no black leaders from the established black colleges appeared on the guest list of participants at the Howard University conference indicates that all currently solvent black colleges are primarily interested in the evolutionary rather than the revolutionary route to black liberation."[17] Yet one must be careful to distinguish between HBCU administrators and HBCU faculty. Nathan Hare would leave Howard to head Black Studies at San Francisco State University and Gerald McWorter, then at Fisk and Vincent Harding then at Spelman would play significant roles in the development of Black Studies.

The presence of large public universities in NCBS leadership might be best explained as a function of resources and numbers. Large universities were more likely to have the funds to subsidize faculty travel to professional meetings, and there were greater numbers of Black faculty at public schools than small private colleges. Moreover, activist leaders such as Nelson at Ohio State and John Bracey at the University of Massachusetts at Amherst were able to gain the support of Black state legislators. In its early development, the NCBS was particularly dependent on its national office and executive director located at Indiana University. Bloomington is intuitively not the place one would expect to find the headquarters of a Black professional organization. However, with the support of Herman Hudson, Russell was able to staff and support the national office. This dependence was highlighted by the fact that when Russell moved to Ohio State in the early 1990s, the national office moved with him.

The move to Ohio State proved to be somewhat controversial when the university's president decided not to support the NCBS at the level Russell thought had been promised. In fact, when I met with him he seemed surprised that we existed at all on the Ohio State campus. Russell stepped down as NCBS executive director and the new leadership on the executive board—Selase Williams and William Little—moved the national office to California State University at Dominguez Hill where they held academic appointments. From this point on the executive director would not play as prominent a role in NCBS affairs as had Russell. When Charles Jones assumed the presidency of the organization in 2006, the headquarters were moved to his school, Georgia State University, where it became even more closely associated with the president rather than the executive director. When Jones left Georgia State for the University of Cincinnati in 2011, the national office followed. It was not until Georgene Bess Montgomery assumed the presidency of the NCBS in 2014 that the organization had a leader from an HBCU as the following table illustrates (Table 4.2).

The absence of scholars from elite private schools from NCBS leadership reflects, in part, the ideological divisions of the early NCBS movement. In a special September 1974 issue of the *Black Scholar* entitled "Black Education: The Future of Black Studies" the editors state, "[a]t present, black studies departments are embattled on campuses throughout the United States in a struggle for survival. For, their basic social and political nature exits in direct conflict to the emphases that predominates

Table 4.2 NCBS Presidents

Bertha Maxwell Roddey	University of North Carolina at Charlotte	1976–1978
William King	University of Colorado	1978–1980
William Nelson	Ohio State University	1980–1982
Carlene Young	San Jose State University	1982–1984
Delores P. Aldridge	Emory University	1984–1988
Selase (Wayne) Williams	California State University, Dominguez Hills	1988–1992
Charles Henry	University of California, Berkeley	1992–1994
William A. Little	California State University, Dominguez Hills	1994–1998
James Stewart	Pennsylvania State University	1998–2002
Shirley Weber	San Diego State University	2002–2006
Charles Jones	Georgia State University	2006–2010
Sundiata Cha-Jua	University of Illinois at Urbana-Champaign	2010–2014
Georgene Bess Montgomery	Clark Atlanta University	2014–present

on 'white' campuses, who would prefer that black students, 'cast down their booklets where they are, and join the white capitalist rat race'."[18] *Black Scholar* editor Robert Allen goes on to note that the number of Black Studies units has declined from around 500 in 1971 to only 200 in 1974.[19]

A year before the creation of the NCBS, Allen ended his analysis with recommendations for saving Black Studies that included "the need for curriculum development and standardization" and "the need to bring pressure to bear on professional organizations to compel full and general recognition of Black Studies and active support of the black presence in higher education."[20] These two recommendations for curriculum development and standardization/accreditation would become the core objectives of the NCBS but not in the absence of ideological struggle within the organization.

Although a crucial founding meeting and subsequent early board meetings took place in Princeton, New Jersey, at ETS, Princeton University was largely absent from the gatherings. Furthermore, although there was sporadic attendance at the early annual meetings, no individual faculty from the resource rich Ivy League schools would play a leadership role in the organization's development. One might assume that the few Black scholars at these elite universities shared the view of Harvard's Martin Kilson that he "smell(ed) a rat," that is, he questioned the intellectual validity of studying the Black experience.[21] And while that view would change decades later with the arrival of Henry Louis Gates, Jr., and the "dream team," the fact remains that neither Cornell West, Gates or other prominent Ivy League faculty assumed the leadership of the field's primary professional organization.

One explanation might revolve around the early fights on the executive board between what Allen and others have termed "cultural nationalists" and "Black radicals/Marxists." The leaders of these two factions on the NCBS board were William "Nick" Nelson and Gerald McWorter (later Abdul Alkalimat), respectively. Conflict between these camps could be intense and continued at least from the first annual meeting at Nelson's Ohio State to the seventh annual meeting at McWorter's University of Illinois at Chicago Circle.[22] Yet there was a larger group of board members who sought to steer the organization away from any close identification with either ideological camp. Neither McWorter nor later Maulana Karenga or Molefi Asante, for example, became president of the NCBS. These activists, however, produced the first textbooks in the field.

The Peoples College, led by McWorter and Ronald Bailey, produced an *Introduction to Afro-American Studies* that was developed over a ten-year period. Growing out of a freshman social science course at Fisk University in 1972, their textbook had undergone four revisions by 1980. One stimulus for the project was a conference on "The Pull the Covers off Imperialism Project" held in Nashville in 1975. The title of the conference suggests the ideological framework of the textbook. A third edition, "Intro-Green" is notable for its inclusion of the problems and struggles of Black women. In the fourth "Intro-Blue" edition the ideological framework is evident in its history of the development of Black Studies.

> The key social force in this spontaneous violence were those young, working class Black people who were being kept out of productive jobs, and kept out of institutions that they felt could help them improve their lives.... But after this thrust of spontaneous violence (1963–1967), a large sector of this youth population was coopted into higher education, purportedly "to civilize the natives and quell the unrest." But things didn't work out for this scheme of bourgeoisification...and these students became a militant social force <u>inside</u> the university by disrupting the normal state of affairs.[23]

The Peoples College textbook is designed to complement more traditional disciplinary-focused books such as Lerone Bennett's *Before the Mayflower* and Nathan Huggins's *Key Issues in the Afro-American Experience.*

Karenga, who has a doctorate in political science and another in social ethics, began to teach Africana Studies at California State University in Long Beach in the 1980s. He used Kawaida theory as the foundation for his widely used textbook, *Introduction to Black Studies* that was first published in 1982. Karenga acknowledges that Kawaida's seven-area focus and definition of culture "coincides with the core focus of Black Studies" and cites Cruse's contention that the demand for Black Studies rests under the ideology of Black cultural nationalism.[24] Consequently, the text is organized around seven core subject areas: (1) Black History, (2) Black Religion, (3) Black Social Organization, (4) Black Politics, (5) Black Economics, (6) Black Creative Production, and (7) Black Psychology. Two facts are immediately obvious in examining the text's organization. First, the content is skewed toward the social sciences with only religion and creative production representing arts and the humanities and no discussion of math and science. Second, rather than developing a new discipline, Karenga has emphasized Black content in traditional disciplines. Black Studies, then, was defined as interdisciplinary rather than as a unique discipline or antidiscipline. In fact, he states that although the development of a paradigm is in process in Black Studies, it has yet to emerge.[25]

By the turn of the century, the Peoples College text was no longer being produced; however, Karenga's text was still in use. Fabio Rojas's survey of seminal Black Studies texts ranked the People's College text at 2.22 on a 5-point scale compared to a 3.29 ranking for Karenga's text. Leading the 18 texts surveyed was Du Bois's *The Souls of Black* Folk at 4.88.[26] A 2000 sampling of introductory courses reveals a number of approaches. Manning Marable at Columbia used a chronological approach to Black history featuring two of his own works as well as classics by Du Bois and Frederick Douglass. Wahneema Lubiano at Duke mixed cultural studies with Black intellectual history and diaspora studies including works by Patricia Williams and Aime Cesaire. At Georgia State University, Akinyele Umoja uses Karenga's text along with a book of readings by Floyd Hayes. Cornell West, then at Harvard, has students read ten books from cover to cover from Du Bois to his own *Race Matters*. Martha Wharton at Ohio State assigns Deirdre Mullane's *Crossing the Danger Water* as the basic text. At Temple, Nathaniel Norment, Jr., uses Karenga's text supplemented with other authors. Ernest Allen at the University of Massachusetts at Amherst reverses the chronology starting with contemporary issues and drawing parallels with earlier periods. His texts include Mullane's anthology and George Curry's edited work on affirmative action. Finally, Anthony Monteiro at the University of Pennsylvania spends half the semester on a close reading of *Souls of Black Folk* followed by selections from more contemporary authors.[27]

Under the leadership of Carlene Young at San Jose State University and her successor Delores Aldridge of Emory, the board conflict subsided and new attention was devoted to curriculum development and accreditation. In 1980, the NCBS adopted a Black Studies core curriculum developed by its committee on curriculum standards chaired by Perry Hall, then of Wayne State University. NCBS was not the only group of Black scholars concerned about curriculum.

During roughly the same period, the Institute of the Black World (IBW) in Atlanta launched its Black Studies Curriculum Project. IBW had been a vital catalyst for the new field since its November 1969 Director's Seminar brought together some 35 Black Studies heads to discuss the explosion of Black Studies units across the country. They followed that successful gather with a Summer Research Symposium in 1971 that focused on some of the cutting edge research being done in Black Studies. Their curriculum project would be the last major effort of IBW prior to its demise.

Under the leadership of historian Vincent Harding and staff director Howard Dodson, IBW surveyed some 250 Black Studies units asking them for sample syllabi and teaching methods. They discussed the results of the survey in three conferences from 1981 to 1982. Six goals were put forth by the project's organizers: (1) to provide Black Studies faculty with new materials and approaches; (2) to encourage the exchange of materials, ideas, and methodologies in the discipline; (3) to supply faculty members with effective course materials; (4) to promote novel approaches to teaching Black Studies; (5) to encourage a higher level of "critical self-evaluation in the field"; and (6) to refine issues and problems in the field of Black Studies.[28] The conferences revealed the virtual absence of attention to the contributions and issues of Black women—a finding that would be repeated in the work of the NCBS. Unfortunately, IBW did not survive long enough to implement its work.

The importance of curriculum in the early development of Black Studies seemed self-evident. In her work on the role of the Ford Foundation in the development of Black Studies, Noliwe Rooks contended that the tension in Black Studies in 1969 was between those who believed that it was a means of racial integration and access to increased opportunity and those who believed that it was tantamount to a revolutionary groundswell capable of overturning the existing social order. Ford chose to fund those forces pushing Black Studies into the mainstream of the institutional structure rather than Black autonomy since their real goal was racial integration and diversification of campuses and curriculum. Yet Ford's notion of curriculum diversification came from the top down rather than the bottom up as illustrated by Ford president McGeorge Bundy's comments at the influential Yale conference on Black Studies in 1968.

If Black Studies were to be more than the simple inclusion or enrichment of Black content courses in traditional departments, a rationale for a core curriculum that transcended any current discipline must be put forward. Moreover, if discrete Black Studies units were to gain academic legitimacy through accreditation, one must distinguish between essential courses and mere desirable courses.

NCBS recognized that the quick growth of the field often produced a chaotic mix of courses—some fundamental and some frivolous—dependent of the availability of faculty and in some cases graduate student instructors. It was necessary, therefore, to produce a core curriculum that cohered and that allowed for sequencing and synthesis created by the structure not the student. Toward this end the NCBS model curriculum set forth the following goals:

1. Training for a professional or scholarly career in Black Studies, or other careers for which Black Studies is an integral part.
2. Liberation of the Black community.
3. Enhancing self-awareness and esteem.
4. Providing a nuclear description of the Black Experience that functions as an indispensable component in general education and liberal studies programs, and so on.[29]

The first and fourth goals might be found in the rationale for any traditional discipline. The second and third goals, however, are directly related to the politics surrounding the creation of Black Studies and have proved contentious. In further elaboration of these goals NCBS states that "Black Studies inaugurates an unflinching attack on institutional oppression/racism with the goals of total eradication of racist ideology in institutions." "Black Studies," NCBS continues, "questions the adequacy, objectivity and universal scope of other schools of thought, it assumes a critical posture."[30]

After an introductory course taken by all majors, the core curriculum sets forth three developmental tracks: a social/behavioral studies area, a history area, and a cultural studies area. Each area coheres through a set of "key constructs" found throughout the courses in that track. Majors pass through two levels of courses together in their chosen track before coming together in a level-four senior seminar that attempts to synthesize and apply the knowledge gained. Any discussion of core courses and "key constructs" automatically leads to a discussion of canon or "great books." The curriculum committee report defers this discussion to a new task force that it recommends explore and identify core literature. Surprisingly, the report says little about pedagogy but does recommend "that NCBS initiate efforts to provide guidelines and illustrations for use of various skills and methods for teaching and researching various areas of Black Studies."[31] Nathan Huggins criticized the core curriculum for ignoring the sciences and research methods associated with the social sciences.[32]

Twelve years after the adoption of its model core curriculum, NCBS undertook the development of new curriculum standards with the support of a Ford Foundation grant administered by NCBS president Delores Aldridge. The new curriculum committee was chaired by William Little, then at Portland State University. The committee differed from the Hall committee in that it was able to collect curricular models and course syllabi from Black Studies units across the country and also include graduate level curricula.

The NCBS final report to the Ford Foundation explicitly compares the new "Holistic Afrocentric Curriculum Developmental Model" to Hall's earlier Black Studies Model. Whereas Hall's model introduces three subfields at Level One—Social/Behavioral Studies, History, and Cultural Studies—the new model presents only an Introduction to Africanology at the First Level. Level Two in the new model has five subfields—African Aesthetic and Expressive Arts and Tradition; African Peoples, Civilization, and Social Development; African World Views and Belief Systems; African Power and Organizational Relationships; and Science and Technology in the African World. Hall's Level Two only had three subfields—Basic Literature Review or Survey (soc. sci.); African Pre-History through Reconstruction; and Basic Literature Review or Survey (fine arts). The Holistic Afrocentric Curriculum Development Model culminates at Level Three with Senior and Graduate Course syntheses or applications of previous study. Hall's Level Three, however, introduces three new study areas focusing on current research/issues in Social Studies, Historical Interpretation, and Cultural Expression.

He reserves Level Four for Senior and Graduate capstone courses.

The Holistic Curricula Model is further defined by Little, Edward Crosby, and Carolyn Leonard to include Methods courses at Level Two followed by courses covering three time periods—Antiquity to the fifteenth century, the fifteenth to the eighteenth century, and the nineteenth century to present. Each of the three time periods has content suggested in eight areas compared to the five content areas of Level Two of the earlier Holistic Model. In the revised Holistic Model, Level Three a capstone course, research methods seminar, and practical research or fieldwork are suggested.

Aside from the change in terminology over the years from Black Studies to Africanology to Africana Studies, the most curriculum development takes place at Level Two. An historical chronology is presented and research methods get a new emphasis. Significantly, the goals of "Black liberation" and "enhancing self-awareness" are omitted from the rationale for the new model although practical research and fieldwork are options at Level Three.[33]

A glaring omission in both the old and new models was the absence of any special attention devoted to Black women and gender inequality. In his book, *In the Vineyard*, Hall criticizes an IBW curriculum conference in 1980 for ignoring gender issues. Yet these issues are not mentioned in the rationale for his core curriculum. This oversight is much harder to explain in the new "holistic" curriculum in 1992 after over a decade of new research on Black women. Although the teaching workshops sponsored by NCBS do address some of these concerns, the workshops are limited to a relatively few participants as we shall see.

In 1984, an NCBS Goals Committee Report identified three priority areas for the organization—professional development, curriculum standards, and program data centralization. NCBS sought support from the Ford Foundation to address these priorities and were rewarded with a three-year, $300,000 grant in 1988.[34] This grant was renewed for an additional three years in 1992. One project supported by the grant was the revision of the Black Studies model curriculum just discussed.

The professional development priority was implemented through a series of summer institutes and workshops. Under the first grant summer faculty institutes of approximately two and one half weeks were held in 1989, 1990, and 1991. The NCBS rationale for the institutes states that "[t]hat the large majority of those who consider themselves to be Black Studies scholars received their training in one of the traditional disciplines and have taken few or no courses in Black Studies [per se]...we should not allow this process to be perpetuated, forcing talented, young, Black scholars to train themselves as we have had to do."[35]

The institutional host was Indiana University in 1989 and Ohio State University the two following years. An average of 14 scholars were given a stipend to participate in lectures and discussions by visiting senior scholars under the direction of James Stewart of Pennsylvania State University. Applicants were chosen by the director, and preference was given to those applicants from HBCUs although they remained a minority of the participants.

Evaluations of the institutes by the participants indicated general satisfaction with the content areas and quality of presentations. Black Male–Female Relationships and Africana Women's Studies were topic areas. Well-known figures such as Maulana Karenga, Molefi Asante, Haki Madhubutti, and James Turner were among the resource persons.

Administrative workshops were also held for three summers under the provisions of the first Ford grant. These workshops were much shorter than the faculty teaching institutes and usually held in conjunction with the NCBS executive board meeting allowing its members to serve as resources for the workshops. Applicants were either potential administrators or in their administrative positions for less than five years. There were an average of 11 participants in the workshops under the direction of the grant administrator Delores Aldridge. Once again preference was given to administrators from HBCUs and Indiana University and Ohio State University served as hosts. The workshops were designed to "[o]rient new and prospective Black Studies administrators to the bureaucratic and political nature of higher education institutions" including managing budgets, personnel, faculty searches, and relationships with external professionals.[36] Participants generally found the workshops helpful and those involved in both the institutes and workshops tended to increase their involvement with NCBS.

The location of the first summer institutes and workshops at Indiana and Ohio State universities underscores the importance of the national office being established there. The second Ford grant, however, permitted NCBS leaders to be more flexible in developing the institutes from 1993 to 1995. Both the annual meeting and summer institute were held at the University of Ghana at Legon in West Africa in the summer of 1993. Places were set aside for Ghanaian scholars as Institute Fellows (participants), and the faculty for the Institute was largely composed of Ghanaian scholars. Jacqueline Wade, who had replaced Joseph Russell as NCBS executive director, served as the Institute director. The shift in Institute faculty also brought a shift in content focus to one centered more on African history, art and worldviews and less on the African American experience.[37]

Another example of the broadening of the African American perspective was our second international conference in Guyana, South America, in June 1994. My colleague at Berkeley, Percy Hintzen, was spending a year on leave consulting with the University of Guyana and the government of Guyana. Following our adventure in Ghana, I asked Percy if he could arrange an NCBS conference in Guyana. Percy put together a local arrangements committee and with the assistance of our executive director, Jacqueline Wade, we held a conference with over 200 participants in June 1994. The president of Guyana, Cheddi Jagan, opened the conference, and it received a great deal of media attention as the first such "Black Studies" conference in the country. Unfortunately, the conference was also an example of racial politics outside the United States. Jagan, who was of Indian ancestry, took the opportunity to criticize the previous regime of Desmond Hoyte, who was of African ancestry, in his speech. Hoyte and his followers, who were in the audience at the National Cultural Center, walked out. The news coverage of the event not only reported on the conflict but also asked how one could have a "Black" Studies conference with no Blacks on the stage. Of course, Jagan was cited as Indian. Hintzen was on the stage as local host and was labeled as "Dougla," that is half Black and half Indian. I, as president of the NCBS, was cited as White! It was a quick lesson in Guyanese race relations.[38]

The administrative workshops followed NCBS executive board member William Little first to West Virginia State University and then to California State University at Dominguez Hills. The national office also moved from Ohio State to California State in 1994 as Selase Williams and Little assumed administrative positions there. The latter served as the administrative workshop director and the goals and objectives of the workshop remained the same although the number of fellows expanded slightly. By one important yardstick, the programs have been an unqualified success. Three future NCBS presidents were workshop participants—Charles Jones, Sundiata Cha-Jua, and Georgene Bess Montgomery.

In addition to support for the administrative workshops and faculty summer institutes, the first Ford funds provided support for research grants in Black Studies in the amount of $5000 per grant. NCBS identified the issues surrounding Black student retention, curriculum development with a focus on theory and methodology for the integration of women and other underrepresented content areas, and assaults on Black Studies as the priority research areas to be funded. No proposals were funded the first year of the grant, and only three grants were made in the subsequent two years. Perhaps the most notable of the three was a study of the early history of the NCBS by William King. The NCBS used its unexpended research funds to hold a Post-Assessment Conference to which it invited all of the participants in its first three institutes and workshops.

Ford's first grant to the NCBS also provided funding for a "program data centralization project." This effort took the form of a survey instrument sent to over 1600 institution with over 1400 responses. Aldridge reports that the survey showed over 170 institutions had an African Studies unit. Of these 170 units, 28 percent were called Minority or Ethnic Studies, while 72 percent were Black Studies programs, centers, or departments. There were 30 departments and 6 research units. In addition, 30 institutions planned new Black Studies units in the next three years. She also identified many new journals and publications in the field. Aldridge's report also criticizes the shift of the administrative workshops and teaching institutes outside the United States because there were no provisions for continued funding.[39]

Undoubtedly, the very limited success of the research grants initiative and the program data centralization project led the NCBS to drop them from its second grant proposal. Curriculum and research development were collapsed into an effort to provide workshop and institute participants with "relevant information packages."[40]

A more successful research initiative was the launch of a new Black Studies journal, *The Afrocentric Scholar*, during the 1991–92 academic year. William Little was the driving force behind the long anticipated journal's creation. As a Black Studies director at West Virginia State University he was able to commit to underwriting the costs of production for three years.[41] The new journal was peer reviewed and published twice a year. Little, who assumed the position of editor, stated that the journal would "explore the African World Experience from an Afrocentric perspective rather than a Eurocentric perspective in an effort to illuminate the contributions of African people to world culture and to provide an alternative intellectual framework to the study of African people."[42] *The Afrocentric Scholar* urged contributors to submit manuscripts that fall within the eight content areas delineated by Little in the NCBS Africana/Black Studies Holistic Curricula Model. Contributors to the first issue included James Stewart, Delores Aldridge, and Molefi Asante.

In 1995, the NCBS board changed the name of the journal to the *International Journal of Africana Studies* to reflect a more global perspective. The eight subject areas guiding submissions were expanded to 12 including public policy, political economy, education, and urban development as topics. John Davis of Loyola Marymount University took over as managing editor, and a series of guest editors were responsible for individual volumes. Currently, the NCBS journal has published 14 volumes and is edited by Bertis English of Alabama State University.

I served as the national coordinator for the NCBS national student essay contest for several years early in its existence. The contest awarded monetary prizes to the best graduate and undergraduate student essays on a Black Studies related theme. In addition, we tried to bring the winners to the annual meeting and sought publication for their work. My job was to advertise the contest and to press NCBS colleagues into service as readers of the essays. As I recall there was no student representation on the Board during those early years.

Their absence began to change when students attending the Berkeley annual meeting in 1983 met to discuss their concerns. They complained that they had little involvement in planning the Berkeley convention, which as coordinator of the meeting I can attest to as being true. Consequently, they formed a Black Studies Student Network whose objective was to ensure greater participation at all levels of the organization and in the Black community—including HBCUs. NCBS founder, Bertha Maxwell, supported the student proposals and promised to include them in the planning of the eighth annual meeting of the NCBS in Charlotte, North Carolina, in 1984.[43]

A basic problem facing an organization such as the NCBS has been the dual allegiance of many faculty teaching Black Studies. With the first generation of Black Studies scholars being trained in traditional departments, there was and remains a real reluctance to cut their ties and devote their professional careers only to this new field.

The Huggins report indicated that few economists or political scientists were willing to define themselves as specialists on African American questions. Yet at the same time traditional departments refused to address these questions, Black Studies was accused of "ghettoizing the broad study of African American life and history in the standard curriculum and offering a way off the hook for faculties and departments reluctant to meet affirmative action criteria."[44] This latter rational was often used to deny Black Studies units additional resources while providing no tangible evidence that traditional departments were moving to add Black faculty or integrate their curriculum. If they did move in that direction it was only with the promise of added resources and positions rather than through regular appointments and budgets.

A majority of Black Studies scholars attempted to do both, that is specialize in the area of race while maintaining ties to traditional departments through joint appointments. Fabio Rojas reports that the entire population of Black Studies professors including joint appointments is only 855 individuals. About 14 percent are White, 19 percent are foreign born, and most have joint appointments. They are roughly equally split between the humanities, social sciences, and schools of education with 88 percent holding a doctorate. Only nine percent of four-year colleges and universities offer a Black Studies degree, and the average program size is seven faculty including joint appointments.

In her Ford Foundation report on Black Studies, historian Darlene Clark Hine divided Black Studies scholars into three categories: traditionalists, authentists/Afrocentrists, and Black feminists. Hine states that she essentially focuses on the scholarship produced by the "traditionalists" in sociology, history, and literary theory. After citing an extensive list of scholars Hine states that in "every established social science and humanities discipline, including art history, music, psychology, political science, and economics, has had to contend with the fresh interpretations and perspectives, innovative methodologies, new sources, and probing questions that characterize the best of traditional Black Studies scholarship."[45]

Despite Hine's high praise few Black Studies scholars are seen as influential as represented in the nation's most prestigious academies. The American Academy of Arts and Letters, for example, has only 11 Black members (4.4 percent) among it 250 scholars. Of the 11, only Henry Louis Gates and Amiri Baraka have been directly linked to Black Studies units. In an examination of three databases measuring the impact of Black scholars by citations, Black Studies scholars fared better with Maya Angelou, Cornell West, and Henry Louis Gates consistently at or near the top. Other Black Studies scholars consistently mentioned included Molefi Asante, Harold Cruse, Asa Hilliard, Leonard Jeffries, Darlene Clarke Hine, Manning Marable, Nell Painter, and Colin Palmer.[46] The inclusion of Asante and Hilliard on these lists indicates that scholars outside the traditionalist category are also having an impact.

Notes

1. Mario L. Small, "Departmental conditions and the emergence of new disciplines," *Theory* and *Society* 28: 659–707. 1999.
2. William M. King, "The Early Years of Three Major Professional Black Studies Organizations," in Delores P. Aldridge and Carlene Young (eds.), *Out of the Revolution*, (Lanham, MD: Lexington, 2000), pp. 127–8.
3. Ibid. p. 129.
4. Ibib. P. 129.
5. Martin Kilson, "Thinking About Black Intellectuals," manuscript later published as *Transformation of the African American Intelligentsia 1820–2012,* (Cambridge: Harvard University Press, 2014), p. 10.
6. National Council for Black Studies, Inc., Constitution and ByLaws, Carolyn M. Leonard and William A. Little, (eds.), (Bloomington: Indiana University, 1988).
7. John Henrik Clarke quoted in Ronald W. Walters, *Pan Africanism in the African Diaspora*, (Detroit: Wayne State University Press, 1997), p. 368.
8. Walters, Op. Cit. p. 369. See also Mario Azevedo, (ed.), *Africana Studies,* (Durham, NC: Carolina Academic Press, 1998), pp. 20–25; and Maulana Karenga, *Introduction to Black Studies,* (Los Angeles: University of Sankore Press, 1993), pp. 28–31.
9. The 1st Annual Convention of the National Council for Black Studies, Ohio State University, Columbus, Ohio, February 16–19, 1977, p. 3.
10. "Vice-Chairperson's Report," NCBS Executive Board, March 18–22, 1979, Sacramento, CA, p. 4.
11. Ibid. p. 6.
12. Conference call from Edward W. Crosby, Department of Pan-African Studies, Kent State University, April 28, 1980. The OCBS itself represented a merger of two smaller consortiums—the Central Ohio Black Studies Consortium and the Northeastern Ohio Black Studies Consortium.

13. Philip T. K. Daniel and Admasu Zike, "The National Council for Black Studies—Northern Illinois University Black Studies Four Year College and University Survey," (Dekalb, IL: Northern Illinois University, May, 1983), p. 13.
14. Nick Aaron Ford, *Black Studies,* (Port Washington, NY: Kennikat, 1973), p. 170.
15. Daryl Zizwe Poe, "Black Studies in Historically Black Colleges and Universities," in Molefi Kete Asante and Maulana Karenga, (eds.), *Handbook of Black Studies,* (Thousand Oaks, CA: Sage, 2006), p. 220.
16. Ford, Op. Cit., p. 52.
17. Ibid. p. 167.
18. "Introduction to Blacks in Higher Education," *Black Scholar,* September 1974, Vol. 6, No. 1.
19. Robert L. Allen, "Politics of the Attack on Black Studies," Ibid, p. 2.
20. Ibid. p. 7.
21. Martin Kilson, Jr., "The Intellectual Validity of Studying the Black Experience," in Armstead L. Robinson, et al., (eds.), *Black Studies in the University,* (New Haven: Yale University Press, 1969) p. 13.
22. There were constant fights in the organizations early years between a Nationalist faction led by William Nelson of Ohio State and a leftist faction led by Gerald McWorter of the University of Illinois at Chicago Circle. These conflicts subsided when McWorter resigned from the National Executive Committee following his defeat in the election for board chair (president). His reasons are mentioned in a letter he sent to the *Black* Scholar dated February 28, 1984: "RE: his resignation as vice-chair person....two main reasons...(1) the current election is illegal...(2)...NCBS

    as it is now constituted is no longer viable and effective as the national Black Studies organization....I contend that the only lasting accomplishment of NCBS so far is the national report on curriculum standards. Though not published by the organization until two years after its passage, it has been popularized and utilized around the U.S. almost in spite of the organization." See The Black Scholar Papers, Bancroft Library, University of California at Berkeley, carton 28, folder NCBS.
23. Teachers' Guide, *Introduction to Afro American Studies,* (Chicago: Peoples College Press, n. d.), p. 3.

24. Maulana Karenga, *Introduction to Black Studies* (Los Angeles: University of Sankore Press, 1993), p. 26.
25. Maulana Karenga, "Black Studies and the Problematic of Paradigm," in Nathaniel Norment, Jr., ed., *The African American Studies Reader*, (Durham, NC: Carolina Academic Press, 2003), p. 286.
26. Fabio Rojas, *From Black Power to Black Studies,* (Baltimore: Johns Hopkins University Press, 2007), p. 202.
27. "Black Studies 101: A Sampling of Approaches," *Chronicle of Higher Education*, May 19, 2000.
28. Derrick E. White, "An Independent Approach to Black Studies," *Journal of African American Studies* (2012), Volume 16, p. 84.
29. Perry Hall, Chairman, "Report of the Curriculum Standards Committee to the National Council for Black Studies," March 26–29, 1980, p. 6.
30. Ibid. p. 7.
31. Ibid. p. 22. An exception is early NCBS board member, Johnnella E. Butler who published *Black Studies: Pedagogy & Revolution*, (Washington, DC: University Press of America, 1981). In addition to attacking the "banking concept of education," Butler argues that "a democratic relationship must be effected between the teacher and students through the dissolution of the student–teacher contradiction" (p. 121).
32. Nathan I. Huggins, "Afro-American Studies," in Nathaniel Norment, Jr., *The African American Studies Reader,* (Durham, NC: Carolina Academic Press, 2001), p. 260.
33. The Holistic Curricula model was developed by William A. Little, Edward Crosby, and Carolyn M. Leonard and was sponsored in part through a grant from the Ford Foundation to the National Council for Black Studies.
34. A meeting between Darlene Clark Hine, who had been contracted by the Ford Foundation to consult on the state of Black Studies, and Selase Williams led to an invitation to an NCBS Executive Board meeting. As a result, Hine and Ford became supportive of NCBS efforts in standardization and curriculum development. See Summer Institute, National Council for Black Studies, Accra, Ghana, West Africa, July 24–August 15, 1993, p. 4.

35. Africana Studies Summer Institute, National Council for Black Studies, Inc. & the University of Ghana-Legon, West Africa, July 9–August 6, 1995, p. 17.
36. Delores P. Aldridge, "Professional Development, Curriculum Standards and Program Data Centralization: Black Studies Advancement Project," *Final Report,* January, 1993, p. 147.
37. An emotional peak of the Ghana conference was a tour of two of the "slave castles" on Ghana's coast. On the tour were several leading Afrocentrists, and it was quickly noted that the "castles" had been stripped of any identification with colonial powers presenting a rather sterile portrait of the past. Another peak was a meeting with Robert Lee, a leader of the ex-patriot African American community that moved to Ghana during the Nkrumah regime as well as a meeting with Ghanian president Jerry Rawlings.
38. Sheron Forde, "Squall at opening of Black Studies conference," *Guyana Chronicle,* June 2, 1994, p. 1.
39. Delores P. Aldridge "NCBS" 2001, pp. 5–21.
40. Delores P. Aldridge, "Professional Development, Curriculum Standards and Program Data Centralization: Black Studies Advancement Project," Continuation Grant Proposal, July 1992, p. 11.
41. "Publication Report," *The Afrocentric Scholar*, NCBS Board of Directors meeting, July 9–12, 1992.
42. *Afrocentric Scholar* v. 1, no. May 1, 1992, p. 1.
43. Letter from David Charles Mills to the Founders of the National Council for Black Studies Student Network, June 3, 1983.
44. Huggins, op. cit., pp. 62–66.
45. Darlene Clark Hine, "The Black Studies Movement," in Nathniel Norment, Jr., (ed.), *The African American Studies Reader*, (Durham, NC: Carolina Academic Press, 2001), p. 242.
46. "Black Members of the American Academy of Arts and Letters," *Journal of Blacks in Higher Education*, No. 39, (spring 2003), p. 36 and "There Are Now Three Databases for Measuring the Impact of Black Studies," *Journal of Blacks in Higher Education,* No. 47, (spring 2005), pp. 84–85.

CHAPTER 5

The Black Scholar: Drum of the Black Studies Movement

At the 40th anniversary celebration of *The Black Scholar* (*TBS*) held on the Berkeley campus of the University of California, a special arrangement was made with students protesting cuts in programs that aid minority students to include the conference as a strike event. That *TBS* would participate in a student strike some 40 years after its founding is apropos of its origins. As its cofounder and publisher Robert Chrisman said at the celebration, "the *Black Scholar* had its inception and inspiration with the Black Power and black student movements that swept the United States in the 1960s."[1] Chrisman notes that of the 292 major student protests in the first half of 1969, nearly half dealt with issues of Black recognition. More specifically, students demanded more courses on the Black Experience, increased Black enrollment, and the hiring of more Black faculty and administrators. *TBS* was there to document it all. Moreover, the founders of *TBS* had been participants in the iconic first struggle for a Black Studies program at San Francisco State University (SFSU).

Cofounder Nathan Hare had been an assistant professor of sociology at Howard University from 1961 to 1967. Among his students were Stokely Carmichael and Claude Brown, and it was his letter of protest to the student newspaper *The Hilltop* which got him fired. In September 1966, Howard president James Nabrit announced in the *Washington Post* a plan to make Howard "sixty percent white" by 1970. Hare vehemently and publicly objected saying virtually every student on campus was opposed to the plan.[2] His teaching contract was not renewed and he

C.P. Henry, *Black Studies and the Democratization of American Higher Education*, DOI 10.1007/978-3-319-35089-9_5

joined the SFSU faculty in 1968 to coordinate the Black Studies program. When Hare arrived in February of that year, there were already 15 Black Studies–oriented courses offered throughout the college. Hare and the Black Studies Union (BSU) proposed increasing the number of courses and moving them into a department that would be as "autonomous" as possible from the administration. Chrisman was an assistant professor at SFSU, and joined Hare and the BSU in what would be a prolonged and well-chronicled struggle to implement the proposal. In March 1970, university president S.I. Hayakawa, who had been hired to end the student protests, fired the Black Studies faculty. Hare was actually fired on stage during a demonstration, and Chrisman was removed from his tenure track teaching position in the English department.[3]

Hare had experienced the costs of free expression when he was fired for expressing his opposition to Nabrit's plan at Howard. In writing about his experience at the historically Black university, he said:

> I have watched them, day by day, young professors with style and promise already losing their spark, grumbling in the dark but falling silent and teethy when administrators walk by, old men now dissatisfied but powerless at this late date to move, driven to drink in bars near the campus discussing the books begun five to ten years ago which their frozen pens will now never finish.[4]

Hare had said that it was impossible, even at Howard, for a liberal arts student to take a course in Negro history unless he was a history major. Now Hare was being punished again for siding with students who wanted a Black Studies department.

Hare, Chrisman, and Alan Ross (a printer and activist) realized that the struggle for Black Power and Black Studies was being reduced to "ten-second sound bites" on the evening news usually accompanied with the appropriate incendiary photograph. They believed that an independent source of information and critique was needed if the struggle was to succeed. In June 1969, the three activists moved into office space in Sausalito, California, used by Ross who printed the 20,000 copies of the first issue for $700 in November of the same year.[5] *The Black Scholar* was born.

Historically, Black scholarly writing has been an exercise fraught with difficulty at best and danger at worst. In a country where slaves were forbidden to read and write, and free Blacks had their schools burned to the ground, to assume Blacks had anything worth publishing was a bold move.

Thus Black scholars were in a particular bind. White academic journals seldom published articles related to race. When they did, the authors were almost always White. The few existing Black academic journals did publish Black authors but were seldom granted any academic legitimacy.[6]

As Chrisman pointed out, the Modern Language Association (MLA) did not accept Black members or the Black literary canon. This exclusion led to the founding of the College Language Association in the 1950s with its own journal.[7] In an examination of race-focused research in two of the most influential journals in political science, Hanes Walton, Jr., and Joseph McCormick, II, found race to be practically invisible. Both the *Political Science Quarterly* over 105 years and the *American Political Science Review* over 85 years published a total of only 27 race-related articles or approximately 2 percent of their coverage from 1886 to 1990.[8]

When articles related to race were published, they invariably supported the racial regime of the time. Anthropologist Lee Baker reports, for example, that the first issue of the *American Anthropologist* published an article by John Wesley Powell entitled "From Barbarism to Civilization." In it Powell explained that his analysis of evolution was necessarily confined "to one great stock of people—the Aryan race." Baker also notes that the organs of the American Philosophical Society, the American Academy for the Advancement of Science, and the Academy of Natural Sciences became regular outlets for Daniel Brinton's scholarship on racial inferiority, ethnology, and the grammar of Native Americans.[9]

Historically, Blacks in professions like law and medicine, when faced with exclusion from professional societies and their official publications, formed their own parallel organizations and journals. By the late 1960s and early 1970s, there were enough African Americans in the social sciences and humanities to form separate disciplinary organizations with official publications. Some Black scholars chose to join the predominantly White disciplinary associations and fight to expand the scholarly horizons of their journals. Others chose to concentrate their efforts on the new groups where they could be sure their academic interests would be addressed. Still others tried to maintain ties to both camps. After all, the established disciplinary societies had funds for graduate student scholarships and conferences. Most importantly, publication in their official journals was a ticket to teaching positions in elite schools and tenure. The journals of the new predominantly Black organizations, however, struggled to survive. Membership in these groups came disproportionately from historically Black colleges and universities. Their institutions did not have the resources, by and large, to support association publications in the same way that White institutions supported academic journals. With small memberships in the low hundreds, the new Black academic associations struggled to hold conferences and produce journals often relying on a handful of members to do the work.

An example of this process was the creation of the National Conference of Black Political Scientists (NCOBPS). In response to pressure inside the American Political Science Association (APSA) during 1969–70, its president, David Easton, enacted several reforms. One reform was the establishment of a special committee on the Status of Blacks in the Profession. That committee, in cooperation with the Ford Foundation and Southern University, sponsored a conference directed by Jewel Prestage on political science curricula in Black colleges in 1969 and an informal Black caucus functioned through the 1969 and 1970 APSA meetings in New York and Los Angeles.[10]

The special committee on the Status of Blacks in the Profession became a formal part of the APSA. In addition, it was decided that an organization independent of the APSA was needed—the National Conference of Black Political Scientists. This new organization would focus on research and teaching centered around Black politics. The first conference was held at Atlanta University in 1970 and Mack Jones of Atlanta University was elected president. While the APSA journal, the American Political Science Review (APSR), continues to publish relatively few articles by Black political scientists, NCOBPS has struggled to produce a journal that better reflects the interests of Black politics scholars.[11] In 1975, NCOBPS joined with the Commission for Racial Justice to produce *The Journal of Political Repression*. Only lasting a few years, this journal was replaced by NCOBPS in 1989 by a new annual journal, *The National Political Science Review* (NPSR). This journal has had a number of editors including two who were president of both the APSA and NCOBPS—Lucius Barker and Matthew Holden. However, publication in the *NPSR* has none of the academic prestige attached to publication in the *APSR*.

Chrisman recognized the institutional realities of producing the typical Euro-American scholarly journal. A publication like the *APSR* is the official organ of a dues-paying, national or regional association dedicated to the discipline. A subscription is part of the professional dues (often paid by the institution or tax deductible) and the journal is guided by distinguished scholar/editors who reflect a general consensus on the nature of the discipline, its goals, objectives, methods, and protocols. These associations and their publishing arms evolve over time and are subject to contestation. "Thus," said Chrisman, "one may well argue that in view of the new and original nature of the black studies discipline, the Euro-American academy should not require it to be an instant clone of its own discipline, offices, and publications."

The Black Scholar cofounder suggested that "we be cognizant of our own unique intellectual, institutional, and cultural traditions, and require our Euro-American counterparts to appreciate that reality."[12] It also meant that we recognize Black studies was still emerging, still embattled, and still struggling for resources. He made a special plea for the legitimacy of independent or nonacademic journals. Chrisman said, "while black publication in journals such as *TBS*, *Renaissance Noir*, *The Crisis*, or *Ebony* might not be deemed acceptable, it is laudatory for a white scholar to publish in *Harper's*, the *Atlantic Monthly*, the *New York Review of Books*, or a Sunday newspaper supplement."[13] White academics must recognize the importance of Black engagement with the world outside the disciplines.

White academics never did fully accept *TBS* as a legitimate publishing venue.[14] *TBS*, however, did not have academic legitimacy as its primary objective. In the words of Black Panther leader Eldridge Cleaver, "*The Black Scholar* is, in fact, part of the revolutionary communications network that exists inside Babylon."[15] As such *TBS* was engaged in a broad range of non-scholarly activity, from distributing petitions on apartheid and publishing the works of political prisoners to organizing trips to Cuba and networking with the African diaspora. Without the oversight of academic referees, *TBS* editors were free to publish activists as well as scholars. In soliciting articles for the early issues of the journal, the editors stated that "[a]lthough we are soliciting radical writers, we will publish anything of quality, we have no taboos."[16]

The editors of *TBS* rejected the notion that academic referees provided "objective" reviews of manuscripts. Hare and Chrisman believed there was no such thing as objectivity and they did not hide their commitment to Black political liberation. Chrisman's philosophy is encapsulated in his poem "Letter of Reference" that concludes with the lines "the voices, murmurings, loomings, Douglass, Du Bois, Coltrane, Parker, Cabral, El Che....Who would be free must strike the first blow."[17] This ideological openness led them to publish the works of cultural nationalists like Maulana Karenga as well as revolutionary nationalists such as Cleaver. Marxists Herbert Aptheker and Angela Davis might be found in the same volume with elected officials such as Ron Dellums and Shirley

Chisholm. A special point of pride was the publication of speeches by African revolutionary leaders such as Kwame Nkrumah, Amilcar Cabral, Julius Nyerere, and Sekou Toure who were seldom featured in American publications.

This broad range of contributors, however, did not mean that *TBS* escaped ideological controversy. Perhaps the most serious dispute in the early years—foreshadowing Hare's departure from *TBS*—involved a critique of Harold Cruse's *The Crisis of the Negro Intellectual.* Cruse's 1967 book, along with a handful of other works, were hugely influential in the late 1960s. For those struggling to establish Black Studies, Cruse's work was proof positive of a Black intellectual tradition long overlooked. In fact, Cruse had been invited to join *TBS* editorial board in 1969 and asked to contribute an article to the first issue or any subsequent issue. Cruse could not make the deadline for the first issue but did agree to join the editorial board stating his "only reservation is will it be a scholarly publication and research vehicle, or will it be a catch-all black publication with material suitable for any other kind of publication."[18]

Cruse's preference for a scholarly journal is telling in that it goes to the heart of Chrisman's critique of his work. In Chrisman's 1969 review entitled "The Crisis of Harold Cruse," he began by praising Cruse's work as "by far the most impressive history of black intellectual development to emerge this decade."[19] He goes on to compare its impact on Black letters and American sensibility to that of James Baldwin's *Notes of a Native Son* and Ralph Ellison's *Invisible Man* to previous generations. But unlike Baldwin, said Chrisman, Cruse emphasizes the collective Black sensibility not the individual.

It is the task of the Negro intellectual and artist to create and maintain this collective Black sensibility or Black culture said Cruse and this was problematic for Chrisman. This insistence that the elite created and maintained Black culture led Cruse to focus on "high" (esthetic) culture rather than "low" (functional) culture. According to Chrisman, this tendency forces Cruse to argue that culture *precedes* political and social change. That is, in his elitist theory, "esthetic culture is a catalyst for social change, with an apolitical, non-activist intellectual in the vanguard."[20] The failure of Negro intellectuals to create a revolutionary culture was blamed on a "communist, Jewish, Zionist, liberal, integrationist conspiracy that has smothered black culture for sixty years," wrote Cruse.[21]

Chrisman would likely agree with an unpublished manuscript submitted to *TBS* by historian Sterling Stuckey that criticized Cruse's attempt to found Afro-American culture in the Harlem ghetto rather than the early slave plantations. Stuckey guessed that "it is Cruse's deep-seated desire to separate himself from Africa. Since the culture of the Negro who worked on the plantations of the South is so obviously stamped by Africa, he is led in desperation to say that black culture was born out of the urban experience—like Athena from the head of Zeus."[22]

While Cruse was invited by Hare to respond publically to the critique, he declined. Avoiding any real substantive response, Cruse, in a private letter, simply stated that "Chrisman underestimates the complexity of our problem. He (Chrisman) apparently thinks that black and white issues are really so simple that any single book, article or review can succeed in making up for just about forty years of scholarly, academic, theoretical and conceptual neglect that has been the dishonorable fate of black studies in this society." He adds that "[n]ot even the advent of *TBS* caused me to have any allusions about any incipient 'unity' of opinion among black intellectuals."[23] Chrisman would agree with Cruse that such unity of opinion is not only impossible, but not desirable. Over the next 40 years, however, *TBS* sought to make sure the opinions were heard.

The dialog between Chrisman and Cruse mirrors the major ideological divide among Black activists in the late 1960s and early 1970s. That is, those seeking to critique the liberal state that emerged after World War II typically sought to make their case from one of two established alternative perspectives. At the outset of *The Crisis of the Negro Intellectual*, Cruse identified Black nationalism as the "rejected strain" of Negro thought that "emerged simultaneously with its opposite—the racial integration—strain."[24] He stated that Frederick Douglass was the prototypical leader of this strain, which marched in almost a direct line to the National Association for the Advancement of Colored People (NAACP) and modern civil rights movement. The leaders of the early Black nationalist strain—Martin Delany, Edward Blyden, Alexander Crummell, Henry M. Turner, and George Washington Williams—are now largely forgotten according to Cruse. Yet all of American Black political history may be seen primarily as a conflict between the forces promoting these two strains of thought. Cruse attributes W.E.B. Du Bois with first making this theoretical formulation; however, Du Bois, he said, never moved toward a synthesis.[25]

The problem with liberalism as Cruse saw it was its idealization of the rights of the individual when in reality the United States was dominated by the social power of ethnic and religious groups. For that reason, Cruse paints a largely sympathetic picture of the history of Black nationalism. The only element capable of reaching outside the group and providing some synthesis are intellectuals and artists. The failure of Black intellectuals and artists to provide this transformative leadership to the Black masses constituted the bulk of Cruse's work.

Black Marxism was the other historical alternative to American liberalism. In addition to emphasizing the role of the capitalist economics, Black Marxism, says political scientist Michael Dawson, also recognized race and spirituality as fundamental categories to a degree not found in traditional Euro-American Marxism. Chrisman, for example, complained that the West Coast Marxist Scholars conference in 1984 lacked race and gender diversity.[26] Moreover, he believed a concern with self-determination and land have often put Black Marxists at odds with White comrades and especially White workers.[27]

As we have seen, Chrisman was critical of Cruse's reliance on a Black intellectual elite for political progress. In a letter to Marxist historian Herbert Aptheker, he called Cruse a bourgeois nationalist and said he (Chrisman) was more than ever convinced that nationalism was a phenomena peculiar to Sixteenth Century Europe, as it emerged into capitalist production, and that racism therefore emerged as its major ideology.[28] Elsewhere he contended that Black intellectuals and activists must overcome three spurious arguments: (1) the idea of social imperialism that weakened the focus on economic inequality; (2) the neo-negritude or cultural nationalist focus on biology that ignored class; and (3) the open endorsement of the capitalist process by Black North Americans.[29]

Although Chrisman was critical of Cruse's elitism, the readership of *TBS* was largely an elite one. He estimated that its readers were affluent, college-educated, and at least 80 percent Black. They worked as teachers, executives, and decision-makers of various kinds. Hare also noted that his journal appealed to college students and Black street intellectuals.[30]

A notice in the March 1975 issue of *TBS* announced Nathan Hare's resignation as president of the Black World Foundation and publisher of the *TBS*. Hare's only explanation for his departure was "my political differences with *TBS* and its current direction."[31] New York's *Amsterdam News* summed up those differences in a headline that read "Black Reds takeover Black Scholar."[32] The split came to a head around the planning for the journal's fifth anniversary in March 1975 that featured Shirley Graham Du Bois as keynote speaker. During a planning meeting, Hare expressed his displeasure with his lack of input in the decisions around the event. In fact, Hare had been less and less involved in the production of the journal as he focused on obtaining a PhD in clinical psychology. In a sense, his professional shift from sociology to psychology mirrored the split with Chrisman. Chrisman was interested in the external forces that shaped the Black experience, while Hare wanted to examine the internal forces that guided Black behavior. Chrisman's move to president of the Black World Foundation and publisher of *TBS* was announced in the September issue. At the same time, Robert Allen was promoted to managing editor.[33]

As we have seen, Chrisman's own views did not lead him to exclude opposing viewpoints from *TBS* and Hare would contribute to future issues. However, the Marxist/nationalist discourse peaked in the early to mid-1970s and then began to fade as other issues moved to the forefront. Political scientist Michael Dawson charted the frequency with which articles reflected one of five ideological orientations—Marxism, Nationalism, Conservatism, Liberalism, and Feminism—over five periods of five years each. He found that Nationalism peaked at 32 articles from 1969 to 1973 and then declined to 25 articles from 1974 to 1978 and 10 articles from 1979 to 1983 and another 10 articles from 1984 to 1988. Marxism, on the other hand, appeared in only 6 articles from 1969 to 1973 but increased to 34 articles from 1974 to 1978 and then declined to 15, 12, and 3 articles in subsequent five-year periods. Feminism grew from 10 articles each in the first two five-year periods to a peak of 23 articles from 1979 to 1983 before declining in subsequent periods. Liberalism with 20 articles peaked as an ideology in *TBS* from 1984 to 1988, while Conservatism never reached more than 5 articles in any five-year period.[34]

Directly related to Chrisman's views is the attention *TBS* devoted to the Cuban Revolution. Like many Black activists of the late 1960s, the Cuban Revolution provided the nearest example of what an American revolution might look like. Moreover, multicultural Cuba more closely resembled the American context than revolutionary Ghana or Tanzania. In fact, Cuban leaders declared an end to racism in Cuba. They backed up their rhetoric with public support for American civil rights leaders and Black militants alike. In addition, they provided material support for those fighting colonialism in Africa.[35]

It was Robert Allen who initially sparked *TBS* link to Cuba. As part of the Venceremos Brigade,[36] Allen and his wife Pam had traveled to Cuba in 1972. He returned to Cuba with Chrisman for three weeks in December 1972 as part of a 12-member delegation of African Americans invited by the Cuban government to study progress made by the Cuban Revolution.

As reported in the February 1973 issue of *TBS*, the group met with academics from the University of Havana, the Cuban Academy of Science, and the revolutionary leadership. They traveled through Havana, Oriente, and Camaguez provinces visiting hospitals, schools, farms, industrial complexes, housing projects, and government agencies. The result was a highly favorable report on the successes of the revolution especially in the areas of literacy, public health, and popular culture.[37]

In a section of their report on "race relations," Chrisman and Allen declared that "[u]nlike the United States, and many parts of Latin America and the Caribbean, Cuba today is a multi-racial society without racial strife."[38] They credit the socialist revolution for making this possible but find the roots of the transformation in Cuban history. Race mixing occurred early on, however, unlike the United States, "the multiraciality of the popular masses became a factor in national formation."[39] Revolutionary leaders like Antonio Maceo and Jose Marti were strongly antiracist and the liberation armies themselves became social laboratories. In addition, the earlier equalitarian ethos was aided in the years following the 1959 Revolution when many of the White racist Cubans fled to the congenial shores of Florida.

The Cuba report was the lead article in the *TBS* issue devoted to pan-Africanism and the Caribbean. Its authors saw Cuba's multiracial character and its fight against imperialism as the major factor promoting its spirit of international solidarity. They outlined a number of Cuban diplomatic and aid initiatives to Guinea-Bissau, Chile, Nicaragua, Barbados, Guyana, Jamaica, and Trinidad. This internationalism along with socialist construction were the main pillars of the new Cuba and gave hope to oppressed people throughout the world, opined the journal's editors.

The peak of *TBS* engagement with Cuba came with two major events in 1976. In the fall of 1976 and at the invitation of the Cuban Institute for Friendship with People (ICAP), Chrisman led a group of eight "cultural workers" on a tour of Cuba—the first such delegation of African Americans since the revolution. Its members included poets Lance Jeffers and Conyus, music critic Phyl Garland, artists Samella Lewis and Therea George, actor William Marshall, singer Bernice Reagon, and novelist Alice Walker. All except Conyus would write about their experience in the summer 1977 special issue of *TBS*.

Chrisman stated the purpose of the trip was to study the development of culture within a revolutionary context, to gauge the changes of emphasis and value that occur for an audience in a socialist society, and to determine the conditions under which art was produced. Moreover, they wanted to observe the interface between the African and non-African components of Cuban culture as it related to the development of a revolutionary national culture.[40]

In a section of his report on "race and gender," Chrisman stated the popular Cuban attitude on the subject:

> Material conditions determine cultural development and having transformed the material base of Cuban society in the first 18 years the Cubans believed that the cultural transformation of blacks and women was inevitable, that blacks and females would produce more and more distinguished leaders, scholars, artists, with full participation in Cuban life.[41]

The delegation noted, however, the disproportionate number of middle-aged White males in key administrative positions. They raised this question of the continued prominence of prerevolutionary leadership with their hosts.

"A revolution is a very complex phenomenon," their host answered. "It is not a contradiction within the revolution," he/she says, "but rather a contradiction within that particular generation."[42] That is, some of the current leaders did not participate in the revolution because they were children but today they fully accept the revolution. Chrisman asked if the generation problem has any effect upon the elimination of racism. He is told that "[r]acism as a problem of the Cuban nation does not exist" and that "Cuba could not be redeemed without the participation of the black movement. Cuba needed integration to be a complete nation."[43]

Chrisman seemed to accept this answer by returning to the topic of prerevolutionary racial stereotypes of the myth of the hypersexual mulatto woman. He moved to a discussion of this trope in American culture and ends blaming the United States for the estimated 100,000 prostitutes in Cuba before the revolution. "In freeing themselves from the imperialist economy of the United States, the Cuban people also rid themselves of the cultural, racial and sexual vampirism that gives life to the private world of imperialism."[44]

As reported in *TBS* on February 26, 1976, three members of the government of Angola convened a three-day Seminar in Havana, Cuba, with 26 representatives from various organizations and the Black press in the United States. The Angolan representatives sought to inform the participants about events in their country, their development, and priorities, and sought diplomatic relations with the United States despite the presence of Cuban troops in their country. In addition, the Angolan spokesperson stated that "[i]f the black movement of America decides to support the M.P.L.A. and Angola, we are certain its support will be strong because United States blacks have a great experience, not only in the struggle to liberate themselves from slavery but also in the struggle to achieve workers' welfare and equality in education."[45] Seminar participants adopted a resolution of support for the Popular Movement for the Liberation of Angola (MPLA).[46]

TBS supported a seminar on Angola held in Chicago in May 1976 and Chrisman made efforts to organize a delegation of Black journalists to visit Angola. The *TBS* publisher even expressed an interest in moving to Angola for six months to a year to help in "the building of revolution."[47] While the move did not happen, the journal would continue to support the revolution in Angola and Cuba in its pages.

Beyond the journal, Chrisman endeavored to produce two books on Cuba. One was to center on "The Culture of Cuba" and the other was a compilation of 20 interviews entitled "Conversations with Cuban Intellectuals."[48] Neither book was completed. He also proposed a West Coast branch of the Center for Cuban Studies and a national tour for two Cuban singers, Sylvio Rodrequez and Pablo Milanese.[49] These proposals were also not implemented; however, Chrisman was more successful with the promotion of Cuban poet Nancy Morejon—whose poetry was frequently published in *TBS*. The journal sponsored national tours of the United States for Morejon in 1983 and again in 1985. Her book of poetry *Where the Island Sleeps Like a Wing* was published by the Black Scholar Press.[50]

Chrisman was a visiting professor of African American Studies at UC-Berkeley in 2001 and, knowing of his interest in Cuba, I asked him about the possibilities of establishing a summer session program in Cuba. The African American Studies Department already had such programs in Barbados and Brazil, and adding Cuba would provide a great addition to our diasporic offerings. The impetus for the course came from my interest in participating in an International Seminar on "Ethics, Culture, Development, International Law and the United Nations" held in Havana on May 16–18, 2001, in the context of the International Year of Dialogue among Civilizations and sponsored by the United Nations Association of Cuba. Through Chrisman's connections with the Cuban interest section in the Embassy of Switzerland, I was invited to participate in the conference speaking on "Continuity and Change in Black Leadership Goals and Tactics." I asked Chrisman and a graduate student, Allen Caldwell, to join me to help make arrangements for a summer session course the following year.

As we developed the course, Chrisman's political contacts included the Jose Marti Foundation, the Federation of Cuban Women, the Committees for the Defense of the Revolution, and the National Political Assembly. On the cultural front, we hoped to work with UNEAC, ICAIC, the Ballet Folklorico, Teastro Nacional de Cuba, and the Fernando Ortiz Foundation among others. I was pleasantly surprised to find a Martin Luther King Center and an Ebenezer Baptist Church in Havana, and we included them on our itinerary. Chrisman's links to Morejon and the leadership of Casa de las Americas were particularly helpful.

In July 2002, some 30 Berkeley students descended on Cuba as a result of our efforts. I taught a course on the relationship of Black Radicals to Cuba and a rotating group of lecturers arranged by Casa de las Americas presented the history and culture of Cuba over a five-week period. In many ways, the course was a revelation for our students and an even larger number joined Professor Percy Hintzen in Cuba the next summer. For example, when our students asked our hosts why more Black Cubans were not included as speakers, the Cubans responded that they were all Cubans and no racial distinctions were made. Yet this official color blindness was contradicted by our daily experience in which we observed Black Cubans disproportionately in menial and low-level jobs. Unfortunately, new restrictions placed on travel to Cuba by the Bush administration ended the program in 2003.

William Brent was one of the speakers in our summer session class in Cuba. Brent was still on the FBI's most-wanted list for having hijacked a plane from Oakland to Cuba during his days with the Black Panthers. Brent, a high school dropout in Oakland, had obtained a PhD in Spanish at the University of Havana and authored a popular autobiography—*Long Time Gone*—that my students read. Brent's appearance illustrated another focus of the *Black Scholar's* work—Black political prisoners.

The journal's international activism was not its only departure from the publishing customs of academic journals. From its earliest days, *TBS* frequently published articles by political prisoners—broadly defined. In a 1971 article entitled "Black Prisoners, White Law," Chrisman states that "[a]ll Black Prisoners…are political prisoners, for their condition derives from the political inequality of black people in America."[51] Because the Black offender is not tried and judged by the black community itself, says Chrisman, "the trial or conviction of a black prisoner, regardless of his offense, his guilt or his innocence, cannot be a democratic judgment of him by his peers, but a political action against him by his oppressors."[52]

The Bay Area was the epicenter of Black radicalism in the late 1960s and early 1970s, and San Quentin was a focal point of prisoner unrest. Therefore, *TBS* was perfectly placed to publish a special issue on "The Black Prisoner" featuring the writing of prisoners themselves in April/May 1971. The lead article on "The Soledad Brothers" was by Angela Davis who was then being held without bail in the Marin County jail. Davis, as well as Fleeta Drumgo, Assata Shakur, Imari Obadele, Maulana Karenga, Marvin X, Conyus, Mumia Abu Jamal, and others would appear repeatedly in its pages. Beyond publication, the journal made private efforts to seek the release of prisoners such Maulana Karenga and Imari Obadele.[53]

Inside prison, *TBS* was popular with inmates when allowed to read it.[54] In response to demands from Black prisoners, the journal launched *TBS* Prisoners Fund with the special issue in April/May 1971. Through contributions to the Fund, individuals outside prison were able to buy *TBS* subscriptions and related readings for Black prisoners. The response was overwhelming with over 1000 prisoners corresponding with the journal. At its peak, the Fund was able to provide 600 subscriptions to inmates across the country.[55]

While the Nationalism v. Marxism or race v. class debate was the most prominent ideological conflict in the Black activist community playing out on the pages of *TBS*, another issue was raised in the earliest volumes. The third issue of the journal, while featuring a tribute to W.E.B. Du Bois, was substantively composed of contributions focusing on Black women. Authors included Alice Walker, Shirley Chisholm, Sonia Sanchez, Earl Conrad, Julia Reed, Robert Staples, Earl Scarborough, Yvonne Chappelle, Lenneal Hendrson, Jr., and William Middleton. Topics ranged from the Black matriarchy to Black Women on Negro college campuses. Alice Walker wrote about her experience creating Black history materials for teachers of Headstart centers in Mississippi. She asked: "How do you teach earnest but educationally crippled middle-aged and older women the significance of their past?"[56] Walker concluded that teaching historical facts was not the most important thing. Rather, it was to give the women a sense of what history was by writing their own autobiographies. In the mid-1970s, Walker's own work on Zora Neale Hurston would help spark new interest in this overlooked anthropologist, writer, and folklorist. Walker's 1982 award-winning novel *The Color Purple* brought attention to the subject of Black patriarchal culture and the following year she coined the term "womanist" to distinguish Black feminism from White feminism.

In her piece "Racism and Anti-Feminism," Shirley Chisholm answered a question that would be raised constantly during her presidential bid two years later—which is the greater obstacle to your success, race or gender? She replied "the harshest discrimination that I have encountered in the public arena is anti-feminism—both from males and brainwashed 'Uncle Tom' females."[57] However, she added that the backbone of America's political organizations are the women who write letters, stuff envelopes, answer telephones, write speeches, organize campaigns, and are the largest number of potential voters.

This early role in gender/sexuality discourse was revealed in two special issues in 1971. "The Black Male" was the focus of the June 1971 issue with a lead article by sociologist Robert Staples. Staples, who was a friend of Chrisman's and taught Robert Allen at the University of California at San Francisco (UCSF), would become a frequent and sometimes controversial contributor to the journal. In his article entitled "The Myth of the Impotent Black Male," he stated that "Black female dominance is a cultural illusion that disguises the triple oppression of black women in this country."[58] Thus, Staples was one of the early proponents of what is now termed the "intersectionality" of race, class, and gender. Staples's edited book on *The Black Family* also examined this issue.

"The Black Male" issue was followed in December 1971 by the "Black Woman" issue featuring a cover photo of and lead article by Angela Davis. Imprisoned Davis joined Staples in an attack on the notion of Black matriarchy. In an article on "The Black Woman's Role in the Community of Slaves," Davis said that "[t]he designation of the black woman as a matriarch is a cruel misnomer" since the term denoted a control and hierarchy that was beyond the power of Black women to exercise in their families."[59] This issue also contained contributions by Chisholm, Joyce Ladner, Jacquelyn Jackson, Johnetta Cole, Kathleen Cleaver, and Chrisman's review of the edited book by Davis and Bettina Aptheker, *If They Come in the Morning*.

Three years later, *TBS* would devote an entire issue to "Black Women's Liberation." In an opening editorial, the staff addressed the issue of the relationship between the expanding women's liberation movement and the Black liberation movement. They stated that "the fallacy of many women's liberation theoreticians has been to emphasize the psycho-sexual aspects of female oppression rather than its political and economic inequities."[60] This tendency, the editors claimed, led to the estrangement of Black women and eliminated sexual oppression as an integral part of the Black liberation struggle. Articles included "Sexism and the Black Male," "The Politics of Sexual Stereotypes," "Frederick Douglass and Woman Suffrage," "The African Woman," "The Black Woman and the Black Middle Class," and "Black Women in Films." An interview with Harlem activist and Universal Association of Ethiopian Women founder Queen Mother Moore concluded the issue.

Gender as an issue in *TBS* would peak over 1978–79. The April issue was devoted to "Blacks and the Sexual Revolution." In a publisher's introduction to the volume, Chrisman raised the issue of civil rights for gays and lesbians for the first time. He said that "[t]he drive for civil rights and self-determination by homosexual men and women has inevitably surfaced during this movement (i.e. the sexual revolution) as well, as perhaps the most conclusive evidence that the fear and intimidation that white male patriarchy in the United States used to inspire, is weakening."[61] However, Chrisman believed the feminist movement and homosexual movement should not assume that gender itself is the basis of political power. These movements must come together with others in a struggle for new equality in class, race, and sexual relations built on love not exploitation. Two articles dealt explicitly with lesbian relationships. Assata Shakur in "Women in Prison" reported that most of the homosexual relationships in prison involved role-playing. The fact that the majority of these relationships were either asexual or semi-sexual is not due primarily to prison prohibitions. Shakur argued that the women involved were basically looking for love, concern, and compassion, not sex. In contrasting the male and female prisoners at Riker's Island, she noted the absence of revolutionary rhetoric among the women.[62]

Audre Lorde's contribution to the volume "Scratching the Surface" emphasized the "red herring of homophobia and lesbian-baiting being… used in the black community to obscure the true double face of racism/sexism."[63] Lorde contended that the increasing attacks on the Black lesbian from both Black men and heterosexual Black women encouraged a kind of horizontal or lateral hostility hiding the real and more pressing issues of oppression.

The rather academic discussions of Black feminism and sexuality occurring on the pages of *TBS* were vastly expanded as the issue reached a popular audience in the late 1970s. In 1977, Ntozake Shange's 1976 choreopoem "For Colored Girls Who Have Considered Suicide When the Rainbow Is Enuf" was nominated for the Tony Award for Best Play on Broadway. A year later, Michele Wallace published *Black Macho and the Myth of the Superwoman*, which was widely heralded in the media and led *Ms.* Magazine to declare it the "book of the 1980s." Both works were critical of Black masculinity as performed in both personal and political spaces in the 1960s and 1970s.

TBS joined the now-expanded discourse in a March/April 1979 article by Staples entitled "The Myth of Black Macho." Staples accused White feminists of hiding behind and manipulating an attack on Black men that well-known Black female activists such as Angela Davis and Joyce Ladner would not condone. Staples attacked both the messenger and the message. On the former, he said: "Both came from very middle-class backgrounds, had some involvement with street brothers, and are now urging black women to go it alone."[64] In regard to the message, he was puzzled why the attack on Black men is happening at a time "when black women threaten to overtake them, in terms of education, occupation and income by the next century."[65] Black men, Staples argued, only have power in the Black church and family, and their "sexist behavior" is nothing more than men acting in ways they have been socialized to behave. "Ultimately," he said, "the issue in America is not that of sexism or racism; it is monopoly capitalism and its impact on human potential."[66]

Staples's piece provoked an overwhelming response. *TBS* published a selection of them in a special issue on "The Black Sexism Debate" in May/June 1979. A lead piece on Amy Jacques Garvey and her work on Black women in the *Negro World* demonstrated the subject was not a new one. The published responses by June Jordan, Maulana Karenga, Audre Lorde, Julianne Malveaux, Harry Edwards, Alvin Poussaint, and others are a fascinating mix of critiques of Staples as well as Wallace and to a lesser extent Shange. Some respondents separated Shange's choreopoem in which Black men are largely absent from Wallace's direct attack on them. While Shange said she loved Black men, Wallace believed Black women should go it alone. Jordan, who had written a critical review of Wallace's book for the *New York Times*, questioned Staples's statistics and wondered why the advancement of Black women would be seen as a problem. Most of the respondents agreed with Staples on two points. First, they were suspicious of the widespread attention Wallace's book enjoyed in mainstream media and wondered why more historically accurate and better-researched works were ignored—one respondent even linked *Ms.* editor Gloria Steinem to the CIA. Second, many respondents believed by focusing on Black male–female conflict, Wallace was blaming the victims of capitalism. This was also the view that resonated most with *TBS* staff.

In the winter/spring of 1991–92 issue on "The Clarence Thomas confirmation," an even larger group of nearly 40 scholars shared their opinions of the Hill-Thomas hearings. The discourse, which included statements by civil rights organizations and the principals themselves, produced such an overwhelming reaction that the editors of *TBS* published an expanded version of this issue as a trade book. In their introduction to the special issue, Chrisman and Allen stated that at the conclusion of the hearings "a vote for Clarence Thomas could be seen as either a liberal or conservative gesture, as a pro-black or anti-black statement or as an absolution of him from charges of sexual harassment."[67] Although the contributors to the special issue took a variety of approaches to the subject, there was general agreement that Thomas was not qualified to hold the seat once occupied by Thurgood Marshall and that Anita Hill rather than Thomas was put on trial.[68]

Other issues of *TBS* were more specialized dealing with "Black Women Writers," "The Black Woman Writer and the Diaspora," "Black Women Writers Dissect Globalization," and "Black Women's Activism." Nor were these special issues the only place concerns over sexuality and the family appeared. Articles with a focus on these issues regularly appeared in the journal and writers such as Angela Davis, Frances Beal, Barbara Smith, Sonia Sanchez, Shirley Chisholm, and Alice Walker were often featured.

TBS was the primary project of a larger enterprise founded by Hare and Chrisman in 1969. In addition to the journal, they established the Black World Foundation, which was the institutional home of the journal, as well as the Black Scholar Speaker's Bureau, the Black Scholar Prisoner Fund, and the Black Scholar Press. While *TBS* was proud of its independence, it did seek funding from the Ford Foundation and from the Carter Administration for a special issue on housing. Two early local projects involving employment training and community development were funded by the Marin county government and CETA. Also early on, *TBS* considered a working relationship with the Institute for the Black World in

Atlanta and shared mailing lists with the National Black United Fund and *Ms.* Magazine.[69] The Black World Foundation also agreed to publish the *Black Law Journal* and the member manuals for Amiri Baraka's Congress of African People.[70]

In December 1971, the Black World Foundation hosted an intellectual retreat "as a first step in calling on black intellectuals to "develop new and appropriate norms and values, new institutional structures, a new and viable black ideology."[71] Participants in the closed retreat included Chuck Stone, Akbar Muhammad (Max Stanford), Carl Bloice, Paul King, Joyce Ladner, James Turner, Robert S. Browne, Johnetta Cole, Dennis Forsythe, S.E. Anderson, Milton White, Mike Thelwell, Gwen Patton Woods, Max Roach, and Allen, Chrisman, and Hare.

Several fundraising events were held in the Bay Area to support the work of the foundation. Shirley Graham Du Bois, widow of W.E.B. Du Bois, was the featured speaker at the first and fifth anniversary celebrations of the founding of the journal. A performance by Maya Angelou was the major attraction of the tenth anniversary fundraiser. In 1989, the foundation purchased a building in Oakland that served as the home of the journal until 2004. Allen took over more of the editing responsibilities, while the production of the journal moved to Ann Arbor, Michigan, where Chrisman was completing his dissertation at the University of Michigan.

In the early 1980s, Chrisman acknowledged that growing conservatism made it more challenging than ever to keep *TBS* afloat. The Reagan administration's attack on the public sector and the programs working toward racial equality as well as the inflation crisis were stark realities. "The black movement has been more quiescent now than anytime since the 1950s," wrote Chrisman, "and the stimulus from the movement to promote interest in *TBS* and its concerns, is not possible as it was when *TBS* began."[72] Recognizing the increasing influence of television and a kind of laid-back hedonism, he believed *TBS* had lost some of the "charisma" that brought it a lot of individual subscriptions and sales in the early days.

Black Studies, too, found that changing conditions produced new challenges for survival. Educational reform, in the form of a return to excellence over equality, swept across the nation's K through 12 schools as well as its universities. Scholars like Allan Bloom and E.D. Hirsch were leaders of the "culture wars" that questioned the move toward multiculturalism. In the mid-1970s, Chrisman had identified Black Studies as a major correction to the ethnocentrism typical of the faculty and curriculum of the typical college. "Black Studies," he contended, "must 1) provide a critique of the 'white' college as it now exists, and 2) black studies must also provide academic instruction, information, research and guidance for those faculty and students who would learn more about the Afro-American experience."[73] *TBS* would continue to defend Black Studies specifically and multiculturalism more generally in such issues as "Black Education 1988" and "The Multicultural Debate" in 1993. Yet Chrisman warned that threats to Black Studies came from the Left as well as the Right.

At the 40th anniversary celebration, he took on the most recent challenge to Black Studies—postmodernism. "Postmodernism," he said, "tends to abolish or subordinate text to theory with a concomitant loss and distortion of historical context; loss of distinction between varieties of black discourse and expression." Citing hip hop culture as a notorious example, he added that "[t]he consequence is the erosion of history and racial consciousness" a consciousness that can serve as "a prism through which social, cultural economic political reality can be viewed and evaluated and improved."[74]

Notes

1. Robert Chrisman, "The Black Scholar: The First Forty Years," *Black Scholar* Vol. 41, No. 4 (Winter 2011): 2.
2. Nathan Hare, "Final Reflections on a 'Negro' College," *Negro Digest*, (March 1968): 43.
3. Robert Chrisman, "The Black Scholar," 2.
4. Nathan Hare, "Final Reflections," 75.
5. Interview with Robert Allen, July 9, 2013.
6. The only older Black-oriented journals are *Phylon*, the *Journal of Negro History* and *Journal of Negro Education*. For many years Atlanta University supported *Phylon* and Howard University supported the latter two journals. The *Journal of Negro* (now African American) *History* is the official organ of the Association for the Study of African American Life and History. During the 1930s and 1940s Nobel Laureate Ralph Bunche, for example, published his research in these journals.
7. Robert Chrisman, "Some Thoughts on Black Publishing in the Academy" (unpublished, n.d.).
8. Hanes Walton, Jr. and Joseph McCormick, II, "The Study of African-American Politics as Social Danger: Clues from the

Disciplinary Journals," *National Political Science Review* Vol. 6 (1997): 61.

9. Lee D. Baker, *From Savage to Negro* (Berkeley: University of California Press, 1998), 41.
10. Charles P. Henry, "African American Politics: The Black Studies Perspective," *Handbook of Black Studies* by Molefi Kete Asante and Maulana Karenga (eds.) (Thousand Oaks, CA: Sage Publishers, 2005): 18.
11. In recent decades the APSA has published two other journals that contain material relevant to the Black experience—*PS* and *Perspectives on Politics.* Neither, however, holds the status of publication in the APSR.
12. Chrisman, "Some Thoughts..."
13. Ibid.
14. This lack of legitimacy extended to the Black Scholar Press. In 1991, I published my *Jesse Jackson: the Search for Common Ground* with the Black Scholar Press. During my subsequent promotion review at UC-Berkeley, I was punished by the university's budget committee for publishing with them. The committee noted that I would have to be a much more senior scholar to publish with such a press and gave me only a half step promotion. They cited no particular problem with the substance of the book. This treatment contrasted sharply with a Black neoconservative who was given an acceleration for a book he published that was admittedly outside his area of expertise.
15. Letter from Eldridge Cleaver to Nathan Hare, July 14, 1971, Carton 23, Folder "Cleaver," Black Scholar Papers, Bancroft Library, University of California, Berkeley.
16. Letter from Nathan Hare to Chuck Stone, July 16, 1969, Carton 5, (S-69-70), Black Scholar Papers, Bancroft Library, University of California, Berkeley.
17. Chrisman in Bettina Aptheker, "Tribute to Robert Chrisman," *Black Scholar* Vol. 44, No. 1 (Spring 2014), p. 136.
18. Harold Cruse to Nathan Hare, October 31, 1970, Carton 1, Folder C-1970, Robert Chrisman to Harold Cruse, July 16, 1969, Carton 1 Folder C-1970, Black Scholar Papers, Bancroft Library, University of California, Berkeley. Cruse also joined the editorial board of the newly established and referred *Journal of Black Studies*

in 1969. Cruse's interest in "scholarly" publications is somewhat ironic given his lack of a college degree.

19. Robert Chrisman, "The Crisis of Harold Cruse," *Black Scholar* (November 1969): 77.
20. Ibid., p. 79.
21. Ibid., p. 79.
22. Sterling Stuckey, 1982 manuscript submitted to the *Black Scholar*, January 14, 1982, Carton 9, Folder "Sterling Stuckey." In his correspondence with Stuckey, Chrisman says Cruse may not be the "gadfly of Athens" but he is certainly the "horsefly of Harlem."
23. Letter from Harold Cruse to Nathan Hare, October 31, 1970, Carton 1, Folder C-1970, Black Panther Papers, Bancroft Library, University of California, Berkeley.
24. Harold Cruse, *The Crisis of the Negro Intellectual* (New York: Morrow, 1967): 4.
25. Ibid., 564. See also Adolph L. Reed, Jr., *W. E. B. Du Bois and American Political Thought* (New York: Oxford University Press, 1997) and Lorenzo Morris and Charles Henry, *The Chit'lin Controversy* (Washington, DC: University Press of America, 1978).
26. Letter from Robert Chrisman to Al Szymanski, April 7, 1984 Carton 5, Folder S-83-87, Black Panther Papers, Bancroft Library, University of California, Berkeley.
27. Michael C. Dawson, *Black Visions* (Chicago: University of Chicago Press, 2001): 18–19. See also Cedric J. Robinson, *Black Marxism* (London, Zed, 1983).
28. Letter from Robert Chrisman to Herbert Aptheker, July 10, 1971, Carton 23, Folder Aptheker, Black Scholar Papers, Bancroft Library, University of California, Berkeley. Chrisman also agreed to contribute a chapter on "Black education to Aptheker's book on Marxism and Education," Letter from Robert Chrisman to Herbert Aptheker, January 16, 1971, Carton 23, Folder Aptheker, Black Scholar Papers, Bancroft Library, University of California, Berkeley.
29. Robert Chrisman, Presentation to the Seminar on Angola, March 1976, Carton 7, Folder Robert Chrisman's Writings, Black Scholar Papers, Bancroft Library, University of California, Berkeley.
30. Letter from Robert Chrisman to Arno Press, May 5, 1975, Carton 1, Folder 1975, Letter from Nathan Hare to Pharnal Longus,

April 17, 1972, Carton 3, Folder 1972, Black Scholar Papers, Bancroft Library, University of California, Berkeley.

31. *Black Scholar*, March 1975, back cover.
32. Allen interview.
33. Allen interview. By 1975, Allen had become a coequal with Hare and Chrisman in producing the journal. *TBS* had reviewed Allen's seminal *Black Awakening in Capitalist America* and when they found out he was in the Bay Area working for the *Guardian* newspaper, they invited him to give a paper at their meeting of Black intellectuals. The offer to join the journal as an editor soon followed.
34. Michael C. Dawson, *Black Visions* (Chicago: University of Chicago Press, 2001), p. 75.
35. For an account of Black radical involvement with Cuba see Ruth Reitan's *The Rise and Decline of an Alliance: Cuba and African American Leaders in the 1960s* (East Lansing, MI: Michigan State University Press, 1999).
36. The Venceremous ("We Shall Overcome") Brigade was formed in the Bay Area town of Redwood City, CA in 1969. Originally a Chicano organization with members from the Maoist Revolutionary Union organization, it moved toward multiracialism and practice over theory. Although active in Bay Area politics for a time, it is best known for its solidarity with Cuban workers (lumpenproletariat). Over its existence some 8000 participants have joined its group travel visits to Cuba to assist workers in agricultural (initially sugarcane harvesting) and industrial projects. These delegations of workers continue today without the approval of the U.S. government. See www.venceremosbrigade.net.
37. Robert Chrisman and Robert Allen, "Race Relations," *Black Scholar* (Feb. 1973): 9.
38. Ibid., p. 9.
39. Ibid., p. 9.
40. Robert Chrisman, "Cuba Report," *Black Scholar* (Summer 1977): 4.
41. Ibid., p. 87.
42. Ibid., p. 87.
43. Ibid., p. 88.
44. Ibid., p. 89. For an opposing viewpoint on racism in Cuba see Carlos Moore, *Castro, the Blacks, and Africa* (Los Angeles:

University of California Center for Afro-American Studies, 1988). Unfortunately, on my two visits to Cuba at the turn of century, one with Chrisman, prostitution was very much evident in the tourist districts of Havana.

45. Robert Chrisman, "Angola News Report," *Black Scholar* (March 1976): 43.
46. Report, 2/2/76 Angola had achieved independence from Portugal on November 11, 1975. Immediately a civil war erupted between three groups involved in the liberation struggle—the National Front for the Liberation of Angola (FNLA) led by Holden Roberto, the National Union for the Total Independence of Angola (UNITA) headed by Jonas Savimbi, and the MPLA and its president Agostinho Neto. While the Organization of African Unity (OAU) and more than 80 countries recognized the MPLA as the legitimate government, the United States and South Africa backed the FNLA and UNITA.
47. Letter from Robert Chrisman to Olga Lima, October 25, 1976, Carton 7, Folder Angola 1976–77, Black Panther Papers, Bancroft Library, University of California, Berkeley. A list of proposed visitors includes Robert Allen, Robert Chrisman, Johnnetta Cole, Belva and Bill Davis, Jean Damu (People's World), Elbert Sampson (KPFA), Moses Newsome (Baltimore Afro-American), Alice Walker (Ms. Magazine), Chuck Stone (Phil. Daily News).
48. Letter to Margarita Delgado, May 5, 1983, Carton 7, Folder Trip to Cuba 1982-n.d., Black Scholar Papers, Bancroft Library, University of California, Berkeley.
49. Memo by Robert Chrisman, n.d., Carton 1, Folder 1978–79, Black Scholar Papers, Bancroft Library, University of California, Berkeley.
50. Letter from Robert Chrisman to Sandra Levinson, April 2, 1983, Carton 8, Folder Morejon Tour 1985.
51. Robert Chrisman, "Black Prisoners, White Law," *Black Scholar* (April/May 1971): 45.
52. Ibid., 46.
53. An example of Chrisman's effort to aid Karenga is enlisting Maya Angelou in the effort to affect his immediate release. Letter from Maya Angelou to Robert Chrisman, January 20, 1975, Carton 23, Folder Maya Angelou. Chrisman contacted Amnesty International on behalf of Imari Obadele in an effort to promote his adoption as

a "prisoner of conscience" and later wrote a letter of recommendation for Obadele for a position at California State University, Dominguez Hills. Letter from Robert Chrisman to Ann Burley, November 7, 1977, Carton 1, Folder 1977. Letter from Robert Chrisman to President Cains, December 27, 1971, Carton 24, Folder Obadele. Black Scholar Papers, Bancroft Library, University of California, Berkeley.

54. Chrisman was concerned that Black prisoners were being denied access to *TBS* in contravention of a recent California Supreme Court decision on prisoner rights. Letter from Robert Chrisman to Philip Ryan, Attorney, December 21, 1971, Carton 4, Folder R-70–71. Black Scholar Papers, Bancroft Library, University of California, Berkeley.
55. Black Scholar Prisoner fund proposal, Carton 9, Folder Prisoner Fund 1971–73. Black Scholar Papers, Bancroft Library, University of California, Berkeley.
56. Alice Walker, "But Yet Still the Cotton Gin Kept on Working," *Black Scholar* (January–February 1970): 20.
57. Shirley Chisholm, "Racism and Anti-Feminism," Ibid., 43. A criticism she would repeat during her failed presidential bid in 1972.
58. Robert Staples, "The Myth of the Impotent Black Male," *Black Scholar* (June 1971): 2. In 1982 the Black Scholar Press published Staples book on *Black Masculinity.*
59. Angela Davis, "The Black Woman's Role in the Community of Slaves," *Black Scholar*, (December 1971): 5. Davis noted in her article that her references and resources were limited in jail. In a letter to Wallace Terry, II, Chrisman indicates that within this issue of the journal "one finds…the seeds of an ideology and perhaps a movement by black women which will expand the thrust of the black liberation struggle." Carton 5, Folder T-71. Black Scholar Papers, Bancroft Library, University of California, Berkeley.
60. Editorial, *Black Scholar* (March 4, 1973).
61. Publisher, "A Critique of the Sexual Revolution," *Black Scholar* (April 1978): 65.
62. Assata Shakur, "Women in Prison," Ibid., 11–12.
63. Audre Lorde, "Scratching the Surface," Ibid., 32.
64. Robert Staples, "The Myth of Black Macho," *Black Scholar* (April 1979):, 25. Angela Davis in "Rape, Racism and the Capitalist Setting," *Black* Scholar (April 1978) contended that the epidemic

of sexual violence in capitalist countries is in stark contrast to its virtual absence in socialist societies (p. 24).

65. Ibid., p. 25.
66. Ibid., p. 31.
67. "Introduction," *Black Scholar* (Winter/Spring 1991/92): p. xii.
68. Ibid., passim. A few notable contributors—Maya Angelou, Niara Sudarkasa and the SCLC—defended the nomination in the hope that Thomas would grow more liberal once confirmed.
69. Chrisman wrote unsuccessfully to the Ford Foundation for funding but was successful in obtaining a local CETA grant from Marin County for employment and training consultation. Letter from Robert Chrisman to Brock Brower, June 30, 1982, Carton 25, Folder Ford Foundation and letter from Glory Bevien and Robert Johnson of the Black World Foundation to Lottie Hall, March 17, 1978, Carton 27, Folder Marin 1977–79. Chrisman and Allen served on the Board of IBW and that organization chose not to publish a journal to avoid competition with *TBS* and *Black World*. Letter from Vincent Harding to Chrisman and Hare, Carton 28, Folder IBW. Black Scholar Papers, Bancroft Library, University of California, Berkeley.

    John Johnson, publisher of the *Black* World was not willing to share mailing lists. Letter from Robert Chrisman to John H. Johnson, November 15, 1977, Carton 3, Folder J-1977. Letter from Vincent Harding to Chrisman and Hare, Carton 28, Folder IBW. Black Scholar Papers, Bancroft Library, University of California, Berkeley.
70. Letter from Nathan Hare to Barbara J. Williams, January 11, 1971, Carton 1, Folder 1970; Letter from Robert Chrisman to Amiri Baraka, April 17, 1971, Carton 1, Folder 1971; Black Scholar Papers, Bancroft Library, University of California, Berkeley.
71. "Editorial," *Black Scholar* (January 1972): 34. In light of Chrisman's critique of Cruse this closed meeting of an intellectual elite to develop new norms and values is somewhat ironic.
72. "The Black Scholar—a black enterprise," n.d., Carton 25, Folder Background information on *TBS*. Black Scholar Papers, Bancroft Library, University of California, Berkeley.

73. Letter from Robert Chrisman to Brother S. Dominic Ruegg, April 10, 1975, Carton 4, Folder R-75.
74. Robert Chrisman, "The Black Scholar: The First Forty Years," *Black Scholar* (Winter 2011): 2. Less than a year before his death in March 2013, Chrisman turned over the leadership of *TBS* to Laura Chrisman, his daughter and a professor of English at the University of Washington. Two new senior editors replaced Robert Allen—Sundiata Keita Cha-Jua and Louis Chude-Sokei. Maize Woodford remained the executive editor.

CHAPTER 6

Democratizing the Disciplines

At the tender age of 13 in 1960, I made the curious decision to obtain a doctorate in political science. As an African American from a working-class family with no college history, this was a rather bold decision. In retrospect, I think it was the combination of the student-led sit-in movement and the election of John F. Kennedy, both in that year, that pushed me in the direction of politics—both electoral and nonelectoral.

My first encounter with Theodore Lowi[1] came as a senior in college in 1968–69. It was the custom of the political science department at Denison University to invite prominent political scientists to campus to administer oral examinations to the graduating majors. That year, Lowi from the University of Chicago and Herbert Shapiro from the University of Pennsylvania were the external examiners. I do not remember anything about the examination and I spent more time talking to Shapiro than Lowi. However, I had already made up my mind to attend (if accepted) the University of Chicago because of its reputation for political theory.

As one of the few African American males on campus during my undergraduate years, I had participated in the formation of a Black Student Union, experimental college, race relations outreach, antipoverty work in the local community, the first Black Studies course on campus, antiwar protests, and many of the other student activities that swept through American colleges in the late 1960s. I looked to political science to provide some perspective and insight on what was happening on campus and in the world. My senior thesis was on "African Socialism" and I hoped Chicago would provide fur-

C.P. Henry, *Black Studies and the Democratization of American Higher Education*, DOI 10.1007/978-3-319-35089-9_6

ther enlightenment. There was only one problem—Chicago accepted me but offered no financial aid. As the son of a retired bricklayer living on social security, I certainly met the need requirement. My faculty adviser, Roy Morey, called Lowi and shortly thereafter I received a full fellowship.

Over the course of my three years in residence (1969–72) at Chicago, I had two of Lowi's public policy courses and he served as my dissertation chair. When he left for Cornell in 1972, he graciously agreed to stay on as chair although sociologist William J. Wilson sat in for him on the oral examination. I think both Lowi and I shared an interest in social movements as an engine of social change (we both saw ourselves as "outsiders"). We also shared a belief that the dominant political theory of the day, pluralism, was an inadequate analytic to capture what was happening. Lowi had also stated that "[r]ace will shape the new leadership and the new techniques, because it is the one issue that cuts across and intertwines with all the issues in our time."[2] All of this led to a dissertation on the civil rights movement from the perspective of its participants using a phenomenological approach.[3] Of course, being in Chicago during this period provided an opportunity to observe and/or participate in some of the key events and organizations of the time including the Chicago Seven Trial, anti-Daley machine work, Operation Breadbasket, the Nation of Islam, and the National Black Political Assembly in Gary in 1972. In addition, given Chicago's lack of student teaching assistants, my first experience as a classroom instructor was at Malcolm X City College, which considered itself in the vanguard of "urban education."

When I left my position in the political science department at Howard for Denison in 1976, I had a joint appointment in Black Studies and political science. Like many other young academics, I tried to maintain my links to the traditional discipline I was trained in as I explored the rapidly evolving world of Black Studies. When Berkeley offered me a position in the department of African American Studies in 1980, I did not fully realize that I was committing disciplinary suicide.[4]

Berkeley's political science department appeared to have no interest in me or my work. When I asked if they would cross-list a course I was teaching on "Black Political Life in the United States," I was told that if they did it for me, they would have to do it for everyone. I wondered how many faculty came to them with such requests! Part of the problem may have been race and part of the problem may have been that I was identified as a "Lowi" student. Young faculty are often linked to their mentors, and Lowi had challenged the dominant paradigm of the discipline.

Richard Merelman in *Pluralism at Yale* defines a legitimating discourse as any body of ideas, images, or practices that portrays a political regime to be functioning as its power holders claim it to be functioning, and, in so doing, provides support to those who exert power in the regime.[5] He argues that the development of the pluralist paradigm at Yale during the period from 1955 to 1970 meets this definition. Pluralism may be summarized as consisting of four basic assertions: (1) that the American policy consists of multiple centers competing for power, (2) that political leaders are tolerant coalition builders, (3) that policymaking is reactive rather than proactive, and (4) that the outcome of this process is graduate, moderate political reform.[6]

The major figures in political science at Yale during this period included Robert Dahl, Robert Lane, Charles Lindbloom, Herbert Kaufman, Harold Lasswell, Karl Deutsch, David Barber, Gabriel Almond, and William Muir among others. Among their students were Nelson Polsby, Raymond Wolfinger, David Mayhew, Aaron Wildavsky, Fred Greenstein, and Theodore Lowi. According to Merelman, the faculty not only "theorized" pluralism but also performed it in most activities. Some of Merelman's respondents contend that this pluralist way of life began to fracture in the late 1960s as a result of internal strains.

One source of stress was the purported moral neutrality or objectivity of pluralism. As a branch of behavioralism, the pluralist researchers' detachment, both personally and professionally, from their research ran counter to student demands for relevancy. For example, Donald Stewart, one of the few African Americans at Yale, saw elements of poverty and disorder in New Haven that upset him. He concluded that pluralism could not handle the question of race and longed "for some identification with social movements and developments that had an impact on people of color."[7]

While Lowi had broken with the paradigm and argued that "students… have been essentially correct in their complaint…and have restored the need to provide a moral basis for action,"[8] many in the political science department at Berkeley had not. They included Polsby, Wolfinger, Muir, and Wildavsky. Of the four, Wolfinger was the only one to write extensively on race and he did so from a pluralist perspective. It was in Black Studies, not mainstream political science, that I found a challenge to the dominant paradigm. And that challenge came wrapped in the politics of that time and place. As Houston Baker states, "[n]ever before in so brief a span of American academic time, had there occurred the type of recovery, revised pedagogy, accelerated cultural and distribution, and scholarly research that was motivated by black cultural nationalism, black studies, and Black Power during the 1970s and 1980s."[9]

In his classic *The Structure of Scientific Revolutions*, Thomas Kuhn states that "all the well-known pre-Darwinian evolutionary theories—those of Lamarck, Chambers, Spencer, and the German Naturphilospher—had taken evolution to be a goal-directed process." "For many men," says Kuhn, "the abolition of that teleological kind of evolution was the most significant and least palatable of Darwin's suggestions."[10] When the dominant paradigm for explaining race and race relations shifted from religion in general and the Christian Old Testament in particular with the publication of Darwin's *Origins of the Species* in 1859, claims about racial inferiority or superiority also shifted from the subjective to the objective. Yet, as Kuhn indicates, Darwinian science implied a randomness or lack of divinely orchestrated direction to racial evolution. If God did not create the races and set them on the path of racial evolution from the lowest to the highest, who did?

While it was morally unsettling to remove God's hand from the equation, a host of theories concerning nature and natural selection quickly assume God's role. Social science soon applied Darwin's theories to race and turned the absence of God into a positive. This "positivism" was more scientific than religion because it was objective—that is, it was value-free. And again, as Kuhn states, "the decision to reject one paradigm is always simultaneously the decision to accept another, and the judgment leading to that decision involves the comparison of both paradigms with nature *and* with each other."[11]

Although the traditional disciplines Black students challenged in the late 1960s were presented as ordained by nature and set in stone, they were relatively recent creations in academia. In fact, they fully emerged during the period of the Darwinian revolution from 1850 to 1914 and institutionalized themselves between World War I and World War II. In writing about the institutionalization of economics during this period, for example, Mark Aldrich examines the activities of progressive economist and leader of the American Economic Association, Walter Willcox, in promoting his work and that of other economists and noneconomists who shared his views:

> Willcox was typical of most economists who studied blacks' economic behavior during this period: virtually all of them made racial inferiority a more or less important explanatory variable in their analyses. It is entirely

> understandable that they should have done this. To economists such as Willcox who thought in the competitive, Social Darwinist manner which made individual success or failure the result of individual merit or demerit, racial inferiority made explicable the plight of an entire people. In so doing, however, the economists had their analyses deflected by scientific racism away from the social system as a primary source of blacks' economic difficulties, and it led them instead to blame its very victims for their trials. Protesting all the while of their objectivity, economists such as Willcox thus added their authority to the scientific consensus which justified the oppression of American blacks.[12]

Not only were the major social science disciplines of history, economics, political science, and sociology as we know them created in a relatively brief time, but they were also geographically limited. At least 95 percent of the practitioners of these disciplines could be found in five countries: Great Britain, France, the Germanies, the Italies, and the United States. According to Immanuel Wallerstein, all four disciplines were confronting the "basic political issue of how to deal with the increasing assertive demands of the growing number of urban proletarians in the wake of considerable industrial development and a marked development of consciousness about popular sovereignty."[13] The response, says Wallerstein, "was the creation of the 'liberal national state' with history and its past orientation based on idiographic prejudices admirably suited to the creation of a national identity" and "social science with its present orientation and its nomothetic prejudice admirably adaptable to policy planning, the necessary tool of rational reformism."[14]

If we see social science as also a civic discourse in which public policies are established or contested, then we may judge scientific theories for their ideological and practical effects. However, the political function of theory operates within, and implicitly projects a basic image of the world. "Positivist social theory," says Richard Harvey Brown, "elaborates the metaphors of society as an organism or a machine, thereby generating theories and data that support social doctoring or social engineering."[15] Unfortunately the language of logical positivism did not include human agency, which created logical and moral contradictions when positivists sought to extend their theories to real world practice.

The debate over whether Black Studies is a discipline or a field obscures the role that politics and ideology played in the establishment of traditional disciplines. It leads immediately to a discussion of boundaries and the policing of boundaries by professionals. Maulana Karenga, for example, skirts the issue of field or discipline by contending that Black Studies has sought to develop an interdisciplinary paradigm. However, do we solve the absence of Black content simply by invoking an interdisciplinary paradigm or placing the adjective "Black" in front of each traditional discipline. This conception of Black Studies as a discipline avoids the question of what paradigm the disciplines operate under. A discussion of paradigms, on the other hand, raises the larger question of who determines the rules of debate when paradigms are in dispute or transition? If, for example, a paradigm is the equivalent of a language or a culture that determines the questions that can be asked and those that are excluded as Bourdieu insists, are there dominant discourses and subordinated discourses? How do paradigms become dominant and what accounts for the differences in status and therefore resources between disciplines and between science and the social sciences and humanities? Beyond the impact of nature and logic, what are the dynamics of persuasive argument and power relationships effective in the professional community and how is that professional community or intellectual network influenced by external forces. As Kuhn indicates, the interpretive enterprise—which is normal science—can only articulate a paradigm, not correct it.[16]

Kuhn's influence is evident in the volume of scholars who both embrace him and critique him. In his effort to democratize science, Brown extends Kuhn's narrow notion of paradigm along several lines. First, he expands its focus on excessively cognitive meaning to also include the practices and politics of intellectual production in particular fields. Second, Brown shifts Kuhn's excessively "internalist" theory of scientific change to focus on the penetrations of the "internal" and "external." Third, he stretches Kuhn's diachronic or sequential narrative to a more synchronic view that permits incremental and revolutionary change to occur simultaneously. Finally, Brown suggests that significant—though not revolutionary—changes occur within normal sciences, such as specialization or fragmentation, that are not accounted for in Kuhn's formulation.[17] With Brown's extension of Kuhn, we are better able to see the obstacles faced in institutionalizing Black Studies and to examine the evolution of the field itself into subspecialties and hybrids.

While we are mainly concerned with the social science disciplines here, including history, science is not immune from the impact of culture as Kuhn demonstrates. Other scholars have examined the characteristics of science "not as inherent or possibly unique, but as part of ideological efforts by scientists to distinguish their work and its product from non-scientific intellectual activities."[18] Kohler's study of biochemistry does not distinguish between science and non-science in the importance of politics to boundary work: "Disciplines are political institutions that demarcate areas of academic integrity, allocate the privileges and responsibilities of expertise and structure claims on resources."[19] Sandra Harding has joined a group of postcolonial science scholars in asking to what extent has modern science borrowed from non-European cultures and are there other culturally distinctive sciences that also "work."[20] Pierre Bourdieu reminds us that the movement of 1968 carried the challenge to academic principles onto the very privileged terrain of the University itself starting with the authority of science.[21] Disciplines, then, can develop within the paradigm; they cannot step outside it and critique or correct it. And the problems disciplines choose to solve are informed by the unquestioned values flowing from the paradigm.

The values of the disciplines discussed here are historically linked to the West in general and the nation-states of Europe and the United States in particular. Wallerstein suggests three consequences that flow from their origins. First, the disciplines of history, economics, political science, and sociology focused almost entirely on the West as worthy of study. From G.F. Hegel's assertion that Africa existed outside history to the absence of a US State Department Bureau dealing with Africa until 1960, Africa was invisible until "discovered" by the West. According to Jacques Depelchin, "the central characteristic of the syndrome of discovery and, one might add, at the root of all forms of oppression and exploitation (among social scientists) is the conviction among its carriers that knowledge as defined, understood and practiced by them cannot be modified by knowledge contained in the 'discovered' societies."[22] Moreover, whereas historians thought their distance in time from the subjects under study gave them objectivity, the more present-oriented social sciences attempted to eliminate the intrusion of the subjective judgments by the researcher by replacing qualitative statements with quantitative data. This shift meant that social science research was limited to those areas that had the "necessary" data—the West.[23]

A second consequence of the rise of social science with the nation-state was its utility in imperial expansion. This necessitated the establishment of a discipline focused on the non-West, hence the creation of anthropology and "Oriental" studies. The past/present cleavage separating history from its sister social science disciplines was irrelevant in "primitive" societies where the past was frozen in the present. However, it did demand new methodological techniques such as ethnography given the absence of "data." Once, however, the ethnographer had established his authority by location (I was there), he/she typically shifts to the third person description that displays dispassion, distance, and scientific objectivity.[24] The study of all "high culture" non-Western civilizations was relegated to Oriental Studies (the first area studies program).[25]

At this early stage of development, economics, political science, and sociology were grouped together (and still are at smaller colleges). As these disciplines professionalized, they sought to differentiate themselves, which meant separating research from social reform components. For example, by 1945, economics concentrated on a set of marketplace rules and excluded the "exogenous." By placing the "free market" or "invisible hand" in the role of determining value, economics avoided the messy moral questions in linking research to practice. In addition, the increasing quantification of the discipline gave it greater legitimacy as the most "scientific" of the social sciences. In his widely discussed *Capital*, economist Thomas Piketty takes on the frequently overlooked problem of the inequality of wealth. He contends that the distribution of wealth has always been deeply political and cannot be reduced to purely economic mechanisms. Piketty even critiques the separation of economics from the other social sciences and its over-reliance on mathematical equations: "To put it bluntly, the discipline of economics has yet to get over its childish passion for mathematics and for purely theoretical and often highly ideological speculation, at the expense of historical research and collaboration with the other social sciences."[26] Piketty sees his work as much a work of history as of economics.

Of course, the most famous economist associated with race and race relations was Sweden's Gunnar Myrdal. Yet the author of *An American Dilemma* eschewed an economic analysis in favor of a psychological quandary. "*American Negro culture*," he said, "*is a distorted development, or a pathological condition, of the general American culture*."[27] The best the Negro could do, according to Myrdal, was act more like Whites to assist them in overcoming the cognitive dissonance created by the gap between American ideals and the American practice of discrimination. His shift toward psychological analysis spawned a host of studies examining the impact of prejudice on Blacks. In *Mark of Oppression*, psychologists Abram Kardiner and Lionel Ovesey contended that at the time of emancipation, the freedman "had no culture…no pride, no group solidarity, no tradition," a condition from which "he has never since freed himself."[28] These and similar post–World War II works on race, such as Richard Hofstader's *The Peculiar Institution*, were considered liberal or pro-Negro in the sense that they sought to explain the Black condition in terms of culture rather than biological inferiority.

Political science faced a great deal of resistance from law in its attempt to establish itself as a separate discipline. As the only traditional discipline to evolve in the United States, it sought to focus on political power rather than jurisprudence. After an early emphasis on political institutions such as Congress and political parties, it shifted toward behavioral studies of voters and rational choice after World War II.[29] This behavioral shift enabled political science to quantify its approaches to problem solving but without the normative-free mechanism of the "invisible hand." But if social scientists were to uncover the meaning behind the behavior of their subjects (data points), it necessitated theorizing. That is, it necessitated generalizing and generalizing only had meaning if one believed in universal truths. If universal truths did not exist, then it did not matter where and when one accumulated data.

As the American-grown discipline, political science generally sought to avoid race altogether despite its centrality to American politics from the very beginnings of the country. When it was discussed, as in the discipline's main journal the *American Political Science Review*, for example, it was always in the context of Blacks' relationship to the White norm.[30] Low Black voter turnout, for instance, was the result of Black alienation or apathy rather than the absence of Black candidates on the ballot.[31] More overt efforts to discourage Black voting were explained as geographically limited to the South or as minor disruptions to the ultimate triumph of American democracy.

While early political science tended to avoid race, American sociologists confronted it head on. In fact, domestic racial tensions were a part of the larger challenges associated with massive European immigration. At the forefront of mainstream sociology in the United States was Robert Park, a former newspaper reporter who was immersed in the race issue as director of public relations and ghost writer for Booker T. Washington's Tuskegee Institute from 1905 to 1914.

When Park moved to the University of Chicago's sociology department in 1914, his views of Blacks as a primitive, rural, southern-based people, a nation within a nation, had been heavily influenced by Washington. Park also adopted Washington's hands-on teaching approach at Tuskegee by sending his students into the real world to conduct empirical research. Significantly, the development of Park's famous race relations cycle of conflict, competition, accommodation, and assimilation drew from Washington's gradualism. Thus, as Park developed the Chicago school of sociology, its major theoretical principles of sociology as an objective science and its unique Social Darwinism combining evolutionary principles with social interaction analysis were heavily indebted to the "Wizard of Tuskegee."[32]

The first generation of Chicago sociologists, led by Albion Small, supposed that the discipline they professed had pledged itself to reassert America's destiny—the nation would be "the city upon a hill."[33] Social scientists were not about to let the status of African Americans interfere with their political belief in American exceptionalism. Influential sociologist Daniel Bell, for example, differentiated between "uniqueness," which every nation can claim, and "exceptionalism," in the sense of being exemplary—"a light unto the nations, immune from the social ills and decadence that have beset all other republics in the past, a nation exempt from the 'social laws' of development that all nations eventually follow."[34] Noting that the founders believed they had created a morally superior state, Bell added that in perhaps the only complete civil society in history, the United States was "an open society [in which] each man was free to 'make himself' and to make his fortune."[35] The institution of slavery is absent from Bell's analysis.

Another prominent social scientist, Seymour Martin Lipset, was equally nationalistic in his praise of American democracy, "however one comes to this debate, there can be little question that the hand of providence has been on a nation which finds a Washington, a Lincoln, or a Roosevelt when it needs him. When I write the above sentence, I believe that I draw scholarly conclusions, although I will confess that I write also as a proud American."[36] Unlike Bell, Lipset acknowledged the status of African Americans had been "qualitatively different" from that of any other racial or ethnic minority in the United States. He attributed the success of the civil rights movement to the American creed although he did not see the hand of providence in the leadership of Martin Luther King or in the need to compete with the Soviet Union for the hearts and minds and resources of a newly independent Africa.

World War II and the following Cold War led to two breakthroughs in regard to research on Africa. At the outbreak of the war, the relative absence of American colonies and subsequent lack of political and scholarly interest in Africa resulted in a dearth of African specialists. When the Office of the Coordinator of Information (later the O.S.S.) in the Library of Congress contacted Harvard University in its search for an African specialist, the name of Ralph Bunche was put forward as the best graduate student "of his race" during his time at Harvard. Bunche, then a political science professor at Howard University, was appointed as senior social science analyst in the Library of Congress in 1941 and later transferred to the State Department in 1943. By the time Bunche joined the United Nations in December 1946, the United States was beginning to encourage and fund "area studies."[37] Thus, for the first time, the traditional social science disciplines crossed the boundary lines they had so carefully constructed to work in the "Third World."

When anthropologist Franz Boas and his disciples Ruth Benedict and Margaret Mead began to challenge the objectivity of Social Darwinism over the objections of industrialists Andrew Carnegie and Richard Gilder among others, the concept of cultural relativity moved to the forefront of racial discourse. Social scientists, however, were quick to state that cultures were not equal. They distinguished between the more advanced cultures of the West where reason and rationality were dominant values and more "primitive" non-Western cultures guided by religion and tribalism. In fact, the concept of development or "modernization" was seen as the gradual erosion of primordial ties and their replacement with science and secular values. Thus, the norms and customs of the West were portrayed as universal values to be striven for by all societies. Tacit methodological norms conflated the notion of culture with the idea of difference.

By the late 1960s, the end of colonialism, both foreign and domestic, led to a questioning of the logical posivitism inherited from the Enlightenment. Boundaries between the social sciences and humanities blurred with forms of social description and even the use of key words drawn from the humanities, such as text, story, and social drama. Anthropologist Clifford Geertz contended that the social sciences underwent deep changes in their conceptions of (1) the object of analysis; (2) the language of analysis; and (3) the position of the analyst.[38] The ideological underpinning of objectivity was deconstructed in order to reveal the cultural. The notion in objectivism that what has already happened had to happen was challenged.

The obvious and not-so-obvious nationalism found in American social science helped forge a consensus among early proponents of Black Studies. These early advocates could agree on (1) a critique of objectivity, (2) the political nature of education, and (3) a critique of Eurocentrism from the perspective of multiculturalism.

It is at least ironic that the social scientist most responsible for introducing empirical research into American social science and rejecting theories based on anecdotal evidence or appeals to racial nature and temperament was excluded from mainstream social science (the dominant discourse) on the grounds that he was too ideological/political. This same figure that introduced empiricism also ranged across disciplines and methodologies, included women and class in his analysis, and utilized a comparative framework. Moreover, his work was guided by the moral imperative of pursuing facts that, he believed, would ameliorate the condition of African Americans. Thus, W.E.B. Du bois is rightly cited as the father of modern Black Studies.

By the late 1960s, only one biography of W.E.B. Du Bois had been published, Francis L. Broderick's 1959 *W. E. B. Du Bois, Negro Leader in a Time of Crisis.* It minimized his contributions to scholarship focusing on his role as a race leader. Du Bois was not taught in sociology, history, economics, or political science although he made significant contributions to each of them. It was not until Black students were challenged by their White professors to come up with content worth inclusion in the curriculum that Du Bois was rediscovered. And, of course, Du Bois had not been offered a teaching position at any predominantly White university despite his sterling credentials. As Dipesh Chakrabarty states in *Provincializing Europe*, nation-states have the capacity to enforce their truth games, and universities, their critical distance notwithstanding, are a part of the battery of institutions complicit in this process.[39]

Today most of Du Bois's voluminous and pioneering research, essays, speeches, and fiction have been published. Moreover, there are a host of biographies including David Levering Lewis's Pulitzer prize-winning two-volume biography. Du Bois's *The Souls of Black Folk* is generally regarded as the most influential work in African American letters. Its posit of the "double-consciousness" of African Americans and the color-line being the foremost problem of the twentieth century are the two most common tropes found across the field. His interdisciplinarity and range across the humanities and social sciences, his empiricism and lyricism, his international activism, and his claim that there is a Black culture worthy of serious analysis mark him as the preeminent Black Studies scholar. More recently, however, his work as a pioneering American social scientist has been recovered.

In *The Scholar Denied*, Aldon Morris claims that his social research was suppressed because it concluded there were no scientific grounds to justify racial oppression. Du Bois insisted that the newly emerging social sciences be built on careful empirical research focused on human action in order to pass the test as genuine science. It was Du Bois's German mentors at the University of Berlin and not his Harvard professors that began to transform his approach to sociology. They rejected grand theories and deductive reasoning insisting on a paradigm shift to inductive reasoning. Social generalizations were to be based on empirical findings rather than on a priori systems of invented "natural" laws and racial "temperments." Moreover, these findings had a public policy dimension—that is they were goal directed. Du Bois put his training to work in researching and writing *The Philadelphia Negro*, now credited as the first empirically based, urban study in the United States.

Morris details the efforts of members of the Chicago school as well as other mainstream scholars to marginalize Du Bois and deny him the resources to carry out projects like the *Encyclopedia of the Negro* project. By denying him foundation funds and limiting his teaching appointments to poorly resourced historically Black colleges, Du Bois was denied access to the elite intellectual networks that are the crucial mechanisms generating and sustaining schools of thought. These networks develop a conservative interest in supporting the dominant paradigm. In Du Bois's words: "So far as the American world of science and letters was concerned, we never 'belonged'; we remained unrecognized in learned societies and academic groups."[40] Yet to some extent, Du Bois was able to work around these networks by using students, Black women's organizations, Black church groups, and the NAACP as resources. In addition, he was able to maintain contact with some of the more progressive scholars such as Max Weber and Franz Boas.[41]

Black Studies was in the vanguard of the postmodern challenge to logical posivitism and its claims of objectivity or neutrality in the late 1960s and early 1970s. They had discovered what Du Bois had seen a half century earlier—that science in pursuit of the truth was not an objective science that ignored the "real world" fearing contamination but rather a critical social science aimed at using knowledge to transform the world through effective research.[42] St. Clair Drake clearly saw Black Studies as an ideological challenge to mainstream scholarship:

> The very use of the term Black Studies is by implication an indictment of American and Western European scholarship. It makes the bold assertion that what we have heretofore called "objective" intellectual activities were actually white studies in perspective and content; and that corrective bias, a shift in emphasis, is needed, even if something called "truth" is set as a goal. To use a technical sociological term, the present body of knowledge has an ideological element in it, and a counter-ideology is needed. Black Studies supply that counter-ideology.[43]

Postmodernists argued that claims to knowledge were also claims to power. In addition, they contested the notion that the pursuit of knowledge was a search for the truth. Societies, they contended, produce meaning not truth and the meanings produced were called "cultures."[44]

As the paradigm for race discourse shifted from biology to culture, it is not surprising that the major form of the Black Studies response would be cultural nationalism. In his *Imagined Communities*, Benedict Anderson states since World War II every successful revolution has defined itself in national terms.[45] The academic revolution proved to be no exception. After all, for all the claims of universities being ivy-covered towers on a hill, they exist in the real world, and their canons and traditions have always reflected the temporal aspects of the larger society in which they rest.

Of course, the question remained of how does one gain critical knowledge of the cultural order that gave it consciousness? Or, as Bourdieu puts it, "how is it possible for a historical activity, such as scientific activity, to produce historical truths, independent of history, detached from all bonds with both place and time and therefore eternally and universally valid?"[46] Marxism stood as the obvious and historical alternative. However, Marxism exhibited several glaring weaknesses for Black Studies advocates. First, Marx was European and his works revealed some Eurocentric biases difficult to reconcile with Black Power. Second, Marxism made "scientific" claims to "truth" at a time when both science and truth were under attack. As Alvin Gouldner states, Marxism "provides no basis in whose terms one can critically examine the assumptions of science itself; science—and social science now become isolated from a larger more encompassing view of reason."[47] Finally, the history of Black intellectuals with Marxism as represented by the Communist Party had been one fraught with difficulties.

What emerges, of course, as the prototype paradigm for a Black Studies critique of the academic status quo is a type of cultural nationalism. It is no accident that Harold Cruse, in his seminal *The Crisis of the Negro*

Intellectual, spends a great deal of time attacking the Communist Party USA, its intellectuals, and its Black fellow-travelers. He argued, for example, that V.F. Calverton's theory of "cultural compulsives" was "possibly the only valid attempt at an original contribution to Marxism by an avowed American Marxist."[48] And, in challenging integration and the notion of an American melting pot, Cruse lays ground work for a critical examination of American higher education from a cultural perspective. He might join Paul Ricoeur in acknowledging "the end of a cultural monopoly, be it illusory or real," is threatening and "suddenly it becomes possible that there are just *others*."[49] Cruse regarded "culture" as the great weakness of American society. He stated "the problem of Negro cultural identity is an unsolved problem within the context of an American nation that is still in process of [cultural] formation."[50]

While Cruse's critique of American society from a cultural nationalist perspective was influential among Black Studies advocates, it failed to offer them a cultural theory on which to build. As Jerry Watts stated, "Cruse continually hits black intellectuals and artists over the head for the abdication of their responsibility to develop a cultural theory that would place black artists and intellectuals in the service of the black struggle"; however, "nowhere…does Cruse put forth his version of this cultural ideology."[51]

Into this void stepped Maulana Karenga who set forth Kawaida theory that offered a continuous critique of the established order and posed correctives. As a critical theory, Karenga said Kawaida did not present itself as a theory of absolute knowledge but rather "a modest ongoing synthesis of the best of nationalist, Pan-Africanist and socialist thought."[52] Kawaida defined "nationalism as the concept and conviction that we are a distinct people with a distinct historical personality and that, therefore, we should unite in order to gain the structural capacity to define, defend and develop our interests as a people."[53] For Karenga, reflecting Cruse, the key crisis was the cultural crisis because views and values flowed from culture. Any analysis of Black status had to be "Afro-centric," and any real solution must involve one of seven basic areas of culture: (1) Mythology; (2) History; (3) Social Organization; (4) Economic Organization; (5) Political Organization; (6) Creative Motif; and (7) Ethos.[54]

Karenga's influence can be seen in the praise of leading Black Studies proponents who later became ideological opponents. Abdul Alkalimat (Gerald McWorter) wrote we "must be committed to *Africanization* for, as Maulana (Ron) Karenga teaches: 'To return to tradition is to take the first step forward'."[55]

Amiri Baraka (Leroi Jones), whose Black Arts and Culture series within the Experimental College at San Francisco State University in 1966 was "the foundation for their new consciousness and identity," described meeting Karenga for the first time.

He said he liked *Blues People*, but that he thought the blues were reactionary. That blues were talking about slavery and submission. I blinked and politely disagreed. But Karenga is nothing if not aggressive. He went on, elaborating his theories on culture and nationalism, talking at high speed non-stop, laughing at his own witticisms and having two members of a chorus, yea-saying, calling "Teach!" when Karenga made some point he considered salient.[56]

Baraka goes on to say that Karenga's doctrine, which he followed for eight years, was very eclectic drawing on Elijah Muhammad, Nkrumah, Fanon, Toure, Nyerere, Garvey, Malcolm, Mao, and even Lenin, Stalin, and Marx. While Baraka and the Congress of African People (CAP) broke with Karenga, the former stated: "I think that there is much in Karenga's doctrines that is valid."[57]

Molife Asante, who has written an intellectual portrait of Karenga, cites his influence on the development of the discourse around African American Studies. "No single individual thinker," says Asante, "has, without media promotion and American mainstream endorsement, molded intellectual discourse and shaped the African American cultural agenda as has Karenga."[58] Asante incorporates key elements of Kawaida into "Afrocentricity" to position the behavioral options of African people in such a manner that Africans would assume full responsibility for emerging from the conditions they found themselves in after the encounter with Europe. He believes Kawaida and Afrocentricity both recognized the need for total systemic change encompassing the entire African community. Ama Mazama, in *The Afrocentric Paradigm*, adds that although Karenga did not grant "paradigmatic status to Afrocentricity," he correctly saw it as rooted in the cultural image and human interest of African people.[59]

While Asante credits Karenga with establishing a systematic ideology and even making tradition *scientifically*, he finds fault with Karenga's concept of history. Stating that Karenga's view of history was too materialistic, Asante says: "When Karenga chastised the Christian element for its 'spookism' his purpose was instructive, but the result was seemingly to isolate the spiritual realities which are in fact parts of our history."[60] Asante labels Karenga a "cultural scientist" concentrating on the structural realities of culture and empirically constructing a set of values when he could not find them in our history. In calling Kawaida "typological as opposed to process," Asante implies that Karenga's "Black Politics," "Black Psychology," and so on are redefinitions of traditional disciplines rather than transformations.[61]

In a later work, Asante contends that African American Studies is more than a mere collection of courses distinguished by its African content. It has become, he states, a method of human studies or a human science equal to any other method of human studies. Unlike most social sciences, it does not distance itself from the subject and it merges its approaches with the humanities. While Africology, as a discipline, centers the methodology in a "particular cultural voice," its seven general subject fields remain remarkably discipline bound and social science oriented. They are social, communication, historical, cultural, political, economic, and psychological.[62]

By reducing the traditional disciplines to subject fields, Asante is able to project Africology as a metatheory that encompasses them rather than replaces them. What distinguishes the student of Africology from a traditional researcher in these areas is the selection of a paradigmatic research approach. According to Asante, there are three such approaches—functional, categorical, and etymological. Thus, for example, a student of Africology might do historical research using the functional paradigm, which represents needs, policy, and action.[63] It is not clear how giving methodology the status of a paradigm makes Africology transformative. However, this is not the most controversial aspect of Afrocentrism.

The study of Kemet (ancient Egypt) has emerged as a source of debate and criticism in relation to Afrocentrism. Asante explains why so much research attention has been devoted to this topic: "The anteriority of the classical African civilizations must be entertained by any Africological inquiry, simply because without that perspective, our work hangs in the air, detached and isolated or becomes nothing more than a sub-set of the Eurocentric disciplines."[64]

Since ancient Greece is the model for the structure of knowledge in the West, it is crucial, says Asante, to establish Kemet in the same role in regard to the African world. Cheikh Anta Diop is the key figure in linking Kemet with the modern African world and Asante merges the classificatory schemes of Diop with those of Karenga. The result is a cultural framework that contains three elements covering all knowledge areas. They are epistemic including ethics, politics, psychology (modes of behavior); scientific including history, linguistics, economics (methods of investigation); and artistic including icons, art, motifs, symbols (types of presentation).[65]

The controversy surrounding Afrocentrism's focus on Kemet involves three issues. First is the claim that Africa is culturally unified flowing primarily from an ancient Black Egyptian civilization. This assertion rests largely on the work of Diop and the earlier work of Edward Blyden on the "African Personality." This claim promotes the view that the early Egyptian civilization was Black—that is civilization flowed up the Nile from the Sudan rather than down the Nile from the Mediterranean. A second claim argues that Greek culture was heavily influenced by these Black Egyptians. A primary focal point for this debate has been the publication of Martin Bernal's work on ancient Egypt starting with *Black Athena*. A final Afrocentric claim seeks to link the cultural unity of Africa with the African diaspora. Asante and, especially, Karenga have devoted a good deal of attention to this linkage.

Each claim has its own set of critics. In one of the more comprehensive critiques, Stephen Howe has questioned the credibility of Diop's sources. Contending that Diop's work and that of UNESCO are outdated, Howe believes most anthropologists do not support unanimism—the belief that Africa is or was culturally homogeneous. Moreover, they also reject diffusionism—the theory that if human phenomena of the same kind are found in different places, they must have spread from a common sources. Howe notes that no significant Egyptian cultural artifacts have ever been discovered in sub-Saharan Africa.[66]

In a sense, the claim that African culture sprang from Egypt is also a claim that the Egyptians were Black Africans. Asante shifts back and forth between biological and geographic definitions of race in *Afrocentricity* and the assertion of a Black Egypt has drawn a great deal of popular attention and ridicule. For example, the question of whether Cleopatra was Black or not garnered the attention of mainstream media.[67] Both Asante and Martin Bernal cite the work of Herodotus as evidence that ancient Egyptians were Black (Ethiopian).[68] A more contemporary Afrocentric perspective contends that in the United States today the physical appearance of most Egyptians would see them categorized as Black. Of course, ancient Egyptians themselves had no conception of the "one drop" rule as applied in America.

Although a number of earlier Black intellectuals such as Chancellor Williams, John G. Jackson, John Hendrik Clarke, J.A. Rogers, Yosef Ben-Jochannen, and George G.M. James, had written about the "Blackness" or

"Africaness" of Egypt and some had addressed the Greek debt to Egypt, none drew both the attention and criticism of Bernal's *Black Athena*. Bernal, primarily a linguist whose father was a distinguished English Africanist, published the first of his three volumes in 1987 at the height of the culture wars in the United States. Perhaps for that reason or perhaps due to his race, Bernal's work was heavily critiqued. Essentially, *Black Athena* contends that in the ancient world, Egypt was widely regarded as an African civilization (Ancient Model). Moreover, it was generally acknowledged that the ancient Greeks had studied in Egypt and borrowed from Egyptian culture. This general view of Egypt was effectively erased in modern times and replaced with an Aryan Model starting with Napoleon's "scientific" expeditions to Egypt at the turn of the nineteenth century and extending through the Aryan supremacy of Nazi Germany in the mid-twentieth century. Thus, according to Bernal, he is reclaiming a lost sociology of knowledge through a revised Ancient Model.[69]

While Bernal did not identify himself as an Afrocentrist, his work was embraced by them and widely condemned by classics scholars. Among the latter, Mary Lefkowitz was among the most prolific. In *Not Out of Africa*, she states, "the only possibility that she (Cleopatra) might not have been a full-blooded Macedonian Greek arises from the fact that we do not know the precise identity of...her grandmother on her father's side."[70] Lefkowitz, however, devotes most of her attention to defending the "integrity" of ancient Greece from the attacks of Afrocentrism that "robs them and their modern descendants of a heritage that rightly belongs to them."[71] Although her actual critique is narrowly focused on Greek philosophy and the older work of James rather than Bernal, she proceeds to level a much broader charge.

> Because of the confusion about the purpose of the university (do we enforce social justice, or do we disseminate knowledge?), we have reached the point where academic discourse is impossible, at least in certain quarters, because the achievement of social goals, such as diversity, has been allowed to transcend the need for valid evidence.[72]

Lefkowitz goes on to say that once we accept the idea that there are many truths or different ethnic truths rather than a single truth, intellectual community is impossible. She suggests that university administrators either eliminate or at least warn students about courses that ignore and/or suppress evidence.

Lefkowitz correctly links Afrocentrism to the postmodern critique of history and historical truths. Asante, for example, challenges the notion that when European philosophers speak of humanism, they mean anything other than expanding to other Europeans or perhaps admitting other peoples into the historical consciousness of Europe. "But for Europeans to enter into a view, a perspective where they will be able to share with others in a world of plural perspectives is to ask them to submit to revolution."[73] Where Lefkowitz sees Afrocentrists as occupying separate enclaves and teaching partial truths, Asante sees a pluralistic community offering multiple perspectives since it is highly improbable that one can step outside one's own history and achieve true historical consciousness.

Afrocentrism is an important part of the postmodern challenge to conventional views on history. It questions the idea that historians can be or should be objective and that reason alone enables historians to explain the past. However, it breaks with more radical variants of postmodernism in its belief that the role of history is to interpret and transmit human culture and intellectual heritage from generation to generation. Afrocentrists take issue with some postmodernists who contend that since there is no truth, there is no objective means to distinguish between right and wrong views.[74] A world without right or wrong would undermine the Afrocentrists and Black Studies activists' goal of social justice.

To the extent that modern reason, a product of the Enlightenment, masks Eurocentrism as universalism, Afrocentrism is one with postmodernism and its critique. Moreover, the assumption made by Lefkowitz and others that there is a best answer that precludes diversity and tolerance is rejected.[75] However, Afrocentrism does not go as far as some postmodernists in its rejection of the state or regulation or the creation of new knowledge. While it "deconstructs" Eurocentrism, Afrocentrism seeks to replace it only in regard to Africans in Africa and the diaspora. Yet, in replacing Eurocentrism with Afrocentrism, it replicates some of the contentious elements of Western civilization.

Erskine Peters argues that Afrocentrism's focus on "classical" African civilization (Kemet) is an "adoption of the highly valorized, Euro-elitist word 'classical', a word which resonates easily as meaning classical like Greece, like Rome, like all the so-called prestigious artifacts of the Europeans."[76] Asante's imperialist gaze is too often cast on the Pharaoh to the exclusion of the common Egyptian, says Peters. As an example of the slighting of African-based conceptual models of social, political, philosophical, and economic being by Afrocentrists, Peters cites Asante's conflation of an ideology of Afrocentrism with an ideology of ethnocentrism. This is problematic, states Peters, because African culture is cosmic not particularistic—"to the extent Afrocentrists focus on the racial identity of Egyptians they overlook the cosmic points that really should be made via true identity with Egypt."[77]

Peters asks why African Americans really desire to claim the pyramids: is it as monuments of their empire or as symbols of an adept process of being and system of knowing? While Peters believes Asante's intention is to claim the latter, many students of Afrocentrism lead one to believe the former. This need for valorization is an old one and directs many diasporic Africans like Paul Gilroy to reject the term "Afrocentric" and replace it with what he calls "Americentrism." Gilroy accuses Afrocentrists of attempting to construct a sense of Black particularity *outside* of a notion of national identity.[78]

The critiques of Peters and Gilroy may be seen as constructive efforts to resolve some of the conceptual conflicts in Afrocentrism. Karenga admits, for example, that research concerning African Americans must be privileged in the development of the discipline.[79] After all, both Karenga and Cruse center their work around the cultural crisis of African Americans. The major goal of Black Studies activists in elucidating the political nature of the university had two thrusts. One was to emphasize the complicity of the academy in everything from slavery to the development of Agent Orange for use in Vietnam. The other thrust was to use the resources of the university, both material and theoretical, to improve the lives of the communities many of the students came from. Afrocentrism proved very useful in the first task of demonstrating the lack of objectivity and bias in the accepted canon. It proved less successful in demonstrating its utility in solving the problems confronting ghetto residents. That is, Afrocentrism as an expression of cultural nationalism had serious problems in its historic treatment of women and gender, and in its applicability to Africa as well as other regions of the diaspora. It is worth quoting Peters at length on this point:

> Gilroy's interest in the way United States African Americans define the Afrocentric is reflected in the complication of Afrocentric representation in Patricia Hill Collin's *Black Feminist Thought*, when from a black feminist perspective reputed African and universal values conflate. Although she refers to African-based emphasis on the use of Dialogue as a humanizing factor for all members of the African indigenous community, still problematic

> in Collins's use of the Afrocentric is the inclination to view the concept more in light of United States African-American oppression instead of in light of traditional African value systems. Thus for Collins to say that "an Afrocentric feminist epistemology is rooted in the everyday experiences of African-American women" is inadequate as Afrocentric, that is, inadequate in establishing within African-American thought systems a foundational relationship with the potency of indigenous cultures, such as emphasis on gaining fundamental understanding and mastery of the female and male cosmic/personal energies, are never discussed or mentioned. The indigenous African ways to "knowledge, consciousness, and…empowerment" (words from the subtitle of Collins's book) are never investigated as gateways to empowerment and liberation.[80]

Patricia Hill Collins and Gilroy were influential figures in expanding or democratizing the scope of Black Studies; however, as Peters suggested, their work also has contradictions.

Like the Black Power movement, the modern feminist movement has roots in the Civil Rights movement. Those women who came to the South to fight for civil rights were largely White and middle-class. Those southern women they joined in struggle were primarily Black and working class. Despite those differences, they could unite to confront the sexual discrimination they faced externally in general society but especially internally in the very civil rights organizations in which they worked. For Black women, it may have been less of a surprise because they had witnessed the patriarchy of the Black church as its preachers led chapters of the National Association for the Advancement of Colored People (NAACP) and the Southern Christian Leadership Conference (SCLC) or new organizations such as the Montgomery Improvement Association (MIA) and Alabama Christian Movement for Human Rights (ACMHR).[81] However, they were shocked as the young radicals in organizations like the Student Nonviolent Coordinating Committee (SNCC) demanded they make coffee and perform clerical duties rather than participate in frontline action. In a 1964 position paper delivered at SNCC's Waveland Conference, White staffers Mary King and Casey Hayden outlined the sexist treatment and harassment of women in the organization. When Ruby Doris Smith, briefly SNCC executive secretary, died a year later, some attributed it to the stress and overwork she was subjected to.[82]

Frances Beale, a founding member of SNCC's Black Women's Liberation Committee, published "Double Jeopardy," one of the most influential early essays in the women's liberation movement in 1970. Targeting one theme that would be repeated for the next two decades, Beale said:

> Unfortunately, there seems to be some confusion in the movement today as to who has been oppressing whom. Since the advent of black power, the black male has exerted a more prominent leadership role in our struggle for justice in this country. He sees the system for what it really is for the most part, but where he rejects its values and mores on many issues, when it comes to women, he seems to take his guidelines from the pages of the *Ladies' Home Journal.* Certain black men are maintaining that they have been castrated by society but that black women somehow escaped this persecution and even contributed to this emasculation.[83]

Beale was careful to point out that Black women were not opposing the rise to power of Black men but they were rejecting a domestic, submissive role that was counterrevolutionary.

Although both branches of Black Nationalism—cultural and revolutionary—claimed Malcolm X as a major influence (and Malcolm's misogyny was available for all to see in his *Autobiography*), most feminists pointed to the early work of Karenga and the cultural nationalists for examples of sexism. In his 1967 *The Quotable Karenga*, for example, he says:

> What makes a woman appealing is feminity and she can't be feminine without being submissive…
>
> The role of the woman is to inspire her man, educate their children and participate in social development…
>
> We say Male supremacy is based on three things: tradition, acceptance, and reason.[84]

In his student days at Los Angeles City College, Karenga had been a supporter of both the Congress of Racial Equality (CORE) and SNCC. The revolutionary nationalists proclaimed support for women's liberation, but were no better than the cultural nationalists in practice. Eldridge Cleaver's emphasis on "pussy power" was perhaps the most blatant insult to the dignity of Black women in the Black Panther Party.[85]

Yet Black women activists were just as incensed by their treatment in the women's liberation movement. Beale charged that any White group that does not have "an anti-imperialist and anti-racist ideology" has nothing in common with Black women. Moreover, activists like Beale saw the

White women's liberation movement as basically middle class ignoring the economic exploitation of Black women and in some cases participating in it.[86]

Black women began to form their own organizations separate from both the Black nationalists and White women's groups. In 1973, the National Black Feminist Organization (NBFO) was founded in New York City. Its statement of purpose reiterated the charges made by Beale.

> Black women have suffered cruelly in this society from living the phenomenon of being both black and female, in a country that is *both* racist and sexist....Because we live in a patriarchy, we have allowed a premium to be put on black male suffering....We have been called "matriarchs" by white racists and black nationalists.... *We*, not white men or black men, must define our own self-image...and not fall into the mistake of being place upon the pedestal which is even being rejected by white women.[87]

Another group, the Combahee River Collective, established in 1974, was an offshoot of the Boston chapter of the NBFO. This organization was instrumental in bringing the oppression of Black gays and lesbians to the forefront. The homophobia of Black nationalists and White feminists was contested through the work of lesbian writers such as Audre Lorde, Cheryl Clarke, and Barbara Smith.[88]

Like Black Studies, Women's Studies can be directly linked to the political activism of the 1960s. Both have roots in the civil rights movement, and the antiwar and counterculture movements of the period. In many cases, Black Studies organizing at places like Cornell University served as a model for Women's Studies.[89] The early ideological struggle between cultural nationalism and Marxists in Black Studies was repeated between radical feminists and Marxists in Women's Studies.[90] Even the Ford Foundation played a role in funding the creation of the National Women's Studies Association in 1977.[91]

The peak period of organizing Women's Studies units lagged behind Black Studies organizing by a few years. For Black Studies the peak period was 1968–72, while for Women's Studies it was between 1970 and 1975, with San Diego State University (SDSU) pioneering as the first official Women's Studies program in 1970. The combination of study with activism was also similar. In writing about Women's Studies as SDSU, Alice Ginsberg states:

It was also explicit within the founding that studying women in an academic setting would directly help make positive social change in the rest of the world for women and other oppressed groups alike.... For the first time, women were not only learning about themselves but were actively *creating* and *owning* knowledge based on their own personal and political experience.[92]

Despite the parallels with Black Studies there were some important differences.

Women's Studies appeared to be much more faculty-driven than Black Studies, which was student-driven. Mari Jo Buhle says: "[T]he founders of Women's Studies more often than not *became* feminists through the process of teaching courses, organizing programs, and developing the curriculum. In addition, some appeared more attached to the traditional disciplines and saw the interest in Women's Studies as temporary."[93] Black Studies units, on the other hand, often ended up purging their activist founders in favor of those with the appropriate academic credentials.

Just as Black feminists challenged the priorities of the women's liberation movement and Black Nationalist movement, female scholars questioned the invisibility of Black women in both Black Studies and Women's Studies. A series of works in the early 1980s changed the discourse in both fields. These works include Angela Davis's *Woman, Race, and Class*; Cherrie Moraga and Gloria Anzaldua's *This Bridge Called My Back*; bell hooks's *Ain't I a Woman*; and Gloria Joseph and Jill Lewis's *Common Differences*. These works advanced the earlier writings of Toni Cade, Shirley Chisholm, Toni Morrison, Audre Lorede, Michele Wallace, and Ntozake Shange.

As early as 1970, Toni Cade had noted that the emerging bibliography by feminists was Eurocentric. An early survey indicated that between 1970 and 1973, courses which concerned minority women or which considered race and class in addition to gender comprised only 4 percent of women's studies courses. A 1978 report on Black Studies found no independent courses on Black women in Western land-grant colleges.[94]

One of the problems was the conceptual framework used to study American women. The minority group model viewed women through the same lens as Blacks—oppressed and victimized. This analogy between race and sex obscured important differences between the groups. Black women, however, did not share the majority status of White women or their class status and access to White men. They were also burdened by the racial caste system while facing the sexism of Black men.[95] This "triple jeopardy" of race, class, and gender resulted in the creation of Black Women's Studies.

The rise of Black Women's Studies quickly raised the issue of whether they would be independent campus units or linked administratively with Black Studies or Women's Studies. The relatively small size of both Black Studies and Women's Studies, and their precarious position within universities led some to perceive them as unwanted competition for scarce resources. At the same time, some saw Black Women's Studies as a threat; this newly visible area was heavily dependent on the institutional support of these more established units. As Barbara Christian wrote, the problem now was not falling through the cracks but rather being spread too thin.

> There is often a black feminist scholar on one university campus who is one-third Afro-American Studies, one-third Women's Studies, and one-third English, let's say, or who is situated in one of these departments with the understanding that she is the liaison person between the three. The one that we are is usually the only *woman* in Black Studies, the *only person of color* in Women's Studies, or in one's traditional department.[96]

This fragmentation created a great deal of stress and demand on one's time, but also provided an opportunity to broaden the scholar's perspective.

Perhaps the most discussed conceptual effort to bridge the disciplines was Patricia Hill Collins's standpoint theory. In her *Signs* article "The Social Construction of Black Feminist Thought" and subsequent book *Black Feminist Thought*, Hill Collins defined it as consisting of "specialized knowledge created by African-American women which clarifies a standpoint of and for Black women."[97] Black women academicians who attempt to rearticulate the standpoint of their nonacademic sisters face the likelihood that their knowledge claims will be rejected by positivist epistemology. Therefore, says Hill Collins, an alternative epistemology must be generated to evaluate their knowledge claims. She then proceeds to delineate the contours of an Afrocentric epistemology that consists of four dimensions: (1) concrete experience as a criterion of meaning; (2) use of dialog in assessing knowledge claims; (3) an ethic of caring; and (4) an ethic of personal accountability. She sees this epistemology as a paradigmatic shift away from the binary thinking of European masculinist thought and toward a paradigm that recognizes race, class, and gender as interlocking systems of oppression.[98]

Hill Collins work has been the subject of numerous critiques. According to Joy James, Hill Collins reconstructs Black women radicals as liberals and conflates teaching and scholarship with political activism. In rearticulating the standpoints of Black women through elite academicians, Hill Collins reinscribes hierarchical norms.[99] Alice Ginsberg argues that the "personal is political approach" or standpoint epistemology "can undercut those who occupy different subject positions and also often assumes all similarly situated people share the same viewpoint."[100] Finally, as Peters stated earlier, Hill Collins's work is more African American centered than African centered.

While Hill Collins seeks to unite a kind of cultural feminism with cultural Black nationalism in her standpoint theory, it leads her back to the kind of universal truths Afrocentrists attack as Eurocentric. E.B. White suggests that Collins falls into a positivist trap when she implies that Black feminists using both Afrocentric and feminist epistemologies may have found the route to "objective generalizations that can stand as universal truths."[101]

In *The Black Atlantic*, Paul Gilroy contends the essentialist (Afrocentrism) and the pluralist (Afrocentric feminism) are, in fact, two different varieties of the same essentialism. Hill Collins, he says, has answered the Western separation of thinking from being by collapsing them back into each other so that they form a functional unity that can be uncritically celebrated. Gilroy states that "another version of racial essentialism is smuggled in through the back porch even as Hill Collins loudly banishes it from her front door. In her transposition, the term 'black' does a double duty. It covers the positions of knowing and being. Its epistemological and ontological dimensions are entirely congruent."[102] For Gilroy, the experience-centered knowledge claims of Afrocentric feminism simply substitute the standpoint of Black women for its forerunner rooted in the lives of White men.[103]

Of course, Gilroy's work marks the popularization of the African diasporic perspective that has been attributed to C.L.R. James, George Shepperson, and Robert Ferris Thompson among others.[104] "Marked by its European origins, modern black political culture," states Gilroy, "has always been more interested in the relationship of identity to roots and rootedness than in seeing identity as a process of movement and mediation that is more appropriately approached via the homonym routes."[105] This concern with rootedness leads Afrocentrists to attempt to figure sameness across national boundaries and between nation-states simply by substituting African American priorities for African priorities.

For Gilroy, "the worth of the diaspora concept is in its attempt to specify differentiation and identify in a way which enables one to think about the issue of racial commonality outside of constricting binary frameworks."[106] Using the work of Martin Delany, W.E.B. Du Bois, Richard Wright, and Black popular music, Gilroy constructs the "Black Atlantic" as a counterculture of the modernity that is the nation-state.

If the pyramids are the motif symbolizing the permanence of African culture for Afrocentrists, it is the sailing ship that symbolizes the fluid nature of global Black culture for the diaspora school of thought. Rather than the cultural nationalism of African Americans, we get a transnationalism that includes Blacks in the Caribbean, Americas, and Europe as well as the United States. It is a kind of transnationalism that was difficult to imagine before the fall of the Soviet Union in 1989. That is, diaspora movement is not unidirectional but can flow not only between the homeland and the diaspora and vice versa but also between diasporas. In short, it is the opposite of particularity or home: it is no home.

Despite their opposition, Afrocentrism and African Diaspora Studies have been charged with similar omissions. Gilroy's *The Black Atlantic* has been constructed without the apparent involvement of Black women. In *Dropping Anchor, Setting Sail*, Jacqueline Nassy Brown has demonstrated the ways in which men and women's connections to the African diaspora are different in the Black Liverpool community.[107] Agreeing with Gilroy that Blackness cannot be limited to a national, cultural, or linguistic border, Michelle Wright adds that it cannot be produced in isolation from gender and sexuality. Gilroy, she says, "limits his survey to mostly African American, hetrosexual, and masculine norms."[108]

Preaching unity without uniformity, as the 1972 Gary National Black Political Assembly did, or promoting a "pluralist" rather than an "essentialist" perspective seems politically safe but lacks practical applicability. And practical applicability, in the form of community assistance, was one of the principle demands of Black Studies activists. Perhaps this is why Karenga clearly states "the priority and centrality of the African American experience in the discipline of Black Studies."[109] He offers three reasons for this privileging. First is due respect for the founders of the discipline who had to achieve their own liberation before they could effectively assist all African people and the Third World. Second, the duality of the African American experience provides a departure point for the systematic study of the Black world in general. Finally, "the priority focus of African Americans makes the praxis dimension of Africana Studies immediate, readily recognizable, and easier to implement."[110]

It is precisely this last point on the practical applicability of Black Studies that both the Afrocentrists and African Diasporists have fallen short. To what extent does the knowledge of ancient Kemet or the role of sailing ships in transmitting culture address the overwhelming numbers of Black imprisoned in the United States or other countries of the African diaspora?

Let us return to the very practical problem of integrating restaurants in the 1960s that opened our work. Would the restaurant have solved the problem by placing ham hocks or chittlin's on the menu? To do so might have pleased our desegregated Negro, but it also makes a number of assumptions. It assumes that a southern regional cuisine is characteristic or representative of all African Americans. What about vegetarians, Muslims, Blacks from other regions, or Blacks from other countries? Is the problem solved by Blacks having their own restaurants and serving only "soul food"? Then we have returned to the pre-1960s state of "separate but equal." What about other people of color who have their own culinary tastes? Does having an ethnic food night—so popular in school cafeterias—meet our needs? This type of weak multiculturalism simply masks the problem. It precludes the possibility of "fusion cuisine" (hybridization). "Sameness" and "difference" are both built on an essentialist logic that fixes or freezes some characteristic. What we really seek is "culinary" and "cultural democracy."

The cultural nationalism implicitly and/or explicitly underlying the first stage of Black Studies evolution was a logical response to the White nationalism so expertly hidden in the objective, universal, and neutral norms of American higher education. When Blacks did appear in the curriculum, they were exoticized, pathologized, or problematized. As Afrocentrism evolved from Black cultural nationalism, it once again seemed logical to "rescue and reconstruct" a glorious and pioneering past that clearly confronted notions of Black inferiority. In short, Afrocentrism proved to be effective in deconstructing Eurocentrism.

Yet Afrocentrism has its own contradictions and exclusions. On the one hand, it shared Eurocentrism's tendency to mark history as the work of great men and its focus was clearly America-centered rather than Africa-centered. On the other hand, it generally excluded the experience of African American women, Black gays and lesbians, and other Africans in the diaspora. This led to the rise of Black Women's Studies and African

Diaspora Studies. The emergence of these topics may profitably be viewed as subspecialties within the field of Black Studies. Their rise to prominence reflects the rather equalitarian and democratic nature of Black Studies. Calls for Black Studies to define itself as a discipline through methodology or prove its worth through job placement ignore the history of disciplines in higher education. Physics and economics, for example, are internally cogent fields with high consistency, even rigidity, in the socialization of their members to an overarching paradigm or general theory and tend toward an unreflexive realist epistemology that needs only internal justification.[111] Sociology and Mathematics, on the other hand, have few start-up costs and are characterized by a multiplicity of perspectives, a personalistic, antibureaucratic style, and currently no interest in an overarching unified theory.[112] Black Studies tends toward the latter fields or what Brown calls "fragmented adhocracies."

In his critique of Kuhn, Bourdieu points out the paradox that the very autonomous fields, such as science and poetry, tend to have no other link with the social world than the social conditions that ensure their autonomy with respect to that world. The social sciences, however, and especially sociology, says Bourdieu, have an object too important, too controversial, for it to be left to their discretion, abandoned to their law alone.[113]

In an attempt to build a discipline, seemingly necessary if one wants to establish graduate programs (i.e., replicate oneself), some Black Studies activists promoted theories and methodologies that were ambiguous at best and contradictory at worst. They established binary systems, claimed at least limited universality, and privileged text over reality. This second stage "race for theory" forgot its community roots. Theory needs to be constructed from the bottom up—grounded theory. It should not be surprising that the key Black Studies texts come from fields that have low entry costs and less hierarchy yet great relevance for African Americans—sociology, history, and literature.

Notes

1. An article in the journal *PS* ranked Lowi as the most influential political scientist of the 1970s.
2. Theodore J. Lowi, *The Politics of Disorder*, (New York: Basic Books, 1971), p. xvii.
3. I have to thank my fellow graduate student and judo partner Jo Freeman for inspiring the dissertation topic. She asked me for a

reference that explained what the civil rights movement meant to those participating and I could not come up with one. At Chicago I found a supportive community of graduate students that included Lorenzo Morris, Dianne Pinderhughes, Linda Faye Williams, Toni Travis, and Margie Barnett.

4. During 1980–81, I was a postdoctoral fellow in African American Studies at Atlanta University. It was my first opportunity to retrain myself in Black Studies and Richard Long, the director of the seminar for the postdoctoral students in African American Studies, proved to be an excellent host. Not only had Long seemingly read everything the field had to offer, he also knew all of the major figures and all the gossip surrounding them making for very interesting discussions. Through Long I was able to share a drink with James Baldwin, listen to Toni Cade Bambara read from her most recent work, and meet Sterling Brown and Romare Bearden. Francis Smith Foster, a fellow postdoctoral student, also became a good friend with whom I would later publish an article on Black Women's Studies.
5. Richard M. Merelman, *Pluralism at Yale: The Culture of Political Science in America* (Madison: University of Wisconsin Press, 2003), p. 9.
6. Merelman, p. 18.
7. Merelman, p. 162.
8. Lowi, Op. Cit., p. 143. For a further discussion of Lowi's views and my critique of them see "Race, Public Policy and the Lowi Canon," in Benjamin Ginsberg and Gwendolyn Mink, eds., *Political Science as Public Philosophy*, (New York: Norton, 2010).
9. Houston A. Baker, Jr., *Betrayal* (New York: Columbia University Press, 2008), p. 160.
10. Thomas S. Kuhn, *The Structure of Scientific Revolutions* (Chicago: University of Chicago Press, 1970), pp. 171–172. Sandra Harding argues that Kuhn's explanation for the distinctive success of modern science is linked to his assumptions about the virtues of European civilization. See her "Is Science Multicultural" in David Theo Goldberg, (ed.), *Multiculturalism* (Cambridge, MA: Blackwell, 1994), p. 351.
11. Ibid., p. 77.
12. Mark Aldrich, "Progressive Economists and Scientific Racism," *Phylon*, 1979, Vol. 40, No. 1, pp. 13–14.

13. Immanuel Wallerstein, "What Are We bounding, and Whom, When We Bound Social Research," *Social Research*, Vol. 62, No. 4 (Winter, 1995), p. 843.
14. Ibid., pp. 843–844. In some universities the department of history is placed in the social sciences in other universities it is placed in the humanities.
15. Richard Harvey Brown, *Toward a Democratic Science*, (New Haven: Yale University Press, 1998), p. 21.
16. Kuhn, *Op. Cit.*, p. 122.
17. Brown, *Op. Cit.*, p. 148.
18. Thomas F. Giery, "Boundary-Work and the Demarcation of Science from Non-Science," *American Sociological Review*, 1983, Vol. 48, (Dec.: 781–782).
19. Ibid., p. 792
20. Harding in Goldberg. *Op. Cit.*, pp. 344–345.
21. Pierre Bourdieu, *Science of Science and Reflexivity*, (Chicago: University of Chicago Press, 2004), p. 17.
22. Jacques Depelchin, *Silences in African History* (Dar Es Salaam, Tanzania: Mkuki Na Nyota Publishers, 2005), p. 7.
23. Wallerstein, *Op. Cit.*, p. 845.
24. Brown, *Op. Cit.*, p. 50.
25. Ibid., p. 847. See also Lee D. Baker, *From Savage to Negro* (Berkeley: University of California Press, 1998) and Edward W. Said, *Orientalism* (New York: Vintage, 1994).
26. Thomas Piketty, *Capital in the Twenty-First Century* (Cambridge, MA: Harvard University Press, 2014), p. 32.
27. Gunnar Myrdal quoted in Lawrence W. Levine, *The Opening of the American Mind* (Boston: Beacon, 1996), p. 151.
28. Ibid., p. 151.
29. Among the early classic works in political science are Harold D. Lasswell, *Politics; who gets, what, when, how* (New York: McGraw Hill, 1936); Woodrow Wilson, *Congressional Government* (Baltimore: Johns Hopkins University Press, 1981); David Truman, *The Governmental Process* (Berkeley: Institute for Governmental Studies, 1971); Heinz Eulau, *Behavioralism in Political Science* (New York: Atherton Press, 1969); Arthur Bentley, *The Process of Government* (Cambridge, MA: Harvard University Press, 1967).

30. See Hanes Walton Jr. and Robert C. Smith, "The Race Variable and the American Political Science Association's *State of the Discipline* Reports and Books, 1907–2002," and Ernest J. Wilson III and Lorrie A Frasure, "Still at the Margins" in Wilbur C. Rich, (ed.), *African American Perspectives on Political Science* (Philadelphia: Temple University Press, 2007).
31. For an excellent treatment of Black political socialization see Harold M. Barger, "The Images of the President and Policeman among Black, Mexican American and Anglo School Children," (Chicago: American Political Science Association annual meeting, 1974). See also Paul R. Abramson, *The Political Socialization of Black Americans* (New York: Free Press, 1977).
32. Aldon D. Morris, *The Scholar Denied*, (Berkeley: University of California Press, 2015), pp. 102–112.
33. A.J. Vidich and S.M. Lyman, "Qualitative Methods," in N.K. Denzin and Y.S. Lincoln, (eds.), *Handbook of Qualitative Research* (Thousand Oaks, CA: Sage, 2000), p. 74.
34. Daniel Bell, "'American Exceptionalism' Revisited," *The Public Interest* 95 (spring 1989), pp. 41–42.
35. Ibid.,
36. Seymour Martin Lipset, *American Exceptionalism* (New York: Norton, 1996), p. 14.
37. Charles P. Henry, *Ralph Bunche* (New York: New York University Press, 1999), pp. 123–129. Bunche retrained himself as an anthropologist in order to do fieldwork in Africa.
38. Clifford Geertz quoted in Renato Rosaldo, *Culture & Truth* (Boston: Beacon, 1993), p. 37.
39. Dipesh Chakrabarty, *Provincializing Europe* (Princeton: Princeton University Press, 2008), p. 41.
40. Du Bois in Morris, *Op. Cit.*, p. 184.
41. Morris, *Op. Cit.*, pp. 134–193.
42. Pierre Bourdieu, *Science of Science and Reflexivity*, (Chicago: University of Chicago Press, 2004), p. 1.
43. St. Clair Drake quoted in Gerald A. Mcworter and Ronald Bailey, "Black Studies Curriculum Development in the 1980s," in Nathaniel Norment, Jr., *The African American Studies Reader* (Durham, NC: Carolina Academic Press, 2001), p. 618.
44. See Pauline Marie Rosenau, *Post-Modernism and the Social Sciences* (Princeton, NJ: Princeton University Press, 1992).

45. Benedict Anderson, *Imagined Communities* (London: Verso, 1991), p. 2.
46. Bourdieu, *Op. Cit.*, p. 1.
47. Alvin Gouldner, *The Dialectic of Ideology and Technology* (New York: Seabury, 1976), p. 14.
48. Harold Cruse, *The Crisis of the Negro Intellectual* (New York: Morrow, 1967), p. 159. See also Richard Wright, *American Hunger* (New York: Harper & Row, 1977).
49. Paul Ricouer quoted in Levine, *Op. Cit.*, p. 173.
50. Cruse, *Op. Cit.*, p. 13.
51. Jerry Watts, (ed.), *Harold Cruse's The Crisis of the Negro Intellectual Reconsidered* (New York: Routledge, 2004), p. 311.
52. Maulana Karenga, *Kawaida Theory* (Inglewood, CA: Kawaida Publications, 1980), p. 15.
53. Ibid., p. 17. These "criteria of culture" were first introduced in *The Quotable Karenga* (Los Angeles: US, 1967), p. 7. Both Karenga and Molefi Asante were influenced by anthropologist Council Taylor at UCLA who promoted the philosophy of "Negritude."
54. Ibid., p. 17.
55. Abd-l Hakimu Ibn Alkalimat, "The Ideology of Black Social Science," in Joyce A. Ladner, (ed.), *The Death of White Sociology* New York: Vintage, 1973), p. 186.
56. Leroi Jones/Amiri Baraka, *The Autobiography of Leroi Jones/Amiri Baraka* (New York: Freundlich, 1984), p. 248.
57. Ibid., p. 253.
58. Molefi Kete Asante, *Maulana Karenga,* (Cambridge, UK: Polity, 2009), p. 1.
59. Asante p. 119 and Ama Mazama, (ed.), *The Acrocentric Paradigm*, (Trenton, NJ: Africa World Press, 2003). The concept of Afrocentrism has gradually grown from an approach to research to disciplinary status. Early definitions of Afrocentrism state it is a "belief in the centrality of Africans in post-modern history" (Asante, 1980, p. 9). Karenga notes that there is no single conception of Afrocentricity, only a general conceptual agreement that Afrocentric means essentially viewing social and human reality from an African perspective or standpoint" (Karenga, 1993, pp. 34–35). In 1980, Asante defined Afrology as an approach, a methodological and functional perspective (p. 67). In 1990, Asante

called Africalogy a discipline sustained by a commitment to centering the study of African phenomena and events in the particular cultural voice of the composite African people (p. 12).

60. Molefi Kete Asante, Afrocentricity (Buffalo, NY: Amulefi Publishing), p. 24.
61. Ibid., p. 24.
62. Molefi Kete Asante, *Kemet, Afrocentricity and Knowledge* (Trenton, NJ: Africa World Press, 1990), p. 12.
63. Ibid., p. 13.
64. Molife Kete Asante, "African American Studies," in Norment, *Op. Cit.*, p. 415.
65. Asante, *Op. Cit.*, 1990, p. 20.
66. Stephen Howe, *Afrocentrism* (London: Verso, 1998). p. 119.
67. The front cover of *Newsweek*'s September 1991 edition asked the question "Was Cleopatra Black?", Howe, p. 130.
68. Asante, *Op. Cit.*, 1990, pp. 121–122.
69. Martin Bernal, *Black Athena* (New Brunswick, NJ: Rutgers University Press, 1987), passim.
70. Mary Lefkowitz, *Not Out of Africa* (New York: BasicBooks, 1996), p. 35.
71. Ibid., p. 35.
72. Ibid., p. 174.
73. Asante, *Op. Cit.*, 1990, p. vi.
74. Rosenau distinguishes between skeptical post modernists who see no social or political "project" worthy of commitment and affirmative post modernists who are oriented toward a process that seeks a nondogmatic, tentative, nonideological intellectual practice that might include postmodern social movements. Rosenau, *Op. Cit.*, pp. 15–16.
75. Ibid., pp. 155–177.
76. Erskine Peters, "*Afrocentricity*," in Norment, *Op. Cit.*, p. 567.
77. Ibid., p. 571. Paul Gilroy notes the moral shift from Black identification with the slaves of the Exodus story to identification with the pharaoh. Gilroy, *Op. Cit.*, p. 207.
78. Peters, *Op. Cit.*, p. 573.
79. Karenga in Norment, *Op. Cit.*, pp. 287–288.
80. Peters in Norment, *Op. Cit.*, p. 573.
81. Septima Clark criticized the sexism in SCLC in her autobiography: "[T]hose men didn't have any faith in women, none whatsoever.

They just thought that women were sex symbols and had no contributions to make....I had a great feeling that Dr. King didn't think much of women either." Clark quoted in Beverly Guy-Sheftall, (ed.), *Words of Fire*, (New York, The New Press, 1995), p. 14.

82. Guy-Sheftall, p. 14. See also Sara M. Evans, *Personal Politics*, (New York: Vintage, 1980).
83. Frances Beale, "Double Jeopardy," in Guy-Sheftall, *Op. Cit.*, pp. 147–148.
84. Karenga, *Op. Cit.*, 1967, pp. 20–21.
85. Komozi Woodard, *A Nation within a Nation* (Chapel Hill, NC: University of North Carolina Press, 1999), p. 123.
86. Beale in Guy-Sheftall, p. 153.
87. National Black Feminist Organization in Ibid., p. 230.
88. Ibid., p. 231. In Afrocentricity, Asante comments on the rise of homosexuality in the African American male's psyche: "An Afrocentric perspective recognizes its existence but homosexuality cannot be condoned or accepted as good for the national development of a strong people (p. 65)." It is implied that homosexuality is the result of European decadence.
89. Florence Howe, (ed.), *The Politics of Women's Studies*, (New York: Feminist Press, 2000), p. 32.
90. Elizabeth Lapovsky Kennedy and Agatha Beins, (eds.), *Women's Studies for the Future*, (New Brunswick, NJ: Rutgers University Press, 2005), p. 31.
91. Howe, *Op. Cit.*, p. xvi.
92. Alice E. Ginsberg, (ed.), *The Evolution of American Women's Studies* (New York: Palgrave Macmillan, 2008), p. 10.
93. Gloria Bowles, "From the Bottom Up," in Howe, *Op. Cit.*, p. 152.
94. Charles P. Henry and Frances Smith Foster, "Black Women's Studies," in Norment, *Op. Cit.*, p. 129.
95. Beverly Guy-Sheftall, "Black Women's Studies," in Norment, *Op. Cit.*, p. 140.
96. Barbara Christian, "But Who Do You Really Belong To—Black Studies or Women's Studies?" in Norment, *Op. Cit.*, p. 184.
97. Patricia Hill Collins, *Black Feminist Thought* (New York: Routledge, 1991), p. 22.
98. Ibid., pp. 206–219.
99. Joy James, *Transcending the Talented Tenth* (New York: Routledge, 1997), pp. 94, 132.

100. Ginsberg, *Op. Cit.*, p. 25.
101. E. Frances White, "Africa on My Mind," in Guy-Sheftall, *Op. Cit.*, p. 521.
102. Gilroy, *Op. Cit.*, pp. 31, 52.
103. Ibid., p. 53.
104. There are at least four schools of thought that might be labeled as diasporic within the common theme of identity. Gilroy represents the African diaspora as a political project resulting from both historical alliances and a confrontation with modernity. This approach, although grounded in Du Bois and Fanon, is distinct from their focus on an existential diaspora grounded in history, memory, and psychology. Still another approach, for example in the work of Michelle Wright, centers on the intellectual tradition of the African diaspora that links the various communities of Africans together. A final approach represented in the work of Brent Hayes Edwards, conceptualizes diaspora as a practice in which diaspora identities are continually being performed especially in artistic productions.
105. Ibid., p. 19.
106. Ibid., p. 120.
107. Jacqueline Nassy Brown, *Dropping Anchor, Setting Sail* (Princeton, NJ: Princeton University Press, 2005), passim.
108. Michelle M. Wright, *Becoming Black* (Durham, NC: Duke University Press, 2004), p. 6.
109. Karenga in Norment, *Op. Cit.*, p. 287.
110. Ibid., p. 288.
111. Brown, *Op. Cit.*, p 142.
112. Ibid., p. 142.
113. Bourdieu, *Op. Cit.*, pp. 15, 87.

CHAPTER 7

Democratizing the National Identity

Ironically the *Brown* decision mandating the integration of public education was also the beginning of the modern Black Studies movement. When National Association for the Advancement of Colored People (NAACP) counsel Robert Carter asked Black psychologist Kenneth Clark for his expert opinion on the effects of school segregation on Negro children, Clark repeated for the Supreme Court the findings of a paper he had delivered at a White House conference in 1953:

> The essence of this detrimental effect (on personality development) is a confusion in the child's concept of his own self-esteem--basic feelings of inferiority, conflict, confusion in his self-image, resentment, hostility towards himself, hostility towards whites, intensification of…a desire to resolve his basic conflict by sometimes escaping or withdrawing.[1]

Clark went on to quote a recent survey that reported 90 percent of the social scientists questioned agreed that segregation negatively impacts the personalities of those victims of segregation and 82 percent agreed that the perpetrators of segregation had feelings of guilt.[2]

The expert witness then moved to report the specific test results he obtained in Clarendon County, South Carolina. When presented with both a brown doll and a white doll, and asked which doll looked "bad" and which doll looked "nice," 11 of the 16 Negro children tested said the brown doll looked "bad" while 10 of them thought the white doll was the "nice" one. Moreover, 7 of the 16 children picked the white doll

C.P. Henry, *Black Studies and the Democratization of American Higher Education*, DOI 10.1007/978-3-319-35089-9_7

as the one like themselves. Clark concluded that these children had definitely been harmed in the development of their personalities and that the signs of instability in their personalities were clear. After a few perfunctory questions from defense counsel Robert Figg, who thought the study was inconsequential, Clark stepped down.[3]

Of course, Clark's study and testimony became a key moment in the most important Supreme Court case of the twentieth century, *Brown v. Topeka Board of Education*. In its unanimous decision overturning the "separate but equal" doctrine it established in *Plessy v. Ferguson* in 1896, the Court cited the increased importance of public education and new social science data (specifically referencing Clark's study) on the impact of segregation on Negro students in its reasoning. The *Brown* decision was rendered in two parts. *Brown I* in 1954 declared school segregation unconstitutional and was enthusiastically embraced by the national Black community. *Brown II* in 1955 mandated the school districts make positive efforts to integrate schools. However, it left the timetable (all deliberate speed) and methods of integration up to local school boards.[4]

The impact of the *Brown* decision can be measured in part by the intensity of the reaction to it. President Eisenhower refused to endorse the decision and the Supreme Court's failure to call for immediate relief, that is, implementation, encouraged resistance. In Congress, 96 Representatives signed a "Southern Manifesto" in 1956 pledging to reverse the decision and prevent the use of force in its implementation. White Citizens Councils were organized throughout the South and state legislatures passed laws aimed at crippling or closing down the NAACP. Private academies sprang up and new state right laws and pupil assignment laws were written.[5] The combined effect led Martin Luther King, Jr., in 1964 to predict that at the current rate of desegregation it would take 100 years to implement *Brown*.[6]

Less well known is Black opposition to *Brown II*. Aside from the firing of Black teachers and the closing of Black schools across the South that implementation would lead to, there was the less tangible objection to the characterization of Black students as psychologically scarred. As Black anthropologist and writer Zora Neale Hurston put it, "[h]ow much satisfaction can I get from a court order for somebody to associate with me who does not wish to be near me?"[7] W.E.B. Du Bois, who was not asked to be a part of the NAACP legal team, shared her concern for the possible mistreatment of Black children in integrated schools and the implication that all-Black schools were inherently inferior.[8]

In fact, Clark's doll test and other studies the two scholars had conducted produced ambiguous results that, had they been known to the defense, would have undermined the NAACP argument. In the first place, the methodology employed in the Clarendon County tests was suspect. Sixteen students is much too small a sample to draw generalizations from. There was also the issue of the terminology used: what is a "good" doll, what is a "bad" doll, why can only one doll be "nice." And, if students picked the white doll as "nice," it is not surprising that they chose to identify with it. As one scholar pointed out in a later analysis, the answers seemed predetermined. If the children said the brown doll was like them, Clark inferred that segregation had made them race-conscious. If the students chose the white doll as like themselves, however, he concluded that segregation had forced them to evade reality.[9] In short, Clark's ideological bias was evident in his interpretation of his research findings. As Black psychologist Reginald Jones said, "the difference between Kenneth Clark and the rest of us was Kenneth Clark was an avowed integrationist, and during that time, we were avowed separatists."[10]

Even more troubling was a study Clark reported on in 1947 that contrasted the results of the doll and coloring test he had administered to 134 Negro children in the segregated schools of Pine Bluff, Arkansas, with 119 Negro children in the unsegregated schools of Springfield, Massachusetts. In this test and another crayon test reported in 1955, Black students in southern schools were significantly more likely to prefer brown than students in northern schools. In short, in terms of the effects of segregation on the self-esteem and self-rejection of Negro children, one could make a credible case that *integration* produced the greater harm.[11]

The use of Clark's doll test marked a milestone in jurisprudence. By using social psychological data against segregation that was seen as custom, the Court demonstrated that law, even constitutional law, was social policy. As such, the justices of the Court joined Gunnar Myrdal and the scholars involved in producing *An American Dilemma* ten years earlier in their belief that social engineering provided a liberal answer to the age-old problem of racial inequality. Yet the Court, like Myrdal, offered little in the way of immediate relief. Most importantly, *Brown*'s embrace of the "damaged Black psyche" similar to that of Myrdal contributed to the development of the concept of Black cultural inferiority or depravation. Rather than promoting integration, this notion of cultural depravation would be used to argue that the plight of Blacks was beyond the scope of government intervention.

In the *Gong Lum v. Rice* case of 1927, the Supreme Court had ruled that the state had the power to categorize by race and place students as it saw fit. In this case, the state of Mississippi had placed a Chinese student in an all-Black school against the wishes of the petitioners who wanted her enrolled in an all-White school.[12] What the mixed Black reaction to *Brown II* foretold was a desire on the part of Blacks to wrest group identification away from federal and state officials. It foretold a desire to see Black institutions in a positive light and Black self-identification as normal, not pathological. In short, it foretold the Black power and Black Studies movement.

The failure of the Supreme Court to grant immediate relief to the plaintiffs in *Brown* raises the question of whether the education of African Americans was seen as a priority or a problem. Of particular interest is the reaction of leading White intellectuals to *Brown*. America's leading theologian Reinhold Neibuhr was glad the Supreme Court gave the southern states time "to adjust themselves."[13] He reinterpreted his own political pragmatism as a moral stance and refused a request from Martin Luther King, Jr., to sign his name to a request that President Eisenhower intervene in the South. In fact, he wondered whether the *Brown* decision by provoking resistance had made things worse.[14] Political philosopher Hannah Arendt argued that schools belonged to the social realm where groups may discriminate against other groups and not the political realm where, in a free society, they may not. "To force parents to send their children to an integrated school against their will," she said, "means to deprive them of rights which clearly belong to them in all free societies--the private right over their children and the social right to free association."[15] Cultural critic Lionel Trilling and sociologist David Riesman urged a turning away from all politics, which implied maintaining the status quo.[16]

The long legal history of school desegregation is most easily summarized in Table 7.1.

Of course, the neglect of Black education was nothing new. For a good part of the nation's history, Blacks lived in states where their education was either illegal or greatly limited by custom. Although the education of the mass of Whites was not prohibited, education was generally private and for elites not the masses.

The common school movement of the mid-nineteenth century was the first significant effort to bring education to the masses. Almost by necessity it was decentralized since in 1860, 80 percent of the population resided in rural areas, and by 1890, the average size of a state office of

Table 7.1 Major court decisions on school desegregation

1849	*Roberts v. City of Boston*	*Black inclusion in Boston Common Schools*
1896	Plessy v. Ferguson	Separate but equal doctrine
1950	Sweatt v. Painter	Separate law school unequal
1950	McLaurin v. Oklahoma State Regents	Separation within graduate school unequal
1954	Brown v. Topeka Bd. of Education	Separate schools inherently unequal
1968	Green v. New Kent Co. Sch. Bd.	Eliminates freedom of choice plans
1971	Swann v. Charlotte-Mecklenburg Bd.	Permits busing and affirmative action
1973	Keyes v. Denver Sch. Dist. #1	Applies remedies to de facto segregation
1973	Milliken v. Bradley	Stops metropolitan integration
1973	San Antonio v. Rodriguez	Denies right to equal funding
1978	UC Regents v. Bakke	Prohibits quotas on admissions
2003	Gratz v. Bollinger Grutter V. Bollinger	Narrowed the means to achieve AA in college and law school admissions

See Richard Kluger, *Simple Justice* (New York: Knopf, 1975) and Waldo E. Martin, Jr., (Ed.) *Brown v. Board of Education* (Boston: Bedford/St. Martin's, 1998).

education comprised two employees. It was primarily lay people who built and supervised public education and young, untrained teachers who did the teaching. These promoters of public education were largely of British-American origin, bourgeois in class status, and evangelical Protestant in religious orientation. Basic education in the three Rs of reading, writing, and arithmetic comprised the curriculum symbolized by McGuffey readers and one-room schoolhouses.[17]

Aside from the brief flowering of education in the Freedman's Bureau schools during Reconstruction—open to both Blacks and Whites—the masses of Blacks in the South were largely ignored by White policymakers. Black schools in some states under Redeemer governments received an equitable share of school tax funds from 1880 to 1890. However, an attempt by Senator Henry Blair of New Hampshire to spend large sums of federal money on public school education in the South was debated for six years before its final defeat in 1890. Blair noted the widespread illiteracy in the South among both Whites and Blacks, and with the removal of federal troops from the South by President Hayes in 1877, the last barriers to North–South political and economic cooperation had fallen. Despite provisions that would have allowed segregated public schools, Southerners could not accept provisions that required federal and state funds to be distributed equally. For their part, Black Southerners in general were willing to accept a real separate but equal educational system.[18]

The urbanization and industrialization of the United States along with the tide of immigration in the late nineteenth and early twentieth centuries prompted the rise of the Progressive movement and with it the development of progressive education. Progressive education meant (1) schools were now directly concerned with health, vocation, family, and community life; (2) new psychological and social science research was used in pedagogy; (3) instruction was tailored to different kinds and classes of children; and (4) there was faith that culture could be democratized without being vulgarized.[19] To accomplish all of the above, progressives believed control had to be centralized in superintendents and state administrators and taken away from parents. Teaching was professionalized as national unions such as the National Educators Association (NEA) were established and new graduate schools of education created credentialing programs.

A shift in focus from intellectual development to functional objectives accompanied professionalization. As secondary education grew to prepare students for their role in society, tools and procedures such as IQ testing and tracking helped teachers and administrators determine what type of education suited each student. Much of the direction for this functional education, however, came from non-elected and private individuals and groups, not teachers. The secular philanthropists of the early twentieth century often regarded the education of Whites as more beneficial to the Negro race than Black education: "[T]he education of 'one untaught white man to the point that knowledge and not prejudice will guide his conduct…is worth more to the black man himself than the education of ten Negroes'."[20]

It was philanthropists/industrialists like Andrew Carnegie, John D. Rockefeller, and the General Education Board that working with Booker T. Washington determined the course of Black education. The famous critique of Washington by W.E.B. Du Bois in *The Souls of Black Folk* highlights the control these forces had over Black education for over a generation. The only real battle was not over vocational v. liberal arts education but over whether the vocational education would include industrial training as well as agricultural education.[21]

The Great Depression and World War II demonstrated how inadequate both private and state/local funding were in meeting the educational needs of all Americans. Just as waves of immigration had prompted the reconstruction of secondary education during the turn of the twentieth century, the Great Depression spurred local school districts to demand federal funds without federal control. Historically, federal intrusion of any kind in education had been condemned by most educators as unconstitutional, inefficient, and antidemocratic. President Roosevelt, himself, was on record as opposing federal aid to education. Thus government funding came not as a conscious and planned effort to educate students to their full potential, but rather as a by-product of poverty and job training programs.

By 1938–39, more than 90 percent of the members of the New Deal's Civilian Conservation Corp (CCC) were enrolled in some instruction, averaging four hours per week. Some two-thirds of these enrollees were in job-related classes, but one-third were in strictly academic classes. Roosevelt's National Youth Administration (NYA) had a more direct educational objective: to permit students in secondary schools and colleges to continue their education by providing them with part-time, often on-campus jobs as clerks, janitors, and research assistants or jobs on construction projects, on playgrounds, and in nursery schools. Due to the efforts of Mary McCloud Bethune and others, the NYA forbade discrimination in student selection or pay. As a result, over 300,000 Black youth participated, with an additional 4000 benefiting from a special fund for Black graduate and college students. Aubrey Williams, head of the NYA, stated: "I can imagine no worse menace to our democratic tradition than the development of a hereditary system whereby only the children of the well-to-do might enter the professions and the children of the now less honored should remain permanently bound to follow in their parents' footsteps."[22] Williams was clearly making a tradition rather than upholding a tradition in that the public school system had been set up precisely to train students for their "station-in-life." Despite this new attitude, the New Deal programs remained separate but equal and did not articulate a policy of equal educational opportunity.[23]

Before World War II, Black educational attainment lagged behind that of second generation immigrants by three to four years for men and two to four years for women. Widespread illiteracy among Blacks was responsible for the fact that the number of Blacks rejected and classified 4-F was about twice that of Whites in the early stages of the war. This educational problem became a national security issue because the segregation of the army meant low-scoring (on Army IQ tests) Black soldiers could not be dispersed among higher-scoring White soldiers.[24] This led to Black units being assigned support roles instead of combat roles.

While Southerners were outraged that potentially a half million illiterate but otherwise draftable Blacks were deferred, Blacks themselves wished to enlist and to fight on the frontlines. By mid-1941, the army increased the limit on the acceptance of illiterates from 5 percent to 10 percent and began to establish remedial illiteracy centers. Two years later, special training units were transformed into an efficient school system employing Black and White teachers. By the end of the war, almost half of all Blacks who entered the army had been subliterate and almost all of these left their stint with new knowledge and a much-expanded sense of postwar possibilities. About half of these veterans sought further schooling under the GI Bill.[25]

Once again the federal government had intervened on behalf of Black education not as a matter of social justice but because of national security. Schooling was not seen as a force for social reform, and equal opportunity for Blacks in education could not substitute for or produce social equality. This thinking would change over the next decade, culminating in the *Brown* decision.

With the launching of Sputnik by the Soviet Union in 1957, education was newly framed as a national security issue and therefore a top priority. According to Diane Ravitch, the Rockefeller Brothers Fund report *Pursuit of Excellence* in 1958 marked a shift away from the school as a community social service center and toward the development of excellence as a national goal.[26] Federal dollars flowed freely into a host of school programs, many targeting math and science education. Some 66 federal category programs were created between 1958 and 1975. Competing with programs devoted to math, science, and the gifted were other federal programs focused on compensatory education, head start, bilingual education, ethnic studies, and sex bias in school athletics.[27]

At mid-century, the United States had finally emerged from the shadow of Europe. Politically, the New Deal meant that power now flowed from the New World to the Old World. And the allied victory in World War II and the subsequent Marshall Plan meant military and economic power now flowed from the United States to Europe and to Asia. The major obstacle blocking the nation's future world historical importance was its domestic race "problem." White supremacy was not a compelling ideological export in a decolonizing world.

These conditions set the stage for the 1944 publication of Gunnar Myrdal's *An American Dilemma* as a paradigm-shifting event. Moreover, Myrdal's outsider status as a Swedish citizen gave the work the veneer of objectivity that continued a tradition started by Tocqueville and extending through James Bryce and John Maynard Keynes. Nikhil Pal Singh cites *An*

American Dilemma "as a symptom of a global shift from Eurocentrism to Americocentrism within the world system in which America and Europe would gradually collude in disavowing the more pernicious legacies of western colonialism."[28]

First, as indicated earlier, Myrdal's work marked a shift from a biologically based paradigm of race status to a psychologically based perspective. This was generally seen as a liberal or progressive development as judged by the reviews of Blacks and Whites alike. The race dilemma pre-Myrdal was between a biologically improbable assimilation and expulsion from the United States that had been physically impossible by the time of the Civil War. Perhaps reflecting the emerging Boasian school of anthropology in the 1920s and 1930s, the army had been careful to indicate that the disproportionately poor performance of Blacks on its mental tests was the result of environment, not heredity.[29]

Second, by emphasizing the talents of top White and Black social scientists (including a young Kenneth Clark), Myrdal's work ostensibly reversed the prevailing social science maximum in the United States that state ways can't change folkways. As the New Deal and army experiments with education demonstrated, greater access to education could be an instrument of social reform. A new generation of social engineers working with groups like the NAACP could plan a rational attack on "irrational" racism.

Finally, *An American Dilemma's* framing of the Negro "problem" was the symbolic pivot on which future claims of the US global mission rested. According to Singh, it was "a massive effort to rationalize an epochal shift in transnational intellectual life in which reformulations of American liberalism were becoming the basis for asserting that the United States had achieved a superior degree of universalization relative to other nation-states, and was therefore the best instrument of rational change not just in the domestic arena, but within the world-system as a whole."[30] In short, the possibility of solving the Negro problem was a Black jeremiad within the American jeremiad that then and future leaders and intellectuals such as King and James Baldwin would embrace.

> What it comes to is that if we, who can scarcely be considered a white nation, persist in thinking of ourselves as one, we condemn ourselves, with the truly white nations, to sterility and decay, whereas if we could accept ourselves *as we are*, we might bring new life to the Western achievements, and transform them. The price of this transformation is the unconditional freedom of the

Negro; it is not too much to say that he, who has been so long rejected, must now be embraced, and at no matter what psychic or social risk. He is *the* key figure in his country, and the American future is precisely as bright or as dark as his. And the Negro recognizes this, in a negative way. Hence the question: Do I really *want* to be integrated into burning house?[31]

For America to achieve its destiny as the one truly exceptional or indis pensible nation, it must extend liberty, equality, and justice to its citizens of color.

This new psychological reformulation of the Negro problem, however, held as many negatives as positives for African Americans. Myrdal's focus on the forces of modernization to resolve the internal conflicts (cognitive dissonance) of individual White Americans removed Blacks from any active role in their advancement. Although he was a trained economist, Myrdal ignored the role of political economy in White attitudes and labeled young colleagues like Ralph Bunche as neo-Marxists. Myrdal also removed the term race from the discourse, preferring to import the concept of "caste" from the Indian subcontinent. Caste was useful in demonstrating that the status of Blacks was in reality an ascriptive practice leftover from pre-modern society. He thereby separated the concept of race from western modernity when others such as Oliver Cox and later race theorists would argue that race constitutes an integral part of modernity.[32]

Most importantly, *An American Dilemma* begins the shift in the conception of race from a biological phenomenon to a cultural phenomenon. In the process, the problem is not really at root a defective White culture but rather the social pathology of Black culture.

We assume that it is to the advantage of American Negroes as individuals and as a group to become assimilated into American culture, to acquire traits held in esteem by the dominant white Americans. This will be the value premise here. *We do not imply that white American culture is "higher"* than other cultures in an absolute sense.…But it does not gainsay our assumption that *here, in America, American culture is "highest"* in the pragmatic sense that adherence to it is practical for any individual or group not strong enough to change it. Also not to be taken in a doctrinal sense is the observation that the peculiarities of the Negro community may be characterized as social pathology.[33]

White culture has now become American culture and if Blacks want to participate in American society—as Moynihan would later state—they must assimilate that culture. Thus, once again the real burden of Black advancement is on the shoulders of Blacks themselves.

Although *Brown II* mandated school integration it did not set a timetable for implementation. Unlike the *Plessy* decision that codified the "Jim Crow" policy already in place throughout the South, *Brown II* attempted to consciously move in a new direction away from customary practice. Unfortunately it did so without planning or funding and a disproportionate share of the burden would be borne by Blacks. New federal dollars did begin to flow into local schools after *Brown* but for national security again, not equal educational opportunity.

Brown highlighted the effects of schooling on students for the first time. But the decision implicitly defined equal educational opportunity as integration rather than any concrete measure of academic success. This led to a split among African Americans, with one side arguing that with increased resources predominantly Black schools could be at least as effective in educating Black students as predominantly White schools where Black students often faced a hostile environment.[34] The slow pace of integration, for example, led parents in the Ocean Hill-Brownsville area of New York in 1966 to demand their school (IS 201) be either integrated or given to them to run. When the school board allowed parents to choose the principal and reassign some of the teachers, the first of three school strikes was launched by the United Federation of Teachers (UFT). After a protracted struggle of nearly four years that included a Ford Foundation pilot program on decentralization, the New York State Commissioner of Education asserted state control reinstating teachers, transferring new principals, and appointing an outside trustee for four months.[35] Eventually the city of New York took the power to appoint principals and assign teachers out of the hands of local school councils but created 32 local elected school boards. Some were led by advocates of African-themed curricula, while others were run by Whites who used community control to protect homogeneity in neighborhood schools.[36] One consequence of the struggle was a new state law curtailing the right of public employees to strike and a splitting of an alliance that had included liberals, Blacks, and Jews. The current charter school movement can trace its origins, in part, to the struggle for parental involvement in Ocean Hill-Brownsville.

A decade after *Brown*, academics responded to the problem of equal educational opportunity by attempting to measure inequality. Sociologist James Coleman's 1966 report "Equal Educational Opportunity" was commissioned by the US Department of Education and involved 650,000 students—the largest study of its kind. This influential study sought to distinguish types of inequality. One type emphasized inputs to the school and included tangible factors such as per pupil expenditures and the racial composition of the school and intangible factors like teacher morale and expectations. The other type of inequality examined outputs including equality of results given the same individual input and equality of results given unequal backgrounds and abilities. Coleman focused on equality of results given the same input since he regarded the latter as unattainable. Controlling all of the variables, Coleman's major finding was that the socioeconomic status of the student's parents, not the school, was the most important factor in determining academic achievement. Given the small Black middle class, this finding implied that Blacks would benefit from a majority White school and provided support for proponents of busing. In 1983, however, Coleman declared, "the assumption that integration would improve achievement of lower-class Black children now has been shown to be fiction."[37]

Whether he intended it or not, Coleman's conclusions helped shift the discourse away from the school's role in insuring equal educational opportunity toward other factors such as family, culture, IQ, and merit. These issues would become central to early Black Studies research.

Coleman's report, especially the finding that tangible factors such as libraries, labs, and per pupil expenditures had the least influence on academic achievement struck at the heart of the NAACP's strategy in *Brown*. Its contention that separate never resulted in equal in terms of bricks and mortar was undermined by Coleman's work. When the strategy shifted to such intangible factors as teacher expectations and psychological damage, the contention that integration was necessary for Black academic advancement was also suspect. By moving the debate away from the school and toward the class status of the family, Coleman reopened the door to a discourse on cultural pathology begun by Myrdal.

Another sociologist working at the same time, Daniel Patrick Moynihan, pointed out the policy consequences of this shift in a report on the Negro family produced by the US Department of Labor in 1965. Moynihan's states that at "the heart of the deterioration of the fabric of Negro society is the deterioration of the Negro family. It is the fundamental source of weakness of the Negro community at the present time.…The white family has achieved a high degree of stability and is maintaining that stability. By contrast, the family structure of lower class Negroes is highly unstable, and in many urban centers is approaching complete breakdown."[38]

Frequently quoting the work of Black sociologist E. Franklin Frazier on the disproportionately high rates of "dissolved" marriages, illegitimacy, welfare rates, and so on in the Black community, Moynihan presents the policy consequences on the first page of the report: "The United States is approaching a new crisis in race relations…in this period the expectations of the Negro Americans will go beyond civil rights. Being Americans, they will now expect that in the near future equal opportunities for them as a group will produce roughly equal results, as compared with other groups. This is not going to happen. Nor will it happen for generations to come unless a new special effort is made."[39] The fundamental problem is that of family structure, said Moynihan, and a new national effort is required that is directed toward the establishment of a stable Negro family structure. However, in an earlier work with Nathan Glazer entitled *Beyond the Melting Pot*, Moynihan had indicated that the problem was deeper than family structure. He said: "It is not possible for Negroes to view themselves as other ethnic groups viewed themselves because—and this is the key to much of the Negro world—the Negro's is only an American, and nothing else. *He has no values and culture to guard and protect* [emphasis mine]."[40]

When Moynihan became an urban affairs assistant to President Richard Nixon, his report served as the basis for a major presidential speech setting forth new domestic policy goals. Most of those goals involved dismantling the programs of Johnson's Great Society rather than any new program initiatives on the family by the new administration. In summary, the social science research of Moynihan provided the basis for what became known as "benign neglect" by the federal government in regard to race issues. The burden of Black advancement once again was shifted from the shoulders of Whites as represented by the federal government to Blacks much as Booker T. Washington had shifted the burden of uplift from Whites to the formerly enslaved. As Moynihan states, "[a]t this point, the present tangle of pathology is capable of perpetuating itself without assistance from the white world. The cycle can be broken only if these distortions are set right."[41]

Not only is Black pathology capable of replicating itself without White help, Moynihan also threatens to withdraw government assistance to lower-class Blacks if they fail to conform to White norms.

> There is no reason why Negroes need conform to anyone's standards but their own.…On the other hand, in order for this to be a *viable* position

> as well as a tenable one, it must reject not only conformity but dependency....So long as exceptional numbers of Negro children are dependent on Welfare...and so long as vast numbers of Negro youth have to be helped along....Negroes will be at the mercy of whites demanding an end to "welfare chiseling" and "immorality." If at the moment educated, middle-class Negroes are much in demand and doing nicely, this is not so for the lower class and is likely never to be. This country is not fair to Negroes and will exploit any weakness they display. Hence they simply cannot afford the luxury of having a large lower class that is at once deviant *and* dependent. If they do not wish to bring it in line with the working class...world around them, they must devise ways to support it from within.[42]

Moynihan, like Gunnar Myrdal, argued that if Blacks expected to receive the full benefits of American citizenship, they must become more like Whites.

However, it is not just the working class that Moynihan takes on. He accuses middle-class Blacks of using violent urban masses to *threaten* White Americans. He concludes that this has been an intoxicating experience in which they demand "Do this or the cities will burn." He continues: "What building contracts and police graft were to the nineteenth-century urban Irish, the welfare department, Head Start and Black Studies programs will be to the coming generation of Negroes."[43]

The Moynihan report generated an enormous response both inside and outside the academy. Of course civil rights leaders objected, but for the first time they could draw on the research of a new group of scholars either directly or indirectly affiliated with Black Studies. Professional conferences featured panels on the report and special issues of journals were devoted to the subject. New courses on the "Black Family" and the "Black Child" were introduced in the offerings of Black Studies programs. Scholars challenged the gender assumptions in Moynihan's portrayal of the stable nuclear family. Robert Staples attacked the myth of Black matriarchy in the *Black Scholar* and edited a book on *The Black Family*.[44] Andrew Billingsley launched a new reexamination of the subject in *Black Families in White America* and published a subsequent analysis for the National Urban League.[45] Perhaps the pinnacle of national attention on the topic came with Alex Haley's publication of *Roots* in 1976 and its subsequent television reenactment watched by a record number of Americans.

The development of the concept of cultural pathology or cultural deprivation served to distance its proponents from discredited theories of Black biological inferiority. However, the old notions of Social Darwinism and eugenics were now replaced with claims that Blacks on average were less intelligent than Whites as measured in intelligence testing (IQ). Of course the obvious policy implications for education were that no matter how much money was allocated for schools, it would be impossible for Black achievement to equal White achievement.

Berkeley psychologist Arthur Jensen fired the initial salvo in what became a very public and very political debate over Black intelligence. In his 1969 essay "How Much Can We Boost IQ and Scholastic Achievement" in the *Harvard Educational Review*, Jensen argued the compensatory educational programs for Blacks were futile given that Blacks were genetically inferior to Whites intellectually. Jensen's relatively cautious policy perspectives were taken to the next level by Stanford physicist and Nobel laureate William Shockley who recommended the establishment of a fund to pay "intellectually inferior" people to allow themselves to be sterilized. On talk shows and in a letter to the National Academy of Scientists, he suggested that $1000 be paid for each point below 100 IQ and that $30,000 be placed in trusts to compensate those with a 70 IQ mentality and the potential to have 20 children not to give birth. Such a policy might save taxpayers $250,000 in reduced costs of mental retardation.[46] Later, Shockley would take the initiative himself to set up a sperm bank for the intellectually gifted.

While Shockley's recommendations were largely ignored by policymakers,[47] Jensen's article sparked a vociferous response. A 1978 list of the decade's most cited social science articles ranked Jensen's sixth. Most of the critiques of Jensen's work focused on his reliance on IQ testing. The long history of such testing in limiting immigration from Eastern and Southern Europe was pointed to as was its role in tracking students in public schools. Lewis Terman, who introduced the Stanford-Binet (IQ) tests in public schools, picked items that boys and girls would test equally on. Items on which girls performed better than boys were thrown out. This screening of questions was not applied to class and race differences. Others attacked Jensen's reliance on the nineteenth century twin studies of Sir Cyril Burt on the influence of heritability, which had been found to be fraudulent. In sum, the critics generally challenged three assumptions: first, that each child proceeds at a uniform rate of development; second, that development stops for all individuals at a certain age; and finally, that something as abstract as general intelligence can be measured in one test and quantified.[48]

Proving that some perspectives never die, the biological paradigm on race resurfaced again in Richard Herrnstein and Charles Murray's 1994 book *The Bell Curve*. The massive volume emerged just as the new Republican majority in Congress was writing a new "contract with America" that gutted what remained of the social welfare state. Like Jensen, Herrstein was a psychologist, not a geneticist or biologist, who had written a 1971 *Atlantic Monthly* essay defending Jensen's work. His coauthor, Charles Murray, was a political scientist attached to the conservative American Enterprise Institute. In his review of the book, Harvard zoologist Stephen Jay Gould stated the book contained no new arguments nor did it present any compelling new data. However, it did emerge at "a historical moment of unprecedented ungenerosity" when its arguments could be used to slash social programs.[49]

The most contentious of Herrnstein and Murrays' claims extended the argument for innate cognitive stratification to a claim that racial differences in IQ are primarily determined by genetic causes. This difference included small differences for Asian superiority over Caucasians, but large differences for Caucasians over people of African descent. Gould called the book a "rhetorical masterpiece of scientism" that hides its politics under hundreds of pages of data obtained through the misuse of statistical methods. He contended that their own data indicate that IQ is not a major factor in determining variation in nearly all the social behaviors they study. This fact does not deter them, however, from predicting the need for a custodial state: "we have in mind a high-tech and more lavish version of the Indian reservation for some substantial minority of the nation's population, while the rest of America tries to go about its business."[50]

The neo-social Darwinism of *The Bell Curve* was only one of several explanations for the continuing disparities between Black and White socioeconomic status. Perhaps the most successful explanation, in terms of public opinion, was the emergence of the underclass concept. This concept's heritage can be directly linked to the culture of pathology model and refers to a group of people—Black urbanites—who are caught in a cycle of generational poverty immune to improvement from external sources, that is, government assistance.

Ken Auletta, who helped popularize the term underclass, estimated there were some nine million persons in this group and he divided them into four categories: (1) the passive poor, usually long-term welfare recipients; (2) the hostile street criminals who terrorize most cities, and who are often school dropouts and drug addicts; (3) the hustlers, who earn their living in an underground economy but rarely commit violent crimes; and (4) the traumatized drunks, drifters, homeless shopping-cart ladies, and released patients.[51]

It is not a coincidence that the Moynihan report with its pathological model of Black family life was revived to explain the existence of the underclass. In short, the number of Black female-headed households was increasing significantly more than the norm and these households were more likely to be poverty-stricken. Moreover, by 1984, 59 percent of all Black births occurred out of wedlock compared to 13 percent of White births. And, the data demonstrated that Black female-headed households were far more likely to remain in poverty over a long period.[52]

The most prominent challenger to conservatives like Murray who claimed that liberal welfare policies enticed lower-class women to have out-of-wedlock births was sociologist William J. Wilson. In *The Truly Disadvantaged*, he argued that Black females delayed marriage and have a lower remarriage rate largely due to the labor-market status of Black males. Wilson suggested that the key to understanding underclass behavior was social isolation, not the culture of poverty. Inner-city Blacks simply lacked contacts with groups of different class or racial backgrounds and were trapped in areas of concentrated poverty with poor schools and few job opportunities.[53]

Although they offered different explanations for the problems of urban African Americans, both liberals and conservatives seemed to accept the existence of an underclass. Yet Auletta's categories of the underclass contain groupings with divergent characteristics. The passive poor on welfare would appear to have very different attitudes than the active hustlers who some have argued are the young capitalists of the inner city. What values do the homeless share with drug dealers who often exhibit lavish lifestyles? Moreover, many census tracts labeled as underclass are *not* in areas of extreme poverty and vice versa.[54] Wealthy individuals exhibit some of the same irrational behavior as those in the culture of poverty with no stigma attached to the "culture of wealth."[55]

As a concept, the underclass, like the notion of IQ, is ambiguous enough to hide a variety of political perspectives. Intelligence testing has the advantage of appearing value neutral but also carries the historical baggage of eugenics and discredited science. The social pathology attached to the underclass can claim liberal proponents such as Myrdal, Frazier, and Moynihan but is a value-committed perspective. That is, it defines integration as assimilation. Without explicitly proclaiming White cultural supremacy, it forces Blacks and other minorities to conform to a White cultural norm if they are to advance. Once federal tax dollars started flowing into local school districts beginning with Sputnik in 1957 and culminating with the passage of the Elementary and Secondary Education Act (ESEA) in 1965 and the creation of a federal Department of Education in 1980, conservatives were not able to turn back the clock and assume complete local control. They did, however, fight to control the content of education—the curriculum—at the local level. In addition, they sought to redirect federal funding away from programs promoting equal educational opportunity toward programs that promoted "excellence" and were coincidentally disproportionately White.

Once again the defining moment in this shift was couched in terms of national security, which trumped the calls for educational equity. In its 1983 report "A Nation at Risk," the National Commission on Excellence in Education (NCEE) chaired by David Gardner, the president-elect of the University of California, stated:

> Our once unchallenged preeminence in commerce, industry, science and technological innovation is being overtaken by competitors throughout the world....If an unfriendly foreign power had attempted to impose on America the mediocre educational performance that exists today, we might well have viewed it as an act of war....We have even squandered the gains in student achievement made in the wake of the Sputnik challenge....We have, in effect, been committing an act of unthinking, unilateral educational disarmament.[56]

Shortly after he was elected president of the United States, Ronal Reagan declared a "crisis" in education and appointed the NCEE that provided the expertise he needed to reverse course on equal educational opportunity. Reagan blamed the civil rights movement for putting too much responsibility on schools and also shifted the burden of support from the federal to state level. Over the period of the 1980s, the federal contribution to urban schools declined from 15 percent to 5 percent. While there was no crisis in the early 1980s when Reagan announced its existence—the National Assessment of Educational Progress showed improvement rather than decline and in a larger, more diverse student population—there was a crisis by the end of his administration.[57]

In fact, as a result of the efforts to equalize educational opportunity in the 1960s and 1970s, school integration peaked in the early years of the Reagan administration. Between 1968 and 1981, the percentage of Black students in predominantly minority schools decreased by nearly 14 percent. Yet from 1981 to 1999, the figures had reversed and climbed nearly seven percentage points. The numbers for Latino students reflected a similar trend. By 1999, racial isolation had increased in all regions, with schools in the Northeast, not the South, being most segregated.[58] Thus the turn away from equal educational opportunity was also a turn away from integration and the spirit of *Brown*.

The turn away from equal educational opportunity in higher education began well before Reagan's election and "A Nation at Risk." In 1978, the Supreme Court's decision in *Bakke v. Regents of the University of California* severely limited the use of affirmative action programs in higher education. These programs along with the Civil Rights Act of 1964 had significantly increased the numbers of minorities and women in higher education. Currently, women comprise more than 50 percent of undergraduate students and 50 percent or more of the students in law, medicine, graduate, and professional schools. Blacks and Latinos, on the other hand, have seen their numbers decline since *Bakke*.

Due to the pressure of the civil rights movement, affirmative action began with bipartisan support in government and—depending on how the question was phrased—majority support in the general population.[59] President John F. Kennedy through an executive order on contract compliance established the Committee on Equal Employment Opportunity. In 1965, President Johnson issued Executive Order 11264 requiring federal contractors to take affirmative action to insure equality of employment opportunity. President Richard Nixon's administration issued specific requirements for enforcing contract compliance that remain in force today. His "Philadelphia Plan" is generally regarded as the first "quota" program.

Title VI of the Civil Rights Act of 1964 and Title IX of the educational amendments of 1972, along with voluntary affirmative action efforts by colleges and universities, resulted in substantial gains in access to higher education for women and minorities. A number of prominent Republicans proclaimed their support for such efforts including Senator Robert Dole and San Diego mayor (later California governor) Pete Wilson. By the late 1970s, however, conservatives began to target minority scholarships and admissions as "reverse racism." Often the conservative groups leading the attack used the rights language of civil rights movement in their rhetoric and even their names, for example, the Center for Individual Rights, the Institute of Justice, the American Civil Rights Institute, and the Center for Equal Opportunity. The rights these groups were defending, however, were for Whites, not Blacks or Latinos. Reagan's assistant attorney general for civil rights focused his concern on "reverse racism" and pulled back from enforcing affirmative action in education.[60] In one of the great ironies of our time, conservatives claimed the mantle of Martin Luther King, Jr., as a weapon against affirmative action.[61]

The *Bakke* decision marks a historic shift from *Brown* in the government's concern for equal educational opportunity. In 1973, in *Rodriguez v. San Antonio*, the Supreme Court had denied that there was a constitutional right to equal educational funding for each student. And, in *Milliken v. Bradley*, the Court ruled that the Constitutional right of Black students to access equal educational opportunity stopped at city borders. Now the Supreme Court reasoned that the 14th Amendment's due process clause applied to Whites as well as Blacks and that limited affirmative action could be allowed on the grounds that it enriched the learning environment of Whites.

Writing the opinion for a plurality of a severely divided Supreme Court in which none of the six opinions had majority support, Justice Lewis Powell ordered that the University of California Medical School at Davis admit Allan Bakke but also declared that race could be one of several factors that the state (University of California) could consider when making admission decisions.[62] The decision was hailed as a victory by both opponents and proponents of affirmative action. Opponents claimed it prohibited quota goals for minority students established by colleges and universities to promote diversity. Proponents contended that the Court preserved race as a factor that could be considered in admissions just as athletic ability and legacy candidates were given special consideration. The Powell opinion remains today the Courts' foundational guideline on race and admissions. What seemed to be lost in the immediate aftermath was a crucial shift in the Court's thinking on race since *Brown*.

First, Powell assumed that Bakke had a right to sue under Title VI of the 1964 Civil Rights Act. In discussing the scope of Title VI he stated that it barred only those racial classifications prohibited by the Constitution. Second, Powell concluded that the long history of racial conscious remedies approved by courts in school desegregation cases did not apply since there was no such history at the University of California at Davis.

In fact, there was a history of racial discrimination in the University of California system and at Davis, but it was not presented by the defendants. Third, in tracing the history of jurisprudence under the Equal Protection Clause of the 14th Amendment, Powell found that it protected all, not merely African Americans or only minorities. This finding was remarkable since the 14th Amendment was ratified in 1868 *specifically* to establish and protect the citizenship rights of Blacks. Nor could Bakke point to a long history of discrimination that he and his ancestors had endured. Finally, said Powell, race remedies could only be used if the state had a *compelling interest* in treating members of different races differently. The compelling interest that the Court found permissible in college admissions was not the redress of previous discrimination against Blacks, but rather that having Blacks in the classroom benefited the education of White students![63] The thinking behind *Brown* had been turned on its head. It was no longer primarily the case that Black students were enriched by sitting next to Whites; it was now White students who were the beneficiaries. Was it the social pathology of the Black students that benefited Whites or was there some cultural trait that Whites were lacking? From that moment on, colleges, employers, and other promoters of affirmative action began to drop that terminology and replace it with the notion of diversity. The term "diversity" was ambiguous enough to cover a wide very of rationales, none of which included social justice.

While proponents of the now-labeled "diversity and inclusion" sought to maintain the presence of "underrepresented" students in the classroom based on their enrichment of the White experience, opponents of diversity wanted to eliminate such influences. That is, they fought to promote and defend the traditional hegemony of White Western culture and deride multiculturalism or cultural pluralism. *Bakke* had slowed the admission of students of color to institutions of higher learning, but the new thereat was the "tenured radicals" of the 1960s who had taken over the university. Thus, the academy became a prime battleground for the "culture wars" of the 1980s and 1990s.[64]

I entered the "culture wars" at a different level when I, and nine other scholars, were appointed to the National Council on the Humanities by President Clinton in 1994. These were the first appointments to the council in 14 years by a Democratic president. As reported in the *Chronicle of Higher Education*, these appointments "could dramatically alter the political dynamics of the 27-member group, which advises the National Endowment for the Humanities (NEH) Chairman on all endowment activities and reviews grant applications."[65] The article noted that for the past decade the NEH council had been composed largely of critics of new fields of scholarship, while many of the new members were "strong advocates of Hispanic, black, and women's studies." [66]

Under President Jimmy Carter's administration, NEH had strongly supported ethnic studies programs at the university level. However, that source of support dried up during Republican administrations. Although NEH chairs had historically remained out of the news, Reagan's appointment of William Bennett as NEH chair marked a new visibility for the post, making him a leader in the "culture wars." One of Bennett's first public acts was to attack Stanford University's changes to its traditional Western civilization requirement. In previous NEH publications, Bennett had criticized multiculturalism and called for a return to a "classical core curriculum."[67]

Bennett's successor, Lynne Cheney, continued his high public profile and was accused of packing the council with enemies of women's and ethnic studies. She believed that liberals and leftists, because they are "politicized," must be controlled by university administrators or outsiders like NEH in order to protect "objectivity." Cheney's view of academic freedom restricted the freedom of radical professors in order to preserve the "disinterested" pursuit of truth, as long as they agreed with higher authorities.[68] Moreover, almost a third of the council was made up of members of the National Association of Scholars, a group that promoted a traditional curriculum. Since not all members rotated off at the same time, a good number of conservative appointees remained on the council. At the center of this "war" was Sheldon Hackney, former president of the University of Pennsylvania, who was finishing his first year as NEH chair. Hackney, a historian and authority on Frederick Douglass, was attempting to carve out a more neutral role rather than take sides in the dialog as Cheney had. However, Stephen Balch, president of the National Association of Scholars, questioned the scholarly quality of the new appointees and said Hackney had wasted an opportunity to show that "he is not a champion of a point of view" in the culture wars.[69] One of the remaining conservative scholars on the council, Peter Shaw, in response to a question about opening up endowment funds to new areas of scholarship, stated: "The aims of these fields may be laudable, advancing self-esteem and a social and political agenda, but they are not scholarly. These fields are explicitly political, lacking in disinterest and objectivity."[70]

Hackney did, indeed, attempt to moderate civil discourse between the conflicting factions on the council. The most contentious discussions occurred at the public meetings of the entire council; however, most of the substantive work was done in committees. I was initially assigned to the "Preservation and Access" committee and spent most of my first year or two learning what the issues in these areas were. After two years, I moved to the "Public Affairs" committee that dealt with more contentious issues such as public television programing. I remember, for example, my Berkeley colleague and Bush appointee to the council, philosopher John Searle, arguing that we should fund obscure research on medieval monks precisely because no one else would fund it. Other committee members contended that we needed to fund more popular programs on television that would appeal to the public and build support for NEH funding. Hackney also created informal discussion groups, which showed promise but were cut short by his departure. By the time most conservatives had left the council in 1996, Hackney was also replaced by another historian, William Ferris. Ferris was more overtly political than Hackney but attempted to reach out to both Democratic and Republican legislators. NEH was, by far, the largest funder of humanities programs and projects in the country; however, its funding was always under threat of cuts—often due to one or two projects that displeased a member of Congress.[71]

The "My History Is America's History" initiative was one way NEH sought to bridge the political divide of the "culture wars." Through the project it sought to encourage all Americans to explore and record their family histories by interviewing relatives, examining personal correspondence and diaries, searching immigration files, and documenting local communities. Participants could share their family histories as well as link up with news articles, maps, photographs, and timelines through an NEH website. Teachers were encouraged to use the website as a tool to make history real for their students.[72]

Although there was consensus on the National Humanities Council that "My History Is America's History" was a worthy project, its origins were somewhat more controversial. It began with the question of what made America exceptional or unique as a nation. The first response was that it was the set of values that Myrdal referred to as the "American Creed" and as embodied in the Declaration of Independence. Yet members of the Council could not agree on all of these values or that they were exclusively American. Moreover, they certainly could not agree that the values were fully reflected in American practice. A second response to the question was that it was the process of fair play and equal opportunity that constituted American greatness—in short, democracy as process rather than result. However, this response felt inadequate to some members. They believed America represented more than just a set of rules. What finally emerged from this discourse was that America was its people in all their diversity and complexity—hence the "My History Is America's History" project.

One of the key texts of the period, James Davison Hunter's *Culture Wars*, highlighted the importance of education: "The education of the public at every level—from elementary school through college—is not a neutral process of imparting practical knowledge and technical skills. Above and beyond that, schools are the primary means of reproducing community and national identity for succeeding generations of Americans."[73] Hunter identifies the adversaries in the culture wars as belonging to one of two camps—those sparked by the impulse toward orthodoxy and those motivated by the impulse toward progressivism. He contended this cleavage was so deep that it cuts across the old lines of religious conflict between Protestants, Catholics, and Jews. At the same time, Hunter undermined the severity of the cleavage by stating that most Americans occupy a vast middle ground between these polarizing impulses.[74]

After discussing a host of educational issues from home schooling to vouchers and curriculum reform, Hunter makes two observations. First, that *pluralism* is the decisive word that links all the issues together but is seen by the conflicting sides in opposite ways. "For the orthodox," says Hunter, "genuine pluralism only exists when there is respect for the integrity of diverse even if exclusive religious and moral commitment." "For progressives," however, "pluralism can only exist when there is an acceptance of all religious an moral commitments as equally valid and legitimate."[75] His second observation notes that the issue of who controls the institutional mechanisms of cultural reproduction is at the heart of the debate over democratic pluralism as reflected in educational policy.[76]

In the battle to control the mission of the modern university, one must distinguish between the ideal of a sanctuary where knowledge and truth might be pursued and imparted no matter how unpopular or difficult the process might be and the reality that universities have always had political and philosophical boundaries. "Depending on the historical and regional context," says Hunter, "academic establishments have always established certain limitations on what is appropriate to teach, to study, to research, and publish, the violation of which could mean professional censure or at least professional obscurity."[77] The origins of many of our most prestigious institutions can be found in narrow theological training. "Modern" writers from Shakespeare to Walt Whitman and Herman Melville were included in the "classical" curriculum only after divisive and prolonged struggles.[78] After a public speech in favor of the emancipation of slaves at the University of Virginia in 1832, the faculty responded with a rule, "there should be no oration on any *distracting* [emphasis mine] question of state or national policy nor on any point of theological dispute."[79] As late as 1936, 21 states plus the District of Columbia required loyalty oaths of their teachers. On the cusp of the "free speech" movement at the University of California at Berkeley in the 1950s, the administration was demanding that faculty sign loyalty oaths.

Historian Lawrence Levine charged opponents of multiculturalism with using two strategies for escaping history. One strategy he terms "Flintstoning" the past where cavemen and women live in an imaginary society that resembles ours in almost every detail. There is room for marginal change generally linked to technology but not for substantial change. The other strategy is avoiding history whereby contemporary society is almost completely severed from the past. Thus the present becomes *sui generis*, where the canons of learning have never been challenged.[80]

Both of these strategies were evident in the most popular attacks on multiculturalism. Liberals and conservatives alike found these strategies appealing. The historian Arthur Schlesinger, Jr., for example, believed that a cult of ethnicity now challenged the melting pot, replacing ideological conflict with ethnic and racial conflict. The Ethnic Heritage Studies Program Act of 1972, which funded the establishment of Ethnic Heritage Studies centers, had according to Schlesinger, "compromised the right of Americans to decide their ethnic identity."[81] If these tendencies continued unchecked, he said, "the result can only be the fragmentation, resegregation, and tribalization of American life."[82] It is not clear in his history when in the past the United States was not fragmented, segregated, or tribalized. Federal Express, however, was impressed enough with his *The Disuniting of America* to make thousands of copies available for free to potential readers.

English professor E.D. Hirsch, author of the best-selling *Cultural Literacy*, stated that as a boy given a traditional education he was literate enough to read Myrdal's *An American Dilemma*, which enabled him to turn against the conservative views of his family and their Southern community. He believed that "our recently fragmented school curriculum"[83] is responsible for a decline in cultural literacy that is particularly devastating for Black students. Cultural literacy was defined as possession of the basic information needed to thrive in the modern world. Hirsch somehow separated the teaching of this basic information from "the complex problem of how to teach values in American schools."[84] That is, while it is fine to teach students to read authors they identify with such as Langston Hughes or Alice Walker, they will be culturally disadvantaged if they have not absorbed traditional writers like Thoreau and Twain. At least these liberal critics of multiculturalism acknowledged a history of oppression and are willing to accept "properly taught" Black history and Black literature courses as supplements to the traditional curriculum.

Conservative classics scholar Allan Bloom painted an even bleaker portrait of the development of multiculturalism in his *The Closing of the American Mind*. Noble laureate Saul Bellow's introduction neatly summarizes Bloom's argument:

> [T]he university in a society ruled by public opinion, was to have been an island of intellectual freedom where all views of were investigated without restriction. Liberal democracy in its generosity made this possible, but by consenting to play an active or "positive," participatory role in society the university has become inundated and saturated with the backflow of society's "problems."[85]

Thus Bellow and Bloom, much like the faculty of Jefferson's University of Virginia who prefer not to hear about slavery, believe the university has only now become saturated with society's problems. In this "Flintstoning" of history, the campus protests of the 1960s are compared unfavorably to the German universities of the 1930s. "Because the student movements were so untheoretical," said Bloom, "the natural sciences were not a target, as they had once been in *high-grade* [emphasis mine] fascism and communism. There were no Lenins thundering against positivism."[86] Accordingly, this allowed the sciences to go along with affirmative action because they did not face minority students in their classes. Since the humanities were seen as irrelevant, stated Bloom, this left the social sciences as the point of attack.

Apparently in the 1950s, the elite universities had achieved their ideal state largely due to the influx of European immigrant intellectuals. Once again adopting the Flintstone view of history, Bloom argued that McCarthyism had no effect whatsoever on curriculum or appointments in major universities.[87] Contending that nothing positive came out of the

1960s, Bloom believes there is much less to study now in the university. He derided, for example, the "Peace Corp mentality," which is not a spur to learning but rather a secularized version of doing good work. The back-to-basics movement in education, Bloom said, is an acknowledgement of the mistake and Black Studies has largely failed because what was serious in them did not interest the students, and the rest was unprofitable hokum.[88]

It took political scientist Samuel Huntington to elevate the "dis-uniting of America" from a domestic problem to a "national security" threat. Widely cited for his 1990s work on the "clash of civilizations,"[89] Huntington attacked multiculturalism in general and specifically Mexican immigration as major causes for concern. He acknowledged that in times of high external threat, such as the Cold War and the aftermath of the terrorist attacks of September 11, 2001, Americans were united. However, when such threats are minimal, ethnic and racial identifications tend to divide the country.

In *Who Are We?* Huntington rejected the old view of America as a "melting pot" and the new view of the multiculturalists of the country as a salad or mosaic. He promoted the perspective of America as a can of tomato soup to which other ingredients may be added but the core of Anglo-Protestant culture remained constant. Multiculturalism, according to Huntington, is essentially anti-European civilization and that along with diversity it has eroded the legitimacy of the remaining central elements of American identity, the cultural core and the American Creed. Proponents of multiculturalism, including many intellectuals and educators, have had their principal impact on schools and colleges.[90]

The primary threat today comes not from the multiculturalism of the 1960s and 1970s but from the biculturalism sparked by waves of Mexican immigration. Huntington believes this immigration differs from past immigration and the current immigration of other groups due to six factors. The proximity or *contiguity* of Mexico has made it possible for unprecedented *numbers* of all classes to immigrate. This immigration is *illegal* and *concentrated* in particular regions of the country. The waves of immigrants are *persistent* with no signs of ebbing. Finally, there is a *historical presence* of Mexicans in the Southwest that no other immigrant group can claim. Therefore, there is a very real possibility, states Huntington, that the United States could become bifurcated with two national languages and a divided loyalty. Although the American public overwhelmingly resists such a deconstruction of the American identity, multiculturalists have been joined by government officials seeking votes and business elites seeking workers and trade in promoting immigration.[91]

Several threads unite both liberal and conservative critiques of Black Studies and multiculturalism. First is a belief that racism was an historic aberration to an American society that is exceptionally good. Citing Myrdal, for example, Huntington declared that the only major historical exception to the American Creed was the South's effort to justify slavery.[92] A second similarity is that America's core Anglo-Protestant culture along with its political creed has remained largely unchanged over three centuries with minor contributions from other groups and variations in saliency. Bloom saw this homogeneous culture as the basis for "man's natural rights" in which class, race, religion, national origin, or culture all disappear or become secondary.[93] Third, Blacks were making good progress toward inclusion until the shift to identity politics and multiculturalism that polarized race relations. Even militants like the Black Panthers, said Hirsch, produced a newspaper that was highly conservative in its language and cultural assumptions in order to communicate effectively. Despite the provocations of multiculturalism, ethnicity is dead and racial blurring is making racial identity passé.[94] Finally, American culture resting on its Anglo foundations is indeed superior to non-Western cultures. That is, the cultural relativism and tolerance promoted by multiculturalists does not allow for distinguishing "good" cultural traits from "bad" or pathological ones. And, it is only in those Western nations influenced by Greek philosophy that there is some willingness to critically examine one's culture. It was, in fact, the assimilation of Western ideas by leaders like Martin Luther King, Jr., that permitted Blacks to progress.

Despite the similarities between liberal and conservative critics of multiculturalism, there are a couple of important differences. Bloom's work is unashamedly elitist and anti-democratic. He limits his analysis to the 20 or 30 "best" universities and charges that democratization of the academy in the 1960s helped dismantle its structure and caused it to lose focus. For Bloom, "democracy took away philosophy's privileges" and a "very great narrowness is not incompatible with the health of an individual or a people, whereas with great openness it is hard to avoid decomposition."[95] In his world, White students no longer hold stereotypes and only pathological lower-class types now hold racist views although the reasons for this progress are not made clear.

Huntington, on the other hand, is careful to align his views with the American public who are overwhelmingly opposed to multiculturalism.

It is the elites who have promoted an unrepresentative democracy. "Overall," says Huntington, "American elites are not only less nationalistic but are also more liberal than the American public"—with the notable exception of business and the military.[96] Huntington is keen to point out the general religiosity of Americans when compared to other nations, but does not address the anti-democratic tendencies of some Christian denominations.

The romantic vision of the ivory tower on the hill teaching a unified, traditional curriculum is just as false as the notion of the stable, unchanging nature of the American Creed. The Great Books and Western Civilization courses so lionized by Bloom emerged briefly after World War I and began to disappear with the advent of electives—not Black and Ethnic Studies—after World War II. Until the opening of universities to a different demographic thanks to the GI bill and affirmative action, the homogeneity of the faculty and students ensured that there was more unanimity about what constituted acceptable ideas and behavior. There was actually more, not less, of what conservatives call political correctness.[97]

"Monoculturalism as an institutional ideology," states David Goldberg, "only emerged in the nineteenth century to create the impression of an intellectual tradition where there was indeed none."[98] Until World War I, Americans generally defined themselves in contrast to England and Europe rather than the proud products of Anglo-Protestant tradition. In fact, it only became popular to refer to the American Creed after World War II, in part due to the influence of Myrdal. George Kennan, the theoretical father of the Cold War's strategy of containing Communism, contemplated the possibility of breaking the United States up into 12 "constituent republics," each having control over its own immigration.[99] Yet Huntington does not accuse Kennan of being unpatriotic.

By insisting that the greatest threat to America both domestically and globally is the "clash of civilizations" rather than ideology, Huntington and his supporters are ensuring the continued need for Black Studies and multiculturalism. In a sense, "the West against the rest" concept is another version of the culture of pathology argument. Western culture is presented as homogeneous, unchanging, and not influenced by non-Western sources. It is worse than the Cold War in the sense that, as Huntington says, it is easier to change one's ideology than one's culture.

It is also easier to allocate values using ideology than it is culture. Ideology can distinguish between good and evil much more readily than culture. Science, despite its claims of objectivity and value neutrality, is ideological because facts are generated that individuals must confront. Whether the issue is IT or climate change, science cannot escape the ideological arena. Natural science, says Bloom, is sovereignly indifferent to the fact that there were and are other kinds of explanations of natural phenomena in other ages or cultures. He believes political science has become, "for the best and worst reasons, the bastion of the reaction against value-free social science and new social science as a whole."[100] But Bloom closes himself off from other kinds of explanations and using other cultures and relies on the ancient Greeks for his discourse of good and evil.

Bloom is not a postmodernist for whom truth is an effect of the rules of a particular discourse. However, he does question reason and its ability to establish values. A value is only a value if it is life preserving and life enhancing, and according to Bloom, "equalitarianism means conformism (and) is founded on reason, which denies creativity."[101] "Since values are not rational, and not grounded in the natures of those subject to them," says Bloom, "they must be imposed."[102]

The imposition of values is at the heart of the origins and development of Black Studies. Who will impose values and is the process by which values are created and maintained open or closed, that is, is it democratic? If, for example, we see American social science as a functioning democratic institution based on intellectual merit as the criterion required to enter the gates and enrich the stock of knowledge, Aldon Morris believes history tells us it has failed.[103] Democracy is more than elections—more than choosing one menu item from another—it is a philosophy or way of life.

Black Studies is a crucial part of the struggle for Black power—the power of self-definition and the power to reach one's full potential. Equal educational opportunity has to mean more than the right to be acculturated. It has to mean more than the right to sit next to a White student in the classroom and vice versa. Equal educational opportunity must include the right to determine curriculum, to decide what is a problem or issue worth studying, and to legitimate knowledge. In his classic public policy book *The Moon and the Ghetto*, Richard Nelson asks how is it we can achieve a landing on the moon but not find the capacity to solve the problems of the ghetto? His short answer is that reaching the moon threatened no significant interests and rewarded some interests while solving the problems of the ghetto rewarded few influential interests but threatened many.[104] That is, solving the problems of the ghetto is a question of power.

Power is an inherent feature of social relations. As Black Studies has attempted to demonstrate over its short life, it is also an integral component in the production of truth. And, as postmodernism has contended, truth is relative to discourse. To claim that truth is relative to discourse does not mean that it is not valid or useful. Rather it means that there is no warrant for the view that science or social science beliefs must be absolute or universal.

In *Toward a Democratic Science*, Richard Harvey Brown argues that the separation of reason and ethics is a historically recent phenomenon. Modern science and narration seem to exclude each other, he says, forcing one to choose between the amoral rationality of science and the seemingly irrational moralism of storytelling. This false choice has led science to become a hegemonic discourse—the language through which the real and true are manifest. As a hegemonic discourse, it meets the criteria of being perceived as specialized (i.e., disciplines); useful to dominant groups; and institutionalized.[105]

Brown also sees the conflict between science and narration as an incompatibility of cognition and identity. That is, cognition through science provides us with a shared external world that provides a framework for our common life but identity depends on constancy of human agency and intentions that is formed through the narration that gives our individual lives meaning. According to Brown, one perspective that synthesizes these worldviews is the approach of science and society as texts. In this approach, social science especially may be seen as a civic discourse, a language in which public policies are established or contested. From Brown's perspective, to the extent that various theoretical approaches articulate the visions and interests of different social groups, a single general theory of society is not desirable.[106]

Claims to knowledge are also claims to power. As we have seen repeatedly, the knowledge claims of social science and science have been used by decision-makers to legitimize policy inimical to Black interests. Humanities knowledge claims are not above politics. The entire conflict over Western civilization courses reflects a distain for values and knowledge claims external to the dominant culture.

Historically, knowledge claims from science have carried more weight because they have been portrayed as value neutral. Yet there is no value-neutral mechanism to move one from a scientific fact to a particular public policy. In fact, what scientists choose to focus their research on is a reflection of what their societies and/or their intellectual networks view as important and worthwhile. Science may note physical differences between "races" but to infer inferiority or superiority from those differences is not science. It is the society that gives meaning to the scientists' fact, not truth.[107] For Pierre Bourdieu, the process of knowledge validation as *legitimation* concerns the relationship between the subject and the object, but also the relationship between subjects regarding the object. And, the more autonomous a science is, the more it tends to be nothing less than the site of a permanent revolution, but one which is increasingly devoid of political or religious implications.[108]

Social science has had less success than natural science in avoiding the appearance of value commitments or subjectivity in its research. Du Bois believed the main reason social scientists became trapped in the search for natural laws was their inferiority complex regarding natural science when in reality there were no universal laws mechanistically governing human behavior. Economics has been the most influential of the social science disciplines in effecting public policy primarily due to the disciplines conceding the role of value allocation to impersonal market forces. Sociology lacks a strong normative tradition and American sociological thought has been dominated by a commitment to the idea that assimilation is the one sure solution to the race problem as evidenced in Kenneth Clark's work. Often race has been blurred into ethnicity with the qualitative distinctions between the nineteenth century immigration and integration of (White) European Americans and the exclusionary subordination of (red/black/yellow) non-European Americans being ignored or played down.[109] Psychology has conceptualized racism as individual prejudice, a hangover from premodern ("caste") assumptions, attributed to ignorance, lack of education, or a certain (authoritarian) personality type; and expected to disappear with modernization.[110] Political science, in an attempt to achieve some of the influence of economics, has increasingly become quantified. There was even a brief flirtation with "rational choice" theory in which the vote was treated like currency in the market place. Even when political scientists focused directly on public policy, it was the policymaking institutions and the implementation of policy rather than value creation or policy innovation that assumed center stage.[111]

Given these social science epistemologies, it is perhaps not surprising that a disproportionate number of Black neoconservative public intellectuals are economists including Thomas Sowell, Walter Williams, and Glen Loury. "Neoconservatism, (as noted in our discussion of the "Bell curve") gained more currency than it justifiably deserved," states Houston Baker, "through resort to regressions, correlations, and a certain social scientism that claimed empirical truth about 'man' as its exclusive province."

Despite their training, however, most Black neoconservative arguments rest on anecdotal evidence.

Given that Blacks have often been voiceless or spoken for, it is not surprising that autobiography has assumed a central place in the Black American intellectual traditions. Being there or "witnessing" carries special explanatory power with respect to race and community.[112] The most influential "texts" or "narrations" in Black letters are the autobiographical works of Frederick Douglass, W.E.B. Du Bois, Booker T. Washington, and Malcolm X. The slave narratives were so significant, Harriett Beecher Stowe chose to construct her novel around a fictional fugitive slave, Uncle Tom. These examples were not lost on contemporary Black public intellectuals. Henry Louis Gates, for example, writes about his family and hometown in *Colored People*, while John McWhorter lowers his academic standard in *Authentically Black* and Stephen Carter expresses the burden of race on Black elites in *Reflections of an Affirmative Action Baby*. Baker accuses Black neoconservatives of profiting from the very Black Power movement they condemn. He does not spare what he calls Black centrist intellectuals like Gates and Cornell West who "rip off what they consider the consumer- and white-approved best of the black arts and act and write as though they had discovered enlightenment for the future of the race."[113]

Arguing that Martin Luther King, Jr., accepted the goals of Black power and took it up in his final years, Baker contends that King was the "most exemplary race man ever born in the United States" and "indisputably a global, Black public intellectual."[114] Baker expressed his disappointment in the post-Civil Rights generation of Black public intellectuals who are far more prone to endorsing the logic of the behaviorists than that of the structuralists like King. They have abandoned King's demands for equality of results, reparations, and unyielding anti-imperialism.

Alone among these disciplinary traditions and their Black public intellectual expressions, Black Studies has taken up the challenge of Martin Luther King, Jr.:

> What has penetrated substantially all strata of Negro life is the revolutionary idea that the philosophy and morals of the dominant white society are not holy or sacred but in all too many respects degenerate and profane....The worst aspect of their (Negro) oppression was their inability to question and defy the fundamental precepts of the larger society.[115]

Black Studies has created an "interpretive" or "critical" community or "intellectual network" that has taken on King's challenge. It has opened doors to new ways of knowing through qualitative research that understands the socially constructed nature of reality, the power differentials between researcher and subject, and the problems of representation and legitimation. It values emotionality, rich description, storytelling, and autobiography. Black Studies promotes a value-critical approach that submits goals to a critical and constant review at every stage. Rather than a clash of civilizations or cultures, Black Studies views hybridity as a constructive alternative. Color blindness, on the other hand, obscures the uniqueness of persons while ignoring the differences in power that often result in discrimination. Perhaps the last word on this subject should go to Alain Locke who wrote nearly a century ago that "[f]or the complete implementation of the pluralistic philosophy it is not sufficient merely to disestablish authoritarianism and its absolutes; a more positive and constructive development of pluralism can and should establish some effective mediating principles for situations of basic value divergence and conflict."[116]

Finding effective mediating principles and constructive spaces of discourse such as Black Studies will only become more important as the United States moves toward a majority minority population.

Notes

1. Richard Kluger, *Simple Justice,* (New York: Knopf, 1976), p. 353.
2. Ibid, p. 354.
3. Ibid. p. 354.
4. See Kluger; Waldo E. Martin, Jr., (ed.), *Brown v. Board of Education,* (Boston: Bedford/St. Martin's, 1998); Derrick A. Bell, *Race, Racism, and American Law,* (Boston: Little, Brown, 1992); Diane Ravitch, *The Troubled Crusade,* (New York: Basic Books, 1993).
5. See Clive Webb, (ed.), *Massive Resistance,* (New York: Oxford University Press, 2005) as well as Martin and Ravitch.
6. Martin Luther King, Jr., *Why We Can't Wait,* (New York: Mentor, 1964), p. 18.
7. Martin, Op. Cit., p. 33.
8. Ibid. p. 33.
9. Kluger, Op. Cit., p. 355.
10. Berkeley psychologist Reginald Jones commenting on his confrontation with Kenneth Clark at the annual meeting of the American Psychological Association when Clark was President. Jones was a founder of the Association of Black Psychologists. Jones oral his-

tory, ROHO, Bancroft Library, University of California, Berkeley, 2005, p. 96. Clark's career benefited from the support of the Ford Foundation that essentially funded the Metropolitan Applied Research Center to promote Clark's research perspective. See my "Big Philanthropy and the Funding of Black Organizations," *The Review of Black Political Economy*, Winter, 1979.

11. Ibid. p. 356. Clark and Marshall were aware of this possible different interpretation of the testing results but decided to use the data any way.
12. Martin, p. 24.
13. Reinhold Neibuhr quoted in Carol Polsgrove, *Divided Minds,* (New York: Norton, 2001), p. 44.
14. Ibid. pp. 46–47.
15. Hannah Arendt quoted in Polsgrave, p. 54.
16. Polsgrave, p. 45.
17. David Tyack and Elisabeth Hansot, *Managers of Virtue,* (New York: Basic Books, 1982).
18. Harold Cruse, *Plural but Equal,* (New York: Morrow, 1987), pp. 12–13.
19. Ravitch, Op. Cit., p. 46.
20. See Henry Allen Bullock, *A History of Negro Education in the South,* (Cambridge: Harvard University Press, 1967); Raymond Wolters, *The New Negro on Campus,* (Princeton, NJ: Princeton University Press, 1975); and Martin Carnoy, *Education as Cultural Imperialism,* (New York: McKay, 1974).
21. Carnoy, pp. 289–294.
22. Aubrey Williams quoted in Paula S. Fass, *Outside In,* New York: Oxford University Press, 1989), p. 126.
23. Ibid.
24. Ibid. p. 116.
25. Ibid. pp. 148–149. See also Ira Katznelson, *Schooling for All,* (Berkeley: University of California Press, 1985).
26. Ravitch, Op. Cit., pp. 229–230.
27. Ibid. pp. 72–75. The Ethnic Heritage Studies Center (later changed to Programs) bill was introduced in Congress by Rep. Roman Pucinski (D-IL) in 1970 and became law in 1972 as part of the Omnibus Higher Education Amendments. It funded community, professional association and college programs including curriculum projects.

28. Nikhil Pal Singh, *Black Is a Country,* (Cambridge: Harvard University Press, 2004), p. 150.
29. Fass, Op. Cit., p. 151.
30. Singh, Op. Cit., p. 149.
31. James Baldwin, *Collected Essays,* (New York: Library of America, 1998), p. 340.
32. See Oliver C. Cox, *Caste, Class & Race,* (New York: Monthly Review Press, 1970); David Theo Goldberg, *Racist Culture,* (Cambridge: Blackwell, 1993); Michelle M. Wright, *Becoming Black,* (Durham, NC: Duke University Press, 2004); Charles W. Mills, *The Racial Contract,* (Ithaca, NY: Cornell University Press, 1997).
33. Gunnar Myrdal quoted in Singh, Op. Cit., p. 145. Myrdal also saw Black church services as abnormal behavior and therefore incapable of performing the vital role they assumed in the civil rights movement.
34. Cruse, Op. Cit., p. 22.
35. See Maurice R. Berube and Marilyn Gittell, *Confrontation at Ocean Hill-Brownsville,* (New York: Praeger, 1969).
36. Thomas J. Sugrue, *Sweet Land of Liberty*, (New York: Random House, 2009), p. 476.
37. James Coleman quoted in Cruse, Op. Cit., p. 69.
38. Daniel Moynihan quoted in Charles A. Valentine, *Culture and Poverty,* (Chicago: University of Chicago Press, 1968), p. 29.
39. Moynihan quoted in Valentine, Ibid. p. 30.
40. Daniel Moynihan and Nathan Glazer quoted in Joyce A. Ladner, (ed.), *The Death of White Sociology,* (New York: Vintage, 1973), p. xxiii.
41. Moynihan quoted in Valentine, Op. Cit., p. 33.
42. Ibid. p. 36.
43. Daniel Patrick Moynihan quoted in Ta-Nehisi Coates, "The Black Family in the Age of Mass Incarceration," *The Atlantic*, October 2015, p. 82.
44. Robert Staples, "The Myth of the Black Matriarchy," *Black Scholar*, Jan/Feb. 1970; Vol. 1, Nos. 3–4, pp. 26–33.
45. Andrew Billingsley, *Black Families in White America,* (Englewood Cliffs, NJ: Prentice Hall, 1968).
46. John Sedgwick, "Inside the Pioneer Fund," in Russell Jacoby and Naomi Glauberman, (eds.), *The Bell Curve,* (New York: Times

Books, 1995), p. 146. See also Michael K. Brown, (et al.), *White-Washing Race*, (Berkeley: University of California Press, 2003), Chapter 3. Psychology faculty at Yale prepared the "Dove Counterbalance Intelligence Test (Soul Folk 'Chitling' Test)" and distributed it to their Yale students and inner-city New Haven residents in the late sixties. Since the content of the test drew on the life experiences of inner-city Blacks the results revealed that the White Yale students scored as having low intelligence while the inner-city residents were brilliant.

47. In the early twentieth century, 31 states passed compulsory sterilization laws for those in public institutions. See Leon J. Kamin, "The Pioneers of IQ Testing," in Jacoby, Op. Cit., pp. 483–486.
48. See Stephan Jay Gould, *The Mismeasure of Man, Hen's Teeth and Horse's Toes,* (New York: Norton, 1996).
49. Stephen Jay Gould, "Mismeasure by Any Measure," in Jacoby, Op. Cit., p. 4.
50. Gould, Ibid. pp. 12–13.
51. Charles P. Henry, "Understanding the Underclass," in James Jennings, *Race, Politics, and Economic Development,* (London: Verso, 1992), p. 71.
52. Ibid. p. 74.
53. Ibid. p. 79.
54. Ibid., pp. 69–71. Also see Steven D. Levitt and Stephen J. Dubner, *Freakonomics,* (New York: Morrow, 2005), especially the chapter "Why Do Drug Dealers Still Live With Their Moms?".
55. Charles P. Henry, *Culture and African American Politics,* (Bloomington, IN: Indiana University Press, 1990), pp. 12–14. For a recent discussion of the "culture of wealth" concept see the controversy around "affluenza" in Manny Fernandez and John Swartz, "Teenager's Sentence in Fatal Drunken-Driving Case Stirs 'Affluenza Debate," *New York Times*, December 14, 2013, p. A11.
56. "A Nation at Risk" quoted in Ira Shor, *Culture Wars,* (London: Routledge & Kegan Paul, 1986), pp. 104–105.
57. "The Bottom Line in Education," part 4 of *School: The Story of American Public Education*"video/c8931.
58. Ronald W. Walters, *White Nationalism Black Interests,* (Detroit: Wayne State University Press, 2003), pp. 200–201.

59. See Louis Harris, "The Future of Affirmative Action," in George E. Curry, (ed.), *The Affirmative Action Debate*, (Reading, MA: Addison-Wesley, 1997), pp. 326–336.
60. Walters, Op. Cit., pp. 116–144; Mary Frances Berry in Curry, Ibid. pp. 299–313.
61. Dinesh D'Souza is an example of this appropriation of King. However, D'Souza goes beyond the normal linking of King to color blindness to also imply King was a believer of culture of poverty type arguments. He states that "[t]he tragedy of King's life is that he was never able to pursue the second dimension of his project: a concerted effort to raise the competitiveness and civilizational level of the black population." He then proceeds to quote King on Black crime and mediocrity. He could just as easily quoted Malcolm X or Barack Obama both of whom lectured Black audiences on character traits. He does cite Booker T. Washington's message of uplift as the correct course of action. Of course, the larger project of King and his shift to economic rights is ignored. See *The End of Racism*, (New York: Free Press, 1995), pp. 198–199.
62. Allan Bakke was a 33-year-old engineer and former Marine captain at the time he sued the University of California Medical School at Davis. He was rejected for admission twice at Davis and a dozen other medical schools in part due to his age. He chose to sue Davis claiming that the School's set aside program for Black applicants violated his right to due process. Writing a plurality opinion for a severely divided court, Justice Lewis Powell stated that the state had a compelling interest in diversity and that it could be considered as one of a number of factors in college admissions, however, the set aside program at Davis was unconstitutional. The Court order Bakke admitted. See Bell, Op. Cit. and Walters, Op. Cit.
63. Regents of UC v. Bakke, 438 U.S. 265, 272-275 (1978) US Supreme Court. Cruse pp. 31–33.
64. See Roger Kimbell, *Tenured Radicals,* (New York: Harper & Row, 1990). See also James Davison Hunter, *Culture Wars,* (New York: Basic Books, 1991) and Shor, Op. Cit.
65. Stephen Burd, "Humanities' New Faces," *The Chronicle of Higher Education*, June 29, 1994, p. A24.
66. Ibid.

67. Richard M. Merelman, *Representing Black Culture,* (New York: Routledge, 1995), p. 136.
68. John K. Wilson, *The Myth of Political Correctness,* (Durham, NC: Duke University Press, 1995), p. 77.
69. Ibid. p. A25.
70. Stephen Burd, "Defiant Conservative Relishes the NEH Fights to Come," *The Chronicle of Higher Education*, June 29, 1994, p. A25.
71. Merelman asserts that despite the highly visible rhetorical roles of Bennett and Cheney the actual grant making process always provided support for multiculturalism citing the independence of scholars who review decisions. This assertion ignores the reality that the Council is advisory to the chair, who has absolute veto power over all grants. Merelman, in fact, cites one NEH official who says 10–15 percent of all grants are overtly political (p. 137). The assertion also overlooks the chilling effect that the NEH chair's public statements have. That is, scholars are less likely to submit grant proposals when the Endowment's leader is attacking multiculturalism on a regular basis. This visibility is particularly important, if, as Merelman states, "few political actors strongly *promote* multicultural education in universities" (p. 147).
72. *Rediscovering America,* (Washington, DC: NEH, 2001), pp. 74–75.
73. Hunter, Ibid. p. 198.
74. Ibid. p. 43.
75. Ibid. p. 211.
76. Ibid. p. 211.
77. Ibid. p. 213.
78. Lawrence W. Levine, *The Opening of the American Mind,* (Boston: Beacon, 1996), p. 15.
79. Hunter, Op. Cit., p. 213.
80. Levine, Op. Cit., p. xv.
81. Arthur M. Schlesinger, Jr., *The Disuniting of America*, (New York: Norton, 1992), p. 43.
82. Ibid. p. 18.
83. E.D. Hirsch, Jr., *Cultural Literacy,* (Boston: Houghton Mifflin, 1987), p. 115.
84. Ibid. p. 25.

85. Saul Bellow in Allan Bloom, *The Closing of the American Mind*, (New York: Simon & Schuster, 1987), p. 18.
86. Bloom, Ibid. p. 348.
87. Ibid. p. 324.
88. Ibid. p. 34, 95.
89. First in an article in *Foreign Affairs* in the summer of 1993 and later in a book, *The Clash of Civilizations*, Huntington presented his theory that in the post–Cold War period, ethnic and religious conflict had replaced ideological conflict as the prime shaper of world affairs. This "civilizational" conflict was more permanent than political regimes and pitted Western civilization against the other world civilizations—he identifies seven such civilizations. He also introduced the idea of "kin" countries and countries torn between the west and the rest (Turkey, Mexico, and the Soviet Union). His theory filled a post–Cold War void but was widely criticized as ignoring the fact that most modern conflicts were intra-civilizational rather than between civilizations with the most notable being between Sunni and Shite Muslims.
90. Samuel P. Huntington, *Who Are We?*, (New York: Simon & Schuster, 2004), pp. 18, 171–173.
91. Ibid. pp. 222–231.
92. Ibid. p. 68.
93. Bloom Op. Cit., p. 27.
94. Huntington, Op. Cit., pp. 303–309.
95. Bloom, Op. Cit., p. 15.
96. Ibid. p. 377.
97. Levine, Op. Cit., pp. 15, 28.
98. David Theo Goldberg, (ed.), *Multiculturalism*, (Cambridge: Blackwell, 1994), p. 3.
99. Levine, Op. Cit., p. 123.
100. Bloom, Op. Cit., p. 366.
101. Ibid. p. 194.
102. Ibid. p. 201.
103. Aldon D. Morris, *The Scholar Denied*, (Berkeley: University of California Press, 2015), p. 223.
104. Richard R. Nelson, *The Moon and the Ghetto*, (New York: Norton, 1977), p. 14.
105. Richard Harvey Brown, *Toward a Democratic Science*, (New Haven: Yale University Press, 1998), pp. 2, 124–125.

106. Ibid., pp. 20–36.
107. See Nelson, Ibid. and Martin Rein, *Social Science & Public Policy*, (New York: Penguin, 1976).
108. Pierre Bourdieu, *Science of Science and Reflexivity*, (Chicago: University of Chicago Press, 2004), pp. 72–73, 86.
109. Charles W. Mills, *Blackness Visible*, (Ithaca, NY: Cornell University Press, 1998), p. 131.
110. Ibid., p. 131.
111. Nelson, Ibid. p. 40; Stanford Lyman in Herbert Hill and James E. Jones, Jr., (eds.), *Racial Equality in America*, (Madison: University of Wisconsin Press, 1993), p. 396. Desmond S. King and Rogers M. Smith, "Racial Orders in American Political Science," *American Political Science Review*, Vol. 99, No. 1, Feb. 2005, pp. 75–92; Paul Frymer, "Racism Revised," *American Political Science Review*, Vol. 99, No. 3, August 2005, pp. 373–385.
112. Baker, Op. Cit., p. 10.
113. Ibid., p. 125.
114. Ibid., pp. 39–42.
115. Martin Luther King, Jr., "The Role of the Behavioral Scientist in the Civil Rights Movement," in John Brigham and Theodore Weisbach, (eds.), *Racial Attitudes in America*, (New York: Harper & Row, 1972), p. 333.
116. Alain Locke quoted in Johnny Washington, *Alain Locke and Philosophy*, (New York: Greenwood, 1986), p. 41.

CHAPTER 8

Postmodernism, Multiculturalism, and the Future of Black Studies

When the Berkeley Academic Senate in its May 10, 1988, Special Meeting voted—213 for and 73 against—to send the proposal for an American Cultures requirement to all faculty members in a mail ballot, those of us who had worked on the requirement for over two years thought the proposal was dead. Even though more faculty had attended the Senate meeting (which includes all ladder-rank faculty) than I had ever seen, some colleagues argued that this issue was too important to pass with only a fraction of the faculty present. Some of us saw this action as a way for faculty who were opposed to the proposal, but were unwilling to publicly vote against it, to have their say. We had worked hard to mobilize faculty to come to the meeting to support the proposal and a straw vote on the sense of the motion indicated that we had succeeded in getting majority support among those present. In that straw vote, 125 were in favor of the proposal and 119 against it.[1]

The proposal, which required all Berkeley undergraduates to take a course that dealt with the experiences and contributions of two American minority groups (from a list that included Afro-Americans, Asian Americans, Chicano/Latino Americans, and Native Americans) in their relations with Euro-Americans, was already a compromise from an earlier proposal. When Asian American historian Ron Takaki approached me sometime during the 1986–87 school year about an Ethnic Studies graduation requirement for all Berkeley undergraduates, I was enthusiastically supportive. After all, I had been centrally involved ten years earlier

C.P. Henry, *Black Studies and the Democratization of American Higher Education*, DOI 10.1007/978-3-319-35089-9_8

in promoting a general education requirement in Black Studies/Women's Studies at Denison and wondered what took Berkeley so long to catch up. Takaki and Mark Min representing students became the coordinators of a Faculty/Student Steering Committee for an Ethnic Studies Graduation Requirement. In our early discussions, the proposal envisioned a requirement in which students took a course in either African American Studies or Ethnic Studies to fulfill the requirement. Of course, such a major infusion of students into our courses would have required that major additional resources be devoted to our respective departments. However, the major impetus for the requirement was the demographic changes occurring in our student body. Just as the influx of Black students on college campuses in the late 1960s and early 1970s drove the demand for curriculum change, California's shifting demographics, especially the rise in the number of Chicano and Asian students, was creating a similar demand for curriculum change. It was frequently repeated that California was becoming the first state in which there was no majority—it was a minority majority state. In 1988, Berkeley's freshman class was 40 percent White, 25 percent Asian, 17 percent Latino, and 12 percent Black. These changes were reflected in the student body until the Regents resolutions (SP-1 on student admissions and SP-2 on hiring) and then the State (Prop. 209) eliminated affirmative action in the late 1990s. By Fall 2003, the undergraduate body was comprised of 42.5 percent Asian Pacific Americans, 30.9 percent White/Caucasians, 10.9 percent Chicano/Latinos, 4.1 percent African Americans, and 0.6 percent Native Americans, with 11.1 percent others. Blacks in the freshman class had declined to less than 100 that year, with only one-third being African American men.[2]

Chancellor Ira Michael Heyman and Provost Rod Park were aware of these demographic shifts and the demands for curriculum change. They sought to get ahead of the issue by appointing a Special or Ad Hoc Committee on Education and Ethnicity that would examine the possibilities of a "cultural pluralism" requirement.[3] By appointing a distinguished group of scholars to the new committee, the administration hoped to win support for the proposal. Members of the committee included William Simmons, Chair (Anthropology), Lawrence Levine (History), David Lloyd (English), Lily Wong Filmore (Education), Guadalupe Valdes (Education), Ling-Chi-Wang, (Asian American Studies), William Shack (Anthropology)—I later replaced Shack, and Emeka Ezera and Mark Min as student members.

During the fall of 1987, there were at least three proposals being discussed. Takaki and the Faculty/Student Steering Committee for the Ethnic Studies Graduation Requirement were in favor of a proposal called the "People's Plan" that required students to choose a course from existing courses in Ethnic Studies or African American Studies. The group met with Provost Park who was absolutely opposed to this plan on the grounds that other departments should also develop courses that would meet the requirement. He devised his own plan that would ask each department in the social sciences (excluding psychology) to develop one or two lower-division courses that specifically satisfied the requirement, eventually resulting in a total of 10–15 lower-division courses. The requirement's criteria would generally exclude a course that emphasized a single ethnic group. Most significantly, Park's proposal would avoid a debate by adding the ethnicity requirement to the existing American History and Institutions requirement. This action would only need an agreement between the new Ad Hoc Committee on Education and Ethnicity and the Committee on Educational Policy.

In the meantime, the Ad Hoc Committee on Education and Ethnicity (Simmons Committee) had begun to shape its own proposal that would require Academic Senate approval. Initially, it focused on about 50 existing courses, both upper and lower division, in which the central component was racial minorities. They debated whether studying one group was too narrow and whether the time period covered in some courses was too short. If the focus was on a single group, what other factors such as gender and class must be considered? Should courses emphasizing European immigrants be counted and who would oversee the selection process?

In March, as Acting Chair of Afro-American Studies, I joined Alex Saragoza, the chair of Ethnic Studies, in requesting a meeting with the Simmons Committee to discuss the emerging proposal. We also mobilized a group of key faculty leaders to sign a letter that would be circulated broadly to all faculty and addressed to Academic Senate Chair Edwin Epstein. The letter was signed by over 70 faculty and expressed support for a curricula that reflected the cultural diversity of California and the nation.[4]

What emerged from the Simmons Committee after a series of workshops, boycotts, and public forums was a "cultural pluralism" requirement primarily centered on the social, economic, and political experience of one or more of the following four US racial/ethnic groups: Afro-Americans,

Asian Americans, Chicano/Latino Americans, and Native Americans. These core groups were to be discussed in relation to their interaction with the dominant American culture. The requirement would be governed by a committee composed of one member from each of the following: Associated Students of the University of California (ASUC) (student government), Ethnic Studies, Afro-American Studies, Women's Studies, and two members selected by the Academic Senate. By the time the proposal came up for a faculty vote in May 1988, it had become the "American Cultures" requirement and courses had to give in-depth coverage of at least two of the four core groups. In addition, the proposal now asked for the establishment of a Center for the Study of American Cultures to support the faculty and graduate student instructors who would be teaching courses for the requirement.

Following the Academic Senate's decision to submit the American Cultures requirement to a mail ballot, it was discovered that the Senate had no authority to enact regulations by mail ballot. While the proposal could have come up again at the November meeting of the Academic Senate, the Committee on Educational Policy asked that the proposal be recommitted to the Simmons Committee to respond to the many suggestions and criticisms the requirement had generated. After considerable debate at the November Senate meeting, the motion to recommit was easily passed.[5]

I believe it was after this Senate meeting that I was appointed to the Simmons Committee to replace William Shack, who was suffering from poor health. I had originally supported the Ethnic Studies proposal that allowed a student to take any course in Ethnic Studies or African American Studies to fulfill the requirement. Richard Merelman calls this approach the "particularistic model" model that confines multicultural education to specific courses or academic fields where its proponents have control over the "perspective" that is taught. Of course, the downside is that it can result in tokenism that leaves other departments untouched by curricular reform.[6] As mentioned, we had instituted a similar proposal (with Women's Studies replacing Ethnic Studies) at Denison ten years earlier and it seemed to be working well there. Moreover, I found it difficult to believe that any one faculty member could master two cultures adequately to teach them let alone the three that some faculty were now suggesting. The arguments I heard against the proposal were also similar to those of a decade ago. Opponents argued that students did not want additional requirements, that the requirement was a special burden on engineering and science students, that the courses would focus on victimhood and oppression, and that other topics ranging from climate change to US intervention in Nicaragua were just as important. I thought there were rational responses for all these objections.

However, as we discussed the proposal in the Simmons Committee, we began to see an opportunity to create something new at Berkeley. There were at least three models for us to consider. The Stanford model that focused on supplementing Western Culture requirements with those of other cultures had received a great deal of backlash—most misguided—and was not seriously considered. We wanted to address identity issues in the United States and the central question was whether to do that with one comprehensive course or a variety of courses. Other universities such as the University of Michigan (had proposed one college-wide course on racism), the University of Wisconsin, Indiana University, and the University of Minnesota (had passed a two-course on US cultural pluralism requirement) were either discussing or had passed requirements involving ethnic studies. Within the UC system, Santa Cruz, Irvine, Riverside, and Santa Barbara were all taking action on an ethnic studies requirement in some form.[7]

As the Simmons Committee discussions progressed, it became clear that the Berkeley proposal would be unique in at least three ways. First, Europeans would be included as one of the core groups that could be studied. Instead of referencing European Americans as the dominant culture with which minority cultures responded to and interacted with, European Americans would now be viewed as an ethnic/racial group. This had the effect of decentering the European American experience while including them in the requirement. This pleased faculty members who had objected to the exclusion of White ethnic groups such the Irish and Italians from the earlier proposal. But it also signaled the new status of such groups in California as one of several "minority" groups. Second, the number of groups to be given attention in American Cultures courses was expanded from two to three. While I had some doubts about any faculty members' ability to seriously examine such a broad range of cultures, I believed Berkeley more than any other institution had the resources to make it work. It could involve team teaching, and it would certainly require the support of a Center for Teaching American Cultures to retrain willing faculty. The Center was also crucial in recommending the third feature of the proposal that was to open the requirement up to all campus departments. The earlier proposal was centered on the social sciences, ignoring the arts and humanities and certainly ignoring the natural sciences. Now it was anticipated that we might see some very innovative courses emerge from unlikely places and indeed that is what happened.[8]

Even with these changes, passage of the proposal was uncertain. A survey conducted by the Simmons Committee in December 1988 found vehement opposition to the requirement by 90 percent of the 147 respondents.[9] Philosophy professor John Searle said the requirement was "political feelgood courses" and another professor stated: "I fear that in practice, the course will lead to an unjust and unwarranted demonization of Western culture."[10] Newspaper columnist John Leo wrote: "[N]ow all Berkeley students are being required to take a course that looks more like an expression of racial division than a cure for it"; and culture wars veteran Stephan Thernstrom worried that any professor who let slip a favorable reference to Moynihan or Glazer or Sowell or Richard Rodriguez would be punished with an INSENSITIVE stamped on their employment record.[11]

Simmons countered, however, that supporters of the requirement were less likely to respond to the questionnaire asking for suggestions than opponents. Nonetheless, student support was as crucial in passing the requirement as it was in demanding the requirement. After all, the student body was becoming more and more heterogeneous but the faculty remained relatively homogeneous—that is White and male. The student (ASUC) senate had passed resolutions supporting an ethnic studies requirement in 1986, 1987, and again in 1988. A poll of Berkeley students indicated majority support and the Graduate Assembly as well as the African Students Association, Asian Student Association, MEChA, and the American Indian Students Association all publically endorsed the proposal. Even the Greek system voted to endorse the requirement.[12] Students also led a mobilization effort to take the fight for American Cultures to the State Capital and organized an April 10 rally featuring then State Assemblywoman Maxine Waters and UFW Vice President Dolores Huerta among others. Prior to the vote, Chancellor Heyman sent a letter to all members of the Academic Senate adding his support. He said: "[A]s a public university and one of the leading research universities in the United States, we are challenged to combine excellence in scholarship with educational and public service responsibilities to the State of California. The proposal presented to us should enhance our capacity to prepare a diverse student body for leadership positions in a state which will increasingly demand a diverse group of leaders."[13] Heyman also committed to providing the resources necessary to offer the some 35 courses envisioned to meet the needs of the requirement when fully implemented.

The final report by the Special Committee on Education and Ethnicity listed annotated proposed courses from the departments of Anthropology, Architecture, Conservation and Resource Studies, Economics, Education, English, Ethnic Studies, Geography, History Journalism, Linguistics, Music, Social Welfare, Sociology, and Women's Studies as well as Afro-American Studies and Ethnic Studies. The report noted the debate in higher education over multiculturalism and the popular attention such opponents of cultural pluralism like Allan Bloom, E.D. Hirsch and former US Secretary of Education William Bennett had attracted. It also cited supporters of multiculturalism such as Stanley Fish and Henry Louis Gates as well as Takaki and Levine who argued for the democratic impulse to open the American Mind. The governing committee for the requirement was also broadened to include the chair from the Committee on Education Policy as well as four faculty members who teach American Cultures courses or have expertise in the areas covered by the requirement. On April 25, 1989, the Academic Senate passed the American Cultures requirement with 227 faculty in favor and 194 against.[14]

A couple of years after the passage of the requirement, Harvard's Henry Louis Gates opened an Opinion-Editorial in the *New York Times* with the following: "I recently asked the dean of a prestigious liberal arts college if his school would ever have as Berkeley has, a 70 percent non-white enrollment. 'Never', he replied. 'That would completely alter our identity as a center of liberal arts'."[15] Gates argues that faculty, like the dean, view the study of our diverse cultures as leading to "tribalism" and "fragmentation." The cultural diversity movement arose in part because of the fragmentation of society by ethnicity, class and gender, says Gates, and to make it the culprit for this fragmentation is to mistake effect for cause. Gates would probably agree with Ralph Ellison who nearly 70 years ago asked:

> Whence all this passion toward conformity anyway?—diversity is the word. Let man keep his many parts and you'll have no tyrant states. Why, if they follow this conformity business they'll end up by forcing me, an invisible man, to become white, which is not a color but the lack of one. Must I strive toward colorlessness? But seriously, and without snobbery, think of what the world would lose if that should happen. America is woven of many strands; I would recognize them and let it so remain.[16]

Moreover, "to insist that we 'master our own culture' before learning others—as Arthur Schlesinger Jr. has proposed—only defers the vexed question: What gets to count as 'our' culture?"[17] Berkeley's American Cultures requirement represented an innovative and tangible effort to answer that question.

The requirement went into effect for the freshman class of 1991. Over a five year period from 1990 to 1995, the Center for the Teaching and Study of American Cultures planned to develop approximately 120 new courses for some 30 disciplines. Bill Simmons agreed to serve as the Center's first director and he chose Ron Choy as associate director. Central to the development of new courses was a summer "American Cultures Fellows" program that enabled interested faculty to work with like-minded colleagues on new courses. I, along with my colleagues William Banks and Barbara Christian in Afro-American Studies, were part of the inaugural class of fellows in 1990. To my surprise, among the nearly 40 fellows from a wide variety of departments was neoconservative political scientist and NAS Board of Advisors member Aaron Wildavsky, who developed and taught a course called "Political Cultures." A current course in the College of Engineering is a prime example of the influence of the Black Studies and Ethnic Studies movement on the entire university curriculum. The class, taught by Professor Khalid Kadir, asks many of the questions that Kadir didn't confront until he was attending graduate school: "What are the politics of engineering? What are the ways in which engineers depoliticize problems—how they draw a box around a thing to exclude questions of power and inequality and just deal with the technical aspects? And how does that reinforce those structures [of inequality]?" Students who take the course's engaged scholar's supplement collaborate with local organizations to do research and develop engineering models that they need.[18]

My initial proposal was for a course on "Ethnic and Racial Succession in Urban Politics." Although there was an emerging literature on the subject, Berkeley already offered a course on urban politics and I began to feel that an undergraduate course on human rights would offer something not available in the undergraduate curriculum and also coincide with work I was doing off campus.

The development of the American Cultures requirement occurred during a period when I was heavily involved in the leadership of the human rights organization Amnesty International (AI). Although I had first become aware of the organization in 1977 when they won the Nobel Peace Prize, I didn't have the opportunity to join a local group until my arrival on the Berkeley campus in the fall of 1981. The Berkeley campus network was the oldest and largest AI group primarily composed of students. As one of the very few faculty involved and one of the very few African Americans involved, I was quickly (affirmative action) pushed to run for the national board of directors.[19] From 1983 to 1989, I served on the board of AIUSA including two years as chair of the board. From 1989 to 1991, I served one term on the international executive committee that met at the organization's headquarters in London.

My AI experience—which included meetings at the United Nations in New York and Geneva, and eventually a brief period working on human rights in the Department of State[20]—taught me a number of lessons that I would attempt to apply in a new American Cultures course at Berkeley. Perhaps the most striking obstacle to AI's work among minority communities in the United States and in developing countries generally was a rule against human rights work in your own country. No doubt the rule was originally instituted to protect human rights activists from harassment and arrest by local authorities as well as insulate them from the influence of national politics. In fact I felt some of that sense of threat for the first time when AI began to actively work against the death penalty. Church groups and others that once welcomed us with open arms now asked why we wanted to protect the rights of murderers. However, as AI grew larger and expanded beyond its European base, the rule served as a major hindrance to activists of color who were willing to work on abuses outside their borders but were primarily motivated by internal injustices. I, along with others, fought a long and ultimately successful battle to introduce some flexibility to the rule.

Another obstacle to AI recruitment was its narrow mandate of working only on political rights to the exclusion of economic rights and social rights. Once again, the logic of a narrow focus on political prisoners and related issues was obvious; however, it was also a reflection of the priority Western nations attached to political rights over economic rights. Moreover, in practice, it was often difficult to separate them. Is the right to organize a union an economic right or a political right or both? Is it universally accepted that a corporation should have the rights of an individual as in the United States? Is the right to own private property an economic, political, or social right? Once again, the mandate gradually expanded to include economic and social rights that were seen as equally important as political rights in much of the world if not in the United States.

The separation and compartmentalization of rights activists was a third experience-based lesson. Among AI activists, there was little connection to civil rights activists and there was often some tension as they competed in fundraising.[21] AIUSA activists were more likely to see Russian physicist Andrei Sakorov as their spiritual leader than Martin Luther King. By the same token, when I worked at the State Department, I tried in vain to get the NAACP to invite the Assistant Secretary of State for Human Rights, Labor and Democracy, John Shattuck, to their annual meeting to discuss US ratification of the International Covenant Against Racial Discrimination. Later I was able to arrange a discussion of the implications of the Covenant in the United States between Shattuck and the Assistant Attorney General for Civil Rights, Deval Patrick, at the Carter Center in Atlanta.

A final lesson involved the abstract nature of many of our board discussions around human rights instruments. The board was composed largely of those with the schedule flexibility to attend meetings—that is lawyers and professors. As a result of this class bias, our discussions could easily become abstract and removed from practical politics. I often argued that no US politician ever lost an election due to their vote on a human rights treaty and, until they did, it was useless to debate over phrases that had no chance of becoming law.

A number of my colleagues on the board taught international human rights law and that was the case at Berkeley. That is, human rights was taught almost exclusively in the law school and not in the undergraduate curriculum. Inspired by both my experience in AI and the opportunity afforded by the American Cultures requirement, I decided to offer a course on "Human Rights and US Foreign Policy: Cultural Perspectives."

Although the course was offered by the African American Studies department, it was cross-listed with the Peace & Conflict Studies (PACS) program. Peace Studies were a product of the antiwar movement of the late 1960s and early 1970s. They enjoyed a resurgence in the early 1980s as the Reagan administration sought to overcome the malaise of Vietnam with a more assertive military posture.[22] Berkeley's program was part of this resurgence and members of the African American Studies department served on the advisory board for most of its existence. Cross-listing my course assured that the class would have a good mix of students with diverse majors and different experiences.

It was a challenge for me to incorporate two other ethno-racial groups in addition to African Americans to meet the AC criteria of three such groups. Over the years—the course was not offered every year—the comparison groups I chose included Native Americans, Cuban Americans, Irish Americans, Japanese Americans, and Chicanos/Latinos. Each group had particular human rights issues they gave priority to, and how those concerns were dealt with by the state and by potential allies or adversaries was at the heart of the course. The syllabus stated:

> Most human rights courses are taught from the perspective of the struggle to achieve international legal standards resting on a base of universal human rights. Traditional foreign policy courses begin with a delineation of the "national interest." This course will examine human rights from the political perspective of three culturally distinct domestic groups—African Americans, Cuban Americans, and Native Americans. While the student will be introduced to the philosophy of human rights and the international legal conventions currently in force, the focus of the course will be on U.S. foreign policy and the attempts by these three groups to influence that policy using human rights as a trump. That is, human rights arguments are used to distinguish the demands of the group from other interest group demands such as trade and national security.
>
> United States foreign policy has historically maintained a distinctive "American exceptionalism." Regardless of party or ideology, "exceptionalism" has been used to justify both isolationism and interventionism. It has also led political leaders in the United States to play a key role in the establishment of international human rights norms while at the same time refusing to endorse the ratification or implementation of such norms at home. The refusal to abide by international human rights norms at home has had a special meaning for each of the three groups under consideration.

Prior to my coming to Berkeley and my experiences with AI and AC, I would have taught a much more narrowly conceived course around "African Americans and Civil Rights." I believe the comparative perspective offered a much richer and more accurate examination of US foreign policy.

A deconstruction of what constitutes the "national interest" in foreign policy quickly revealed the power of ethno-racial groups to mask self-interested concerns as "national" concerns. Why, for example, are Jewish American concerns over Israel given higher priority than Liberia, which was founded as a refuge for American slaves? Or why do we have a different level of concern about human rights violations in Communist

Cuba than we do in Communist Vietnam or China? Samuel Huntington's concept of "kin countries" was useful in sorting through these questions although Huntington and I often drew different conclusions. The "kin country" concept, however, was less useful in explaining the complicated US foreign policy around Irish American support for the Irish Republican Army. This example challenged the monolithic conception of European Americans just as a focus on Haitian Americans reveals differences in the African diaspora.[23]

In looking at genocide in Rwanda, the concepts of "linked fate" and the "African diaspora" could be concretely tested. I argued provocatively that African Americans seemed much more concerned about human rights violations perpetrated by White settlers against Africans than those of Hutu against Tutsi.[24] Native American claims for reparations based on territorial conquest were contrasted with African American claims for unpaid labor.

African American demands for reparations were also compared to the successful Japanese American claims for compensation for their unjust internment during World War II. The case of Japanese Americans highlighted the meanings and rights we attach to citizenship. Are the citizenship rights of some groups conditional? After Hurricane Katrina, news media described the fleeing citizens of New Orleans as refugees (a term applied to foreigners) rather than internally displaced migrants.

The issue of refugees was an important part of discussions around Cuban Americans. US foreign policy makes a distinction between political refugees (Cubans) and economic refugees (Haitians). To what extent are such distinctions justified? Are those fleeing right-wing dictatorships welcomed with the same embrace as those escaping Communist countries? Obviously immigration policy was central to our discussions of Mexican American immigration. It also raised the question of why we limit our human rights concerns to citizens. If we truly believe in "human" rights shouldn't they be universal?

The United States is a leading proponent of universal human rights, yet it has failed to ratify a number of key human rights instruments. When it does so, it is always with the reservation that nothing in the document should supersede US law. Every year, the US State Department reports to Congress on human rights in every country in the world but no such report covers human rights abuses in the United States. Through its actions rather than its words, the United States is implicitly saying universal human rights stop at its borders. And within its borders, human rights is a measure of the value we place on group difference.

Another example of the difficulty in establishing human rights in the abstract is the trope of idealism and realism in US foreign policy. Certain presidential administrations are labeled idealistic (Wilson, Carter), while others are seen as realistic (Nixon, Clinton). In reality, all US foreign interventions have been justified on the high ground of moral idealism, while real politics was often the primary motivation. By the same token, US isolationism has been justified by the same appeal to American exceptionalism.

My students read pragmatist philosopher Richard Rorty who challenged the notion that there was a trans-historical view or catholic religious principle on which we could ground universal rights. He argued that such universalism is always the projected imposition of local values often gendered and ethno-racial. This does not mean, however, said Rorty, that all values are the same and that we should not promote a Western idealized conception of human rights. Rorty suggested that rather than appealing to an abstract set of human rights laws, we should seek to expand the circle of "we." He believed communal "solidarity" could perform the functions for which people once turned naively to the ideal state of "objectivity."[25] Rorty's perspective, like those of the founders of Black Studies, are postmodern. They refuse to accept a meta-narrative or localized values masquerading as universal truths. But also like Rorty, they seek to promote certain values over others. They are "affirmative" postmodernists rather than "skeptical" postmodernists. That is, while accepting that there are multiple ways of viewing history and plural truths, not all truths are equal. If the truth of the racist is equal to the truth of the antiracist, there is no hope for social justice.[26]

In *Achieving Our Country*, Rorty is concerned with our nation's self-identification rather than African American identity. He attacked, for example, Randall Robinson's contention that slavery—something contemporary Blacks did not experience—is truly a part of their history. Moreover, Rorty believed that the history that does shape us is really irrelevant for the purpose of making our society more just. In order to build a more just and expansive "we," he might suggest the adoption of "color blindness."[27]

"Color blindness" has a number of negative consequences, says philosopher Iris Young. The assimilation into a "we" implies coming into a game with the rules already set. It ignores the disadvantaged groups whose experiences, culture, and resources differ from those who set the rules. Young states that "feelings, desires, and commitments do not cease to exist and motivate just because they have been excluded from the definition of moral reason."[28] In addition, when oppressed groups assert a positive meaning for their own identity, they seize the power of naming difference itself and explode the implicit definition of difference as deviance from a norm. When external forces label the difference as deviant, it often produces an internalized devaluation by members of the group itself. It is possible, though seldom achieved, to acknowledge racial identity without resorting to racial hierarchy.

I believe that the goal Black Studies and other emancipatory movements have been working toward is a kind of democratic cultural pluralism. Historically, the terms equality and integration were rather late additions to the Black activist lexicon. Freedom and social justice are objectives with more traditional resonance. Both terms are relational rather than substantive just as racism should not be understood as a set of feelings that are rational or irrational but rather as a sense of group position.[29]

In *Freedom and the Making of Western Culture*, sociologist Orlando Patterson demonstrated the relational aspects of freedom as a concept. Personal freedom, he said, means one can do as one pleases within the limits of not harming others—"the golden rule." Soverneignal freedom, on the other hand, means the power to act as one pleases regardless of its impact on others. Finally, civic freedom refers to the capacity of adults to participate in governance.[30]

While Patterson has been criticized for claiming freedom as a Western value and for ignoring other types of freedom such as spiritual freedom and legal freedom, the discourse itself shows how difficult it is to know what the concept means in the absence of context or history. The soverneignal freedom of a journal to publish whatever it sees fit may conflict with the personal freedom of religious followers who feel harmed by what is published. Stanley Fish, for example, contends that free speech is not only partial but also political. "It is always the freedom of those who possess power to proscribe the speech of others," he says, "in favor of speech representing the values they prefer to the exclusion of the values of those lacking such power."[31] States have the soverneignal freedom to pass voting laws that assure fairness but they should not prevent individuals from enjoying their civic freedom to participate in governance.[32] The International Convention Against Torture, along with other human rights instruments, protects the personal freedom of individuals to be free from torture, yet many states, including the United States, exercise the sovereign freedom to torture on the grounds of national security. And, of course, sovereign states may impose their freedom on other sovereign states.[33]

While my course revealed the hypocrisy and cynicism behind some claims for universal human rights, it also demonstrated the need to have some standard of behavior or ideal beyond the particular that one could appeal to. For example, although there were fewer than 50 nations participating in the drafting of the Universal Declaration of Human Rights, virtually all of the nearly 200 nations in the modern world subscribe to the values it sets forth and literally thousands of rights groups utilize its language in their own work.

Once again, W.E.B. Du Bois may serve as a model for resolving the conflict between the particular and the universal. Ross Posnock contends that "Du Bois sets the organic and cosmopolitian, the mass and elite, the particular and universal, into a deliberately unstable synthesis that enables him to move among positions as warranted by historical circumstances. And exigency."[34] This pragmatist cosmopolitan tradition, says Posnock, includes Du Bois, Alain Locke, Zora Neale Hurston, Ralph Ellison, Albert Murray, and James Baldwin. Yet if Du Bois is truly pragmatic, he must also be willing to embrace a particular racial identity as the situation dictates.

Rogers Smith, in *Civic Ideals*, states that there are two variants of democratic cultural pluralism: universal integrationists and separatists pluralists. Du Bois is placed in both categories. In a sense, Du Bois is a bridge between the cultural pluralism of the World War I era and the multiculturalism of the post–World War II era. While the cultural pluralism of the earlier period as reflected in ethnic group political theory, for example, was something to overcome through assimilation into the melting pot, multiculturalists have been much more successful in convincing the state that it should sustain rather than diminish ethno-racial cultures. Cosmopolitanism, says David Hollinger, is much more likely to understand that the individual is a member of a number of groups simultaneously. "It is this process of consciously and critically locating oneself amid these layers of 'we' that most clearly distinguishes the postethnic from the unreconstructed universalist."[35]

We are all born "other." While our family, and/or our communities, may impose identities on us, we should ultimately be free to accept or reject affiliation. Thus democratic pluralism must be able to protect us from group discrimination while at the same time allowing cultural affiliation for positive affirmation. But just as individuals are not born equal, groups are also not created equal. To treat all groups the same by ignoring their history is unjust.

Young suggests that democratic cultural pluralism requires a dual system of rights with a general system that is the same for all and a more specific system of group-conscious policies and rights.[36] Will Kymlicha, for example, proposes three groups in the United States—African Americans, Chicanos, and Native Americans—be designated national minorities with distinct rights.[37]

Using Du Bois as a model, Black Studies activists of the 1960s and 1970s attacked the prevailing assimilative standard established by White elites. When liberals responded with a weak cultural pluralism that allowed for change on the margins but retained control of the institutions and mechanisms that set and maintained "common" or "traditional" values, Black Studies challenged both the mechanisms and values through a narrow focus on Afrocentrism and a broad focus on the diaspora. What remains is to work toward a more nuanced and critical multiculturalism that can see beyond a particular time and place but refuse to universalize its perspective.

In moving away from universalism that purports to establish the necessity of natural or natural-like law and toward generalization that abstracts from particular instances to the probability of broad commonalities, David Goldberg states:

> Multicultural relativism is ready and able to fashion general judgments, that is, revisable inductive generalizations as the specificity of (particular) circumstances and relations warrant. These circumstances and relations will include often, though not necessarily always, racial, class, and gendered articulation. Thus multiculturalists are able to condemn a specific form or racism, say apartheid, in terms of a general judgment that racist exclusions are unacceptable because they are unwarranted in a specifiable scheme of social value to which we do or should not adhere for specifiable (and perhaps, generalizable) reasons. But there is no transcendental proof or grounds, no universal foundation for this scheme or any other.[38]

This is a more nuanced and useful conception of racism than the traditional liberal attack against "irrational" prejudice.

The writing and rewriting of history—both African and American history—was the essential first step in the evolution of Black Studies. History writing assumes plural ways of being in the world and democracy requires that neglected histories be given their voice.[39] Presenting competing perspectives on history is not a disorder or an attack on truth but rather an approach to order that is not acceptable or foreseen.[40] It is a way of talking about "facts" without prejudging them as "facts." As James Baldwin states, no one is certain when and how identities are formed, but it is a challenging process, especially if you're Black:

> No one knows precisely how identities are forged, but it is safe to say that identities are not invented: an identity would seem to be arrived at by the way in which the person faces and uses his experience. It is a long drawn-out and somewhat bewildering and awkward process....Black is a tremendous spiritual condition, one of the greatest challenges anyone alive can face—this is what the blacks are saying.[41]

The political philosopher Judith Shklar states: "[I]f democracy means anything it signifies that the lives of all citizens matter, and that their sense of their rights must prevail."[42] In the fall of 2014, a movement responding to the police killing of unarmed Black men, women, and children arose with the slogan "Black Lives Matter." Almost immediately, there was a liberal response that "all lives matter." It was typical of a type of color blindness that refuses to recognize the long history of police brutality toward Blacks. If anything, Black Studies is the intellectual manifestation of the value that "Black Lives Matter."

Notes

1. Minutes of Meetings, Berkeley Division, Special Meeting, Academic Senate, May 10, 1988, p. 31.
2. "Diversity Briefing for New Chancellor Vice Provost Christina Maslach", June 2004, pp. 1–2.
3. The committee was actually appointed by the Academic Senate's Committee on Committees. Sociologist Russ Ellis, who Heyman had helped get on the Committee on Committees, was tasked with finding a chair for the new committee. He reports that he first approached sociologist Robert Bellah who declined and then approached anthropologist William Simmons who accepted. Oral History of Russell Ellis, Bancroft Library, p. 370.
4. The cover letter, dated March 7, 1988, was signed by Howard Bern (Zoology), Carol Christ (English and later Provost), Troy

Duster (Sociology and later director of the American Cultures Center), Leon Henkin (Mathematics), Karl Pister (Civil Engineering and later Chancellor of UC-Santa Cruz), Alex Saragoza (Ethnic Studies), Ron Takaki (Asian American Studies), Chang-lin Tien (Mechanical Engineering and later Chancellor), and me.

5. Notice of Meeting, Berkeley Division, Academic Senate, November 28, 1988.
6. Richard M. Merelman, *Representing Black Culture*, (New York: Routledge, 1995), p. 155.
7. See Heather Jones, "All UC campuses considering ethnic studies," *Daily Californian*, February 28, 1989. Also "Ethnic Studies," *Notice*, Academic Senate, University of California, Vol. 12, no. 7, May 1988 and "Flurry of Senate Activity on Ethnic Studies," *Notice*, Academic Senate, University of California, Vol. 13, No. 7, May 1989.
8. Berkeley's requirement would appear to be a version of what Merelman calls the "infusion model" that attempts to project subordinate group culture and experience throughout the university. He believes this is a more ambitious model and cites no empirical examples of its implementation (p. 154).
9. Heather Jones, "Survey uncovers faculty opposition," *Daily Californian*, February 2, 1989. Also "Response Ranges Widely On 'Cultures' Questionnaire," *Berkeleyan*, Vol. 17, No. 13, February 8, 1989.
10. John K. Wilson, *The Myth of Political Correctness*, (Durham, NC: Duke University Press, 1995), p. 82.
11. Ibid., p. 83.
12. Jennifer Packer, "Campus Greek system endorses American cultures requirement," *Daily Californian*, May 6, 1988.
13. Chancellor Heyman letter to Members of the Berkeley Division of the Academic Senate, April 17, 1989, p. 5.
14. Minutes of the Special Meeting, Berkeley Division Academic Senate, April 25, 1989.
15. Henry Louis Gates, Jr., "Whose Culture Is It, Anyway?" *New York Times*, May 4, 1991.
16. Ralph Ellison, *Invisible Man*, (New York: Vintage Books, 1972), p. 563.
17. Ibid.

18. Sarah Burke, "Tumbling the Ivory Tower," *East Bay Express*, September 23, 2015.
19. I was privileged to have Laola Hironaka, a long time staff member of the Center for Japanese Studies and campus coordinator, as my first mentor in AI doctrine (James David Barber, who preceded me as chair, used to call it the "church of AI"). I was equally fortunate to have as an early mentor Ginetta Sagan, a founder of AIUSA in the western United States, a torture survivor and a human dynamo. I would later chair AIUSA's "Ginetta Sagan Fund."
20. I was director of the office of external affairs and long range planning in the Bureau of Human Rights, Labor and Democracy from 1994 to 1995. My most important task was to act as liaison between nongovernmental organizations (NGOs) working on human rights and the government.
21. Death penalty abolitionists, for example, were suspicious of AI's new interest in the issue but gradually came to accept our involvement and especially the resources we brought to the table.
22. One of my more memorable assignment as a member of AI's international executive committee was to go to Grenada to plead to the government for the lives of those persons jailed for the 1983 assassination of Maurice Bishop, Prime Minister of Grenada. The assassination was quickly followed by a US invasion of the country on the pretext of protecting American students attending medical school on the islands.
23. Huntington defines a "kin country" as those countries that share a Western cultural heritage. See Samuel P. Huntington, "The Clash of Civilizations," *Foreign Affairs*, Summer 1993, pp. 35–38.
24. See my "The Rise and Fall of Black Influence on U.S. Foreign Policy," in Michael L. Clemons, ed., *African Americans and Global Affairs*, (University of New England Press, 2010).
25. Richard Rorty, "Response to Appiah," in Matthew J. Gibney, (ed.), *Globalizing Rights*, (New York: Oxford University Press, 2003); and David A. Hollinger, *Postethnic America*, (New York: Basic Books, 1995), p. 67.
26. See Pauline Marie Rosenau, *Post-Modernism and the Social Sciences*, (Princeton: Princeton University Press, 1992) and the differences between skeptical postmodernism and affirmative postmodernism as well as contradictions in postmodernism itself.

27. On color blindness, see Ian F. Haney-Lopez, *Dog Whistle Politics*, (New York: Oxford University Press, 2014); Walter Benn Michaels, *The Shape of the Signifier*, (Princeton: Princeton University Press, 2004) and Eduardo Bonilla-Silva, *Racism without Racists*, (Lanham, MD: Rowman & Littlefield, 2010).
28. Iris Marion Young, *Justice and the Politics of Difference*, (Princeton: Princeton University Press, 1990), p. 103.
29. Martha Minnow quoted in Young, p. 171; See Charles W. Mills on the norming of space done in terms of the *racing* of space in *the Race contract*, (Ithaca, NY: Cornell University Press, 1997), pp. 42–51. Paul Gilroy "mourn[s] the disappearance of the pursuit of Freedom as an element in black vernacular culture" in *Against Race*, (Cambridge: Beknap/Harvard, 2000), p. 184.
30. Orlando Patterson, *Freedom*, (New York: Basic Books, 1991), pp. 3–4.
31. Stanly Fish quoted in David Theo Goldberg, (ed.), *Multiculturalism*, (Cambridge, MA: Blackwell, 1994), p. 11.
32. See Frances Piven, et. Al., *Keeping Down the Black Vote*, (New York: The New Press, 2009) on voting laws.
33. See, for example, Edward W. Said, *Culture and Imperialism*, (New York: Vintage, 1994).
34. Ross Posnock, *Color & Culture*, (Cambridge: Harvard University Press, 1998), p. 41: See also Lorenzo Morris and Charles Henry, *The Chit'lin Controversy*, (Lanham, MD: University Press of America, 1978); Adolph L. Reed, Jr., *W. E. B. Du Bois and American Political Thought*, (New York: Oxford University Press, 1997).
35. Hollinger, Op. Cit., p. 106.
36. Iris Young, Op. Cit., p. 174.
37. Kymlicha also argues that *Brown's* formula for racial justice has been invoked against the rights of American Indians, native Hawaiians, and the rights of national minorities in international law. "Under the influence of *Brown*," says Kymlicha, "these national groups have been treated as a 'racial minority', and their autonomous institutions have been struck down as forms of 'racial segregation' or 'racial discrimination'." Will Kymicha, *Multicultural Citizenship*, (New York: Oxford University Press, 1995), p. 59.
38. Goldberg, Op. Cit., 1994, p. 19.

39. Dipesh Chakrabarty, *Provincializing* Europe, (Princeton: Princeton University Press, 2008), p. 100.
40. John W. Murphy and Jung Min Choi, *Postmodernism, Unraveling Racism, and Democratic Institutions*, (Westport, CN: Praeger, 1997), p. 7.
41. James Baldwin, *No Name Street*, in *Collected Essays*, (New York: Literary Classics of the United States, Inc., 1998), p. 470.
42. Judith Skhlar quoted in Lawrie Balfour, *The Evidence of Things Not Said*, (Ithaca, NY: Cornell University Press, 2001), p. 76.

Bibliography

A Critique of the Sexual Revolution. *Black Scholar* (April 1978): 65.
Black Members of the American Academy of Arts and Letters. *Journal of Blacks in Higher Education*. No. 39 (Spring 2003) 36.
Black Studies 101: A Sampling of Approaches. *Chronicle of Higher Education* (May 19, 2000).
DU Experimental College To Aid In LEADS Courses. *Newark Advocate* (October 16, 1968): 2.
Editorial. *Black Scholar* (January 1972): 34.
Introduction to Blacks in Higher Education. *Black Scholar* 6 no. 1 (September 1974).
Introduction. *Black Scholar* (Winter/Spring 1991/92).
Regents of University of California v. Bakke. 438 U.S. 265, 272-275 (1978) *U. S. Supreme Court*.
Teacher's Guide. *Introduction to Afro American Studies*. Chicago: Peoples College Press, n.d.
The Bottom Line in Education, Part 4 of *school: The Story of American Public Education:* video/c8931.
There Are Now Three Databases for Measuring the Impact of Black Studies. *Journal of Blacks in Higher Education*. No. 47 (Spring 2005): 84–85. 1997.
Abramson, Paul R. 1977. *The Political Socialization of Black Americans*. New York: Free Press.
Afro-American Student Union. 1968. Proposal for Establishing a Black Studies Program. Spring.
Aldrich, Mark. 1979. Progressive Economists and Scientific Racism. *Phylon* 40(4): 13–14.

C.P. Henry, *Black Studies and the Democratization of American Higher Education*, DOI 10.1007/978-3-319-35089-9

Alkalimat, Abdul Hakimu. 1973. The Ideology of Black Social Science. In *The Death of White Sociology*, ed. Joyce A. Ladner. New York: Vintage.

Allen, Robert L. 1974. Politics of the Attack on Black Studies. *Black Scholar* 6(1): 2–7.

Anderson, Benedict. 1991. *Imagined Communities*. London: Verso.

Aptheker, Bettina. 2014. A Tribute to Robert Chrisman. *Black Scholar* 44(1): 136.

Asante, Molefi Kete. 1980. *Afrocentricity: The Theory of Social Change*. Buffalo: Amulefi Publishing.

———. 1990. *Kemet, Afrocentricity and Knowledge*. Trenton: Africa World Press.

———. 2001. African American Studies. In *The African American Studies Reader*, ed. Nathaniel Norment Jr. Durham: Carolina Academic Press.

———. 2009. *Maulana Karenga: An Intellectual Portrait*. Cambridge: Polity.

Asante, Molefi Kete, and Ama Mazama. 2003. *The Afrocentric Paradigm*. Trenton: Africa World Press.

Azevedo, Mario, eds. 1998. *Africana Studies*. Durham: Carolina Academic Press.

Baker, Lee D. 1998. *From Savage To Negro: Anthropology and the Construction of Race, 1896–1954*. Berkeley: University of California Press.

Balfour, Lawrie. 2001. *The Evidence of Things Not Said*. Ithaca: Cornell University Press.

Ballard, Allen B. 1973. *The Education of Black Folk*. New York: Harper & Row.

Banks, William M. 1996. *Black Intellectuals: Race and Responsibility in American Life*. New York: Norton.

Banks, William. 2010. *An Oral History. ROHO*. Berkeley: Bancroft Library.

Beale, Frances. 1995. Double Jeopardy. In *Words of Fire*, ed. Beverly Guy-Sheftall. New York: The New Press.

Bell, Daniel. 1989. American Exceptionalism Revisted. *The Public Interest* 95: 41–42.

Bell, Derrick A. 1992. *Race, Racism, and American Law*. Boston: Little, Brown.

Bentley, Arthur. 1967. *The Process of Government*. Cambridge, MA: Harvard University Press.

Bernal, Martin. 1987. *Black Athena: The Afroasiatic Roots of Classical Civilization*. New Brunswick: Rutgers University Press.

Berube, Maurice R., and Marilyn Gittell. 1969. *Confrontation at Ocean Hill-Brownsville*. New York: Praeger.

Billingsley, Andrew. 1968. *Black Families in White America*. Englewood Cliffs: Prentice Hall.

Biondi, Martha. 2012. *The Black Revolution on Campus*. Berkeley: University of California Press.

Bloom, Allen. 1987. *The Closing of the American Mind*. New York: Simon and Schuster.

Bonilla-Silva, Eduardo. 2010. *Racism Without Racists*. Lanham: Rowman & Littlefield.

Bourdieu, Pierre. 2004. *Science of Science and Reflexivity.* Chicago: University of Chicago Press.

Bowles, Gloria. 2008. From the Bottom Up. In *The Politics of Women's Studies*, ed. Florence Howe. New York: Palgrave Macmillan.

Branch, Taylor. 2006. *At Canaan's Edge: American in the King Years 1965–68.* New York: Simon & Schuster.

Brechin, Gary. 1999. *Imperial San Francisco.* Berkeley: University of California Press.

Brigham, John C., and Theodore A. Weisbach, eds. 1972. *Racial Attitudes in American.* New York: Harper & Row.

Brown, Richard Harvey. 1998. *Toward a Democratic Science.* New Haven: Yale University Press.

Brown, Scott. 2003. *Fighting for US: Maulana Karenga, the US Organization, and Black Cultural Nationalism.* New York: New York University Press.

Brown, Jacqueline Nassy. 2005. *Dropping Anchor, Setting Sail.* Princeton: Princeton University Press.

Bullock, Henry Allen. 1970. *A History of Negro Education in the South.* New York: Praeger.

Bunche, Ralph J. 1936. Education in Black and White. *Journal of Negro Education* 5: 356.

Burd, Richard. 1994a. Defiant Conservative Relishes the HEH Fights to Come. *The Chronicle of Higher Education,* June 29.

Burd, Stephen. 1994b. Humanities' New Faces. *The Chronicle of Higher Education,* June 29.

Burke, Sarah. 2015. Tumbling the Ivory tower. *East Bay Express,* September 23.

Butler, Johnnella E. 1981. *Black Studies: Pedagogy & Revolution.* Washington, DC: University Press of America.

Carmichael, Stokely. 2003. *Ready for Revolution: The Life and Struggles of Stokely Carmichael.* New York: Scribner.

Carnoy, Martin. 1974. *Education as Cultural Imperialism.* New York: McKay.

Chakrabarty, Dipesh. 2008. *Provincializing Europe.* Princeton: Princeton University Press.

Chisholm, Shirley. 1970. Racism and Anti-Feminism. *Black Scholar* 1: 43.

Chrisman, Robert. 1969. The Crisis of Harold Cruse. *Black Scholar* 1(1): 77.

———. 1971. Black Prisoners, White Law. *Black Scholar* 7(6): 45.

———. 1976. Angola News Report. *Black Scholar* 7(6): 43.

———. 1977. Cuba Report. *Black Scholar* 8: 4.

———. 2011. The Black Scholar: The First Forty Years. *Black Scholar* 41(4): 2.

Chrisman, Robert. n.d. Some Thoughts on Black Publishing in the Academy. Unpublished paper.

Chrisman, Robert, and Robert Allen. 1973. Race Relations. *Black Scholar* 9: 12–23.

Christian, Barbara. 2003. But Who Do You Really Belong To—Black Studies or Women's Studies? In *The African American studies reader*, ed. Nathaniel Norment Jr. Durham: Carolina Academic Press.

Churchill, Ward. 2001. To Disrupt, Discredit and Destroy. In *Liberation, Imagination, and the Black Panther Party*, ed. Kathleen Cleaver and George Katsiaficas. New York: Routledge.

Coates, Ta-Nehisi. 2015. The Black Family in the Age of Mass Incarceration. *The Atlantic* 316(3): 82.

Cox, Oliver C. 1970. *Caste, Class & Race*. New York: Monthly Review Press.

Cronin, E. David. 1969. *Black Moses: The Story of Marcus Garvey and the Universal Negro Improvement Association*. Madison: University of Wisconsin Press.

Cruse, Harold. 1967. *The Crisis of the Negro Intellectual*. New York: Morrow.

———. 1987. *Plural but Equal*. New York: Morrow.

Daniel, Philip T. K., and Admasu Zike. 1983. *The National Council for Black Studies—Northern Illinois* University Black Studies Four Year College and University Survey. Dekalb, Illinois.

Davis, Angela. 1971. The Black Woman's Role in the Community of Slaves. *Black Scholar* 3(4): 5.

———. 1978. Rape, Racism and the Capitalist Setting. *Black Scholar* 9(7): 24.

Davis, David Brion. 2006. *Inhuman Bondage*. New York: Oxford University Press.

Dawson, Michael C. 2001. *Black Visions*. Chicago: University of Chicago Press.

Depelchin, Jacques. 2005. *Silences in African History*. Dar Es Salaam: Mkuki Na Nyota Publishers.

Du Bois, W.E.B. 1989. *The Souls of Black Folk*. New York: Penguin.

Dudziak, Mary. 2000. *Cold War Civil Rights*. Princeton: Princeton University Press.

Duster, Troy. 2002. *An Oral History with Troy Duster. ROHO*. Berkeley: Bancroft Library.

Edwards, Harry. 1980. *The Struggle That Must Be*. New York: Macmillan.

Eulau, Heinz. 1969. *Behavioralism in Political Science*. New York: Atherton Press.

Fass, Paula S. 1989. *Outside In*. New York: Oxford University Press.

Fernandez, Manny, and John Swartz. 2013. Teenager's Sentence in Fatal Drunken Driving Case Stirs Affluenza. Debate. *New York Times*, December 14. Page A11.

Fikes, Robert Jr. 2004. Black Presidents of Predominantly White Academic Associations. *Journal of Blacks in Higher Education* 44: 108.

Ford, Nick Aaron. 1973. *Black Studies*. Port Washington: Kennikat.

Forde, Sheron. 1994. Squall at opening of Black Studies conference. *Guyana Chronicle,* June 2: 1.

Franklin, John Hope. 1967. *From Slavery to Freedom*. New York: Knopf.

———. 2005. *Mirror to America*. New York: Farrar, Straus and Giroux.

Frymer, Paul. 2005. Racism revised. *American Political Science Review* 99(3): 373–387.

Gates, Jr., Henry Louis. 1991. Whose Culture Is It, anyway? *New York Times*, May 4.

Giery, Thomas F. 1983. Boundary-Work and the Demarcation of Science from Non-Science. *American Sociological Review* 48: 781–782.

Gilroy, Paul. 1993. *The Black Atlantic: Modernity and Double Consciousness*. Cambridge, MA: Harvard University Press.

———. 2000. *Against Race*. Cambridge: Beknap/Harvard.

Ginsberg, Alice E., eds. 2008. *The Evolution of American Women's Studies*. New York: Palgrave Macmillan.

Goldberg, David Theo. 1993. *Racist Culture*. Cambridge, UK: Blackwell.

———, eds. 1994. *Multiculturalism*. Cambridge: Blackwell.

Gordon, Milton M. 1964. *Assimilation in American Life: The Role of Race, Religion, and National Origins*. New York: Oxford University Press.

Gould, Stephan Jay. 1996. *The Mismeasure of Man, Hen's Teeth and Horse's Toes*. New York: Norton.

Gouldner, Alvin. 1976. *The Dialectic of Ideology and Technology*. New York: Seabury.

Guy-Sheftall, Beverly, eds. 1995. *Words of Fire*. New York: The New Press.

———. 2003. Black Women's Studies. In *The African American Reader*, ed. Nathaniel Norment Jr. Durham: Carolina Academic Press.

Hall, Perry A. 1999. *In the Vineyard*. Knoxville: University of Tennessee Press.

Hamilton, Charles V. 1967. The Place of the Black College in the Human Rights Struggle. *Negro Digest* 16: 8.

Haney-Lopez, Ian F. 2014. *Dog Whistle Politics*. New York: Oxford University Press.

Harding, Sandra. 1994. Is Science Multicultural. In *Multiculturalism*, ed. David Theo Goldberg. Cambridge, MA: Blackwell.

Hare, Nathan. 1968. Final Reflections on a 'Negro' College. *Negro Digest* 17: 43.

Harlan, Louis R. 1972. *Booker T. Washington: The Making of a Black Leader 1856–1901*. New York: Oxford University Press.

Harris, Louis. 1997. The Future of Affirmative Action. In *The Affirmative Action Debate*, ed. George E. Curry. Reading: Addison-Wesley.

Henderson, Stephen E. 1968. The Black University: Towards Its Realization. *Negro Digest* 17(5): 19.

Henry, Charles P. 1979. Big Philanthropy and the Funding of Black Organizations. *The Review of Black Political Economy* 9: 174–190.

———. 1990. *Culture and African American Politics*. Bloomington: Indiana University Press.

———. 1991. *Jesse Jackson: The Search for Common Ground*. Oakland: Black Scholar Press.

———. 1992. Understanding the Underclass. In *Race, Politics and Economic Development*, ed. James Jennings. London: Verso.

———. 1995. *Ralph Bunche: Selected Speeches and Writings*. Ann Arbor: University of Michigan Press.

———. 1999. *Ralph Bunche: Model Negro or American Other?* New York: New York University Press.

———. 2005. African American Politics: The Black Studies Perspective. In *Handbook of Black Studies*, ed. Molefi Kete Asante and Maulana Karenga. Thousand Oaks: Sage.

———. 2010a. Race, Public Policy and the Lowi Canon. In *Political Science as Public Philosophy*, ed. Benjamin Ginsberg and Gwendolyn Mink. New York: Norton.

———. 2010b. The Rise and Fall of Black Influence on U. S. Foreign Policy. In *African Americans and Global Affairs*, ed. Michael L. Clemons. Boston: Univerity of New England Press.

Henry, Charles P., and Carlos Munoz. 1986. The Rainbow Coalition in Four Big Cities. *PS: Political Science & Politics* 19: 598–609.

Higginbotham, Leon A. 1978. *In the Matter of Color*. New York: Oxford University Press.

Hill Collins, Patricia. 1991. *Black Feminist Thought: Knowledge, Consciousness, And The Politics Of Empowerment*. New York: Routledge.

Hine, Darlene Clark. 2003. The Black Studies Movement. In *The African American Studies Reader*, ed. Nathaniel Norment Jr. Durham: Carolina Academic Press.

Hirsch, E.D. Jr. 1987. *Cultural Literacy*. Boston: Houghton Mifflin.

Hollinger, David A. 1995. *Postethnic America*. New York: Basic Books.

Holloway, Jonathan Scott. 2002. *Confronting the Veil*. Chapel Hill: University of North Carolina Press.

Horne, Gerald. 1997. *Fire This Time: The Watts Uprising and the 1960s*. New York: Da Capo Press.

Howe, Stephen. 1998. *Afrocentism: Mythical Pasts and Imagined Homes*. London: Verso.

Howe, Forence, eds. 2008. *The Politics of Women's Studies*. New York: Palgrave Macmillan.

Huggins, Nathan I. 2003. Afro-American Studies. In *The African American Studies Reader*, ed. Nathaniel Norment Jr. Durham: Carolina Academic Press.

Huggins, Nathan. 2007. *Inclusive Scholarship: Developing Black Studies in the United States*. New York: Ford Foundation.

Hughes, Langston, and Arna Bontemps, eds. 1983. *The Book of Negro Folklore*. New York: Dodd, Mead.

Hunter, James Davison. 1991. *Culture Wars*. New York: Basic Books.

Huntington, Samuel P. 1993. The Clash of Civilizations. *Foreign Affairs* 72(3): 22–49.

———. 2004. *Who are We?* New York: Simon & Schuster.

Jackson, Walter. 1990. *Gunnar Myrdal and America's Conscience*. Chapel Hill: University of North Carolina Press.

James, Joy. 1997. *Transcending the Talented Tenth: Black Leaders and American Intellectuals*. New York: Routledge.

Jones, Heather. 1989a. All UC Campuses Considering Ethnic Studies. *Daily Californian*, February 28.

———. 1989b. Survey Uncovers Faculty Opposition. *Daily Californian*, February 2.

Jones, Reginald. 2010. *An Oral History. ROHO*. Berkeley: Bancroft Library.

Jones, Heather. 1989. Response Ranges Widely on 'Cultures' Questionnaire. *Berkeleyan* 17(13): 3.

Jones, Leroi, and Amiri Baraka. 1984. *The Autobiography of Leroi Jones/Amiri Baraka*. New York: Freundlich.

Jordon, Winthrop D. 1968. *White Over Black*. New York: Norton.

Joseph, Peniel E. 2006. Black Studies, Student Activism, and the Black Power Movement. *Journal of African American History* 88(2): 188.

Kalb, Claudia, and Mark Starr. 1996. Up From Mediocrity. *Newsweek* 127(8): 64.

Karenga, Maulana. 1980. *Kawaida Theory*. Inglewood: Kawaida Publications.

———. 1993. *Introduction to Black Studies*. Los Angeles: University of Sankore Press.

———. 2003. Black Studies and the Problematic of Paradigm. In *The African American Studies Reader*, ed. Nathaniel Norment Jr. Durham: Carolina Academic Press.

Katznelson, Ira. 2005. *When Affirmative Action Was White*. New York: Norton.

Kennedy, Elizabeth Lapovsky, and Agatha Beins, eds. 2005. *Women's Studies for the Future*. New Brunswick: Rutgers University Press.

Kilson, Martin. 2014. *Transformation Of The African American Intelligentsia 1880–2012*. Cambridge, MA: Harvard University Press.

Kimbell, Roger. 1990. *Tenured Radicals*. New York: Harper and Row.

King, Martin Luther Jr. 1964. *Why We Can't Wait*. New York: Mentor.

King, Martin Luther Jr. 1972. The Role of the Behavioral Scientist in the Civil Rights Movement. In *Racial Attitudes in America*, ed. John C. Brigham and Theodore A. Weissbach. New York: Harper & Row.

King, William M. 2000. The Early Years of Three Major Professional Black Studies Organizations. In *Out of the Revolution*, ed. Delores P. Aldridge and Carlene Young. Lanham: Lexington.

King, Desomd S., and Rogers M. Smith. 2005. Racial Orders in American Political Science. *American Political Science Review* 99(1): 75–92.

Kluger, Richard. 1976. *Simple Justice: The History of 'Brown v. Board of Education' and Black America's Struggle for Equality*. New York: Knopf.

Kuhn, Thomas S. 1970. *The Structure of Scientific Revolutions*. Chicago: University of Chicago Press.

Kymicha, Will. 1995. *Multicultural Citizenship*. New York: Oxford University Press.

Lasswell, Harold D. 1936. *Politics; who gets what, when, how*. New York: McGraw Hill.

Lau, Edie. 1984. Ethnic Studies now gives doctorates. *Daily Californian*, September 21: 3.

Layman, Stanford, Herbert Hill, and James E. Jones Jr., eds. 1993. *Racial Equality in America*. Madison: University of Wisconsin Press.

Lefkowitz, Mary. 1996. *Not Out of Africa: How Afrocentrism Became An Excuse To Teach Myth As History*. New York: Basic Books.

Levine, Lawrence W. 1996. *The Opening of the American Mind*. Boston: Beacon.

Levitt, Steven D., and Stephen J. Dubnet. 2005. *Freakonomics*. New York: Morrow.

Lewis, David Levering. 1993. *W. E. B. Du Bois: Biography of a Race 1868–1919*. New York: Holt.

Lipset, Seymour Martin. 1996. *American Exceptionalism*. New York: Norton.

Lorde, Audre. 1978. Scratching the Surface. *Black Scholar*. 13(4–5): 20–24.

Lowi, Theodore J. 1971. *The Politics of Disorder*. New York: Basic Books.

Lyman, Stanford M. 1993. Race Relations as Social Process. In *Race in America*, ed. Herbert Hill and James E. Jones. Madison: University of Wisconsin Press.

Magner, Denise. 1993. 60s Dissident at Cornell Should Not Be a Trustee. *Chronicle of Higher Education*, March 3.

Malcomson, Scott L. 2000. *One Drop of Blood*. New York: Farrar Straus Giroux.

Mansbridge, Jane, and Aldon Morris, eds. 2001. *Oppositional Consciousness: The Subjective Roots of Social Protest*. Chicago: University of Chicago Press.

Marable, Manning. 2000. Black Studies and the Racial Mountain. *Souls* 2(3): 17–36.

Martin, Waldo E. Jr., eds. 1998. *Brown v. Board of Education*. Boston: Bedford/ St. Martin's.

May 6, 1988.

Mazama, Ama. 2006. Interdisciplinary, Transdisciplinary, or Unidisciplinary? In *The Handbook of Black Studies*, ed. Molefi Kete Asante and Maulana Karenga. Thousand Oaks: Sage.

McWorter, Gerald A. 1968. Struggle, Ideology and the Black University. *Negro Digest*: 17(8).

McWorter, Gerald A., and Ronald Bailey. 2001. Black Studies Curriculum Development in the 1980s. In *The African American Studies Reader*, ed. Nathaniel Norment Jr. Durham: Carolina Academic Press.

Merelman, Richard M. 1995. *Representing Black Culture*. New York: Routledge.

———. 2003. *Pluralism at Yale: The Culture of Political Science in America*. Madison: University of Wisconsin Press.

Michaels, Walter Benn. 2014. *The Shape of the Signifier*. Princeton: Princeton Univeristy Press.

Miller, Karen Karlette. 1986. Black Studies in California Higher Education, 1965–1980. University of California at Santa Barbara: unpublished Ph.D. dissertation.

Mills, Charles W. 1997. *The Racial Contract.* Ithaca: Cornell University Press.
Mills, Charles. 1998. *Blackness Visible.* Ithaca: Cornell University Press.
Mills, C. Wright. 2000. *The Power Elite.* New York: Oxford University Press.
Moore, Carlos. 1988. *Castro, the Blacks, and Africa.* Los Angeles: UCLA Center for Afro-American Studies.
Morris, Aldon D. 2015. *The Scholar Denied: W. E. B. Du Bois And The Birth of Modern Sociology.* Berkeley: University of California Press.
Morris, Lorenzo, and Charles Henry. 1978a. *The Chit'lin Controversy: Race and Public Policy in America.* Washington, DC: University Press of America.
Morris, Lorenzo, and Charles P. Henry. 1978b. *The Chit'lin Controversy.* Lanham: University Press of America.
Moses, Wilson J. 1978. *The Golden Age of Black Nationalism, 1850–1925.* New York: Oxford University Press.
Murphy, John W., and Jung Min Choi. 1995. *Postmodernism, Unraveling Racism and Democratic Institutions.* New York: Times books.
Napper, George. 1973. *blacker than thou.* Grand Rapids: Eerdmans Publishing.
Nelson, Richard R. 1977. *The Moon and the Ghetto.* New York: Norton.
Packer, Jennifer. 1988. Campus Greek System Endorses American Cultures Requirement. *Daily Californian*: 7.
Painter, Nell Irvin. 2007. *Creating Black Americans.* New York: Oxford University Press.
Patterson, Orlando. 1991. *Freedom.* New York: Basic Books.
Peters, Erskine. 2003. Afrocentricity. In *The African American Studies Reader*, ed. Nathaniel Norment Jr. Durham: Carolina Academic Press.
Piketty, Thomas. 2014. *Capital in the Twenty-First Century.* Cambridge, MA: Harvard University Press.
Piven, Frances. 2009. *Keeping Down the Black Vote.* New York: The New Press.
Poe, Daryl Zizwe. 2006. Black Studies in Historically Black Colleges and Universities. In *Handbook of Black Studies*, ed. Molefi Kete Asante and Maulana Karenga. Thousand Oaks: Sage.
Polsgrove, Carol. 2001. *Divided Minds.* New York: Norton.
Posnock, Ross. 1998. *Color & Culture.* Cambridge, MA: Harvard University Press.
Ravitch, Diane. 1993. *The Troubled Crusade.* New York: Basic Books.
Redmond, Lea, and Charles P. Henry. 2005. The Roots of Black Studies. In *Afrocentric Traditions*, ed. James L. Conyers Jr., 10. New Brunswick: Transaction.
Reed, Adolph L. Jr. 1997. *W. E. B. Du Bois and American Political Thought.* New York: Oxford University Press.
Reitan, Ruth. 1999. *The Rise and Decline of an Alliance: Cuba and African American Leaders in the 1960s.* East Lansing: Michigan State University Press.
Roberts, Virgil P. 2002. *Oral History Interview.* Los Angeles: UCLA-CAAS.
Robinson, Cedric J. 1983. *Black Marxism.* London: Zed.

Robinson, Armstead L., et al., eds. 1969. *Black Studies in the University*. New Haven: Yale University Press.

Rochon, Thomas R. 1998. *Culture Moves*. Princeton: Princeton University Press.

Rodgers, Ibram H. 2012. *The Black Campus Movement*. New York: Palgrave Macmillan.

Rojas, Fabio. 2007. *From Black Power to Black Studies*. Baltimore: Johns Hopkins University Press.

Rooks, Noliwe M. 2006. *White Money/Black Power*. Boston: Beacon.

Rosaldo, Renato. 1993. *Culture & Truth*. Boston: Beacon.

Rosenau, Pauline Marie. 1992. *Post-Modernism and the Social Sciences*. Princeton: Princeton University Press.

Rosenfeld, Seth. 2012. *Subversives: The FBI's War on Student Radicals, and Reagan's Rise to Power*. New York: Picador.

Roty, Richard. 1999. Response to Appiah. In *Globalizing Rights*, ed. Matthew J. Gibney. New York: Oxford.

Rustin, Bayard, et al. 1969. *Black Studies: Myths & Realities*. New York: A. Philip Randolph Educational Fund.

Said, Edward W. 1994a. *Culture and Imperialism*. New York: Vintage.

———. 1994b. *Orientalism*. New York: Vintage.

Schlesinger, Jr. Arthur M. 1992. *The Disuniting of America*. New York: Norton.

Sedgwick, John. 1995. Inside the Pioneer Fund. In *The Bell Curve*, ed. Russell Jacoby and Naomi Glauberman. New York: Times Books.

Shakur, Assata. 1978. Women in Prison. *Black Scholar* 9(7): 8–15.

Shor, Ira. 1986. *Culture Wars*. London: Routledge and Kegan Paul.

Singh, Nikhil Pal. 2004. *Black Is a Country*. Cambridge, MA: Harvard University Press.

Singleton, Robert. 1999. *Oral History Interview*. Los Angles: UCLA-CAAS.

Small, Mario. 1999. Department Conditions and the Emergence of New Disciplines. *Theory and Society* 28(5): 659–708.

Southern, David W. 1987. *Gunnar Myrdal and Black-White Relations*. Baton Rouge: Louisiana State University Press.

Staples, Robert. 1971. The Myth of the Impotent Black Male. *Black Scholar* 2: 2.

———. 1979. The Myth of Black Macho. *Black Scholar* 10(6–7): 24–33.

———. 1982. *Black Masculinity: The black male's role in American society*. San Francisco: Black Scholar Press.

Stewart, James B. 2004. *Flight in Search of Vision*. Trenton: Africa World Press.

Takaki, Ronald. 2008. *A Different Mirror*. New York: Back Bay Books.

Taylor, Ula. 2010. African American Studies at the University of California at Berkeley: A Historical Narrative. In *Forty and Counting*, ed. Ronald Williams II. Berkeley: Department of African American Studies.

Truman, David. 1971. *The Governmental Process*. Berkeley: Institute for Governmental Studies.

Turner, Darwin T. 1968. The Black University: A Practical Approach. *Negro Digest* 17(5): 19.

Tyack, David, and Elisabeth Hansot. 1982. *Managers of Virtue*. New York: Basic Books.

Tyler, Bruce. 1983. Black Radicalism in Southern California, 1950–1982. UCLA: unpublished Ph.D. dissertation.

Valentine, Charles A. 1968. *Culture and Poverty*. Chicago: University of Chicago Press.

Vidich, A.J., and S.M. Lyman. 2000. Qualitative Methods. In *Handbook of Qualitative Research*, ed. N.K. Denzin and Y.S. Lincoln. Thousand Oaks: Sage.

Von Eschen, Penny. 1997. *Race Against Empire*. Ithaca: Cornell University Press.

Walker, Alice. 1970. But Yet Still the Cotton Gin Kept on Working. *Black Scholar* 1(3–4): 20.

Wallerstein, Immanuel. 1995. What Are We Bounding, and Whom, When We Bound Social Research. *Social Research* 62(4): 4.

Walters, Ronald W. 1997. *Pan Africanism in the African Diaspora*. Detroit: Wayne State University Press.

———. 2003. *White Nationalism Black Interests*. Detroit: Wayne State University Press.

Walton, Hanes Jr., and Joseph McCormick II. 1997. The Study of African-American Politics as Social Danger: Clues from the Disciplinary Journals. *National Political Science Review* 6: 61.

Walton, Hanes Jr., and Robert C. Smith. 2007. The Race Variable and the American Political Science Association's 'State of the Discipline' Reports and Books, 1907–2002. In *African American Perspectives on Political Science*, ed. Wilbur C. Rich. Philadelphia: Temple University Press.

Washington, James M., eds. 1986a. *A Testament of Hope*. San Francisco: Harper & Row.

Washington, Johnny. 1986b. *Alain Locke and Philosophy*. New York: Greenwood.

Watts, Jerry, eds. 2004. *Harold Cruse's The Crisis of the Negro Intellectual Reconsidered*. New York: Routledge.

Webb, Clive, eds. 2005. *Massive Resistance: Southern Opposition to the Second Reconstruction*. New York: Oxford University Press.

White, E. Frances. 1995. Africa on My Mind. In *Words of Fire*, ed. Beverly Guy-Sheftall. New York: The New Press.

White, Derrick E. 2012. An Independent Approach to Black Studies. *Journal of African American Studies* 16: 76.

Wilmore, Gayraud S. 1986. *Black Religion and Black Radicalism*. Maryknoll: Orbis Books.

Wilson, Woodrow. 1981. *Congressional Government*. Baltimore: Johns Hopkins University Press.

Wilson, Francille Rusan. 2006. *The Segregated Scholars: Black Social Scientists and the Creation of Black Labor Studies, 1890–1950*. Charlottesville: University of Virginia Press.

Wilson III, Ernest J., and Lorrie A. Frasure. 2007. Still at the Margins. In *African American Perspectives on Political Science*, ed. Wilbur C. Rich. Philadelphia: Temple University Press.

Winston, Michael R. 1971. Through the Back Door. *Daedalus* 100(3): 678–719.

Wolters, Raymond. 1975. *The New Negro on Campus*. Princeton University Press: Princeton.

Woodard, Komozi. 1999. *A nation within a nation: Amiri Barada (Leroi Jones) & Black Power Politics*. Chapel Hill: University of North Carolina Press.

Wright, Richard. 1977. *American Hunger*. New York: Harper & Row.

Wright, Michelle M. 2004. *Becoming Black: Creating Identity In The African Diaspora*. Durham: Duke University Press.

Young, Iris Marion. 1990. *Justice and the Politics of Difference*. Princeton: Princeton Uniersity Press.

Index

A
AALSC. *See* Afro-American Lounge Steering Committee (AALSC)
AASU. *See* Afro-American Student Union (AASU)
Academy of Natural Sciences, 123
ACC. *See* American Commons Club (ACC)
Ad Hoc Committee on African and African American Studies in the curriculum, 8
Ad-Hoc Committee on Education and Ethnicity (Simmons Committee), 231
affirmative action, 74, 107, 115, 191, 205–7, 212, 215, 219, 224n59, 230, 237
African Diaspora Studies, 75, 176
African Heritage Studies Association (AHSA), 49, 98, 99
African Methodist Episcopal Church, 28
African Studies Association (ASA), 98, 99
Africology, 165
Afro-American Association, 37
Afro-American Lounge Steering Committee (AALSC), 5
Afro-American Student Union (AASU), 65, 66, 68, 69, 91n17
Afro-American Studies Department, 6
Afrocentric, 30, 53n38, 95, 98, 99, 109, 113, 119n41, 164, 166, 169, 170, 174, 175, 182n59, 184n88
The *Afrocentric Scholar*, 113, 119n41
AHSA. *See* African Heritage Studies Association (AHSA)
AI. *See* Amnesty International (AI)
Ain't I a Woman (hooks), 173
American Academy for Advancement of Science, 123
American Academy of Arts and Letters, 115, 119n46

Note: Page number followed by "n" denotes endnotes

C.P. Henry, *Black Studies and the Democratization of American Higher Education*, DOI 10.1007/978-3-319-35089-9

American Anthropologist, 123
American Association of Physical Anthropology, 9
American Commons Club (ACC), 2, 19n3
American Communist Party (CPUSA), 43, 44
American Cultures, 75, 79, 229, 232–7, 246n4, 246n12
American exceptionalism, 158, 181n34, 239, 241
American Historical Association, 9
American Journal of Psychology, 42
American Negro Academy, 97
American Philosophical Society, 123
American Political Science Association (APSA), 9, 13, 124, 141n11, 181n30, 181n31
American Political Science Review (APSR), 123, 124, 141n11, 157, 222n111
American Psychological Association, 9, 220n10
Amnesty International (AI), 144n53, 236–9, 247n19
An American Dilemma (Myrdal), 31, 43, 194, 211
Anna T. Jeanes Fund, 29
APSA. *See* American Political Science Association (APSA)
APSR. *See* American Political Science Review (APSR)
ASA. *See* African Studies Association (ASA)
ASAALH. *See* Association for the Study of Afro-American Life and History (ASAALH)
Asian American Studies, 73, 82, 85, 230, 246n4
assimilation, 3, 39–41, 56n81, 67, 158, 195, 204, 214, 218, 241, 243
Assimilation in American Life (Gordon), 3, 56n81
Association for the Study of Afro-American Life and History (ASAALH), 96, 97
Atlanta University (AU), 18, 61, 104, 124, 140n6, 179n4
Atlantic Monthly, 49, 125, 202
AU. *See* Atlanta University (AU)
Authentically Black (McWorter), 219

B

Bakke v. Regents of the University of California, 205
Before the Mayflower (Bennett), 105
The Bell Curve (Herrnstein and Murray), 202
Beyond the Melting Pot (Glazer and Moynihan), 199
Black Academy of Arts and Letters, 10
Black Athena (Bernal), 167
The Black Atlantic (Gilroy), 175, 176
Black Awakening in Capitalist America (Allen), 44, 143n33
Black Bourgeoisie (Frazier), 102
black cultural nationalism, 36, 93n47, 106, 152, 177
black culture, 4, 5, 93n44, 126, 127, 160, 176, 196
Black Families in White America (Billingsley), 200
The Black Family (Staples), 135, 200
Black feminism, 45, 50, 135, 137
Black Feminist Thought (Hill Collins), 169, 174
Black Law Journal, 139
Black Macho and The Myth of The Superwoman (Wallace), 137
Black Marxism, 128, 142n27
Black Panther Party (BPP), 13, 38, 64, 76, 77, 93n50, 171

Black power, 1–3, 20n9, 32, 38, 40, 47, 54n57, 54n60, 56n82, 60, 72, 87, 93n51, 98, 121, 122, 152, 162, 170, 171, 190, 216, 219
Black Power (Carmichael and Hamilton), 3, 11, 69n82
Black scholar, 9, 10, 15, 18, 25, 31, 37, 48, 53n46, 56n72, 57n90, 66, 68, 73, 89, 96, 97, 99, 103, 104, 107, 111, 115, 117n18, 117n22, 121–47, 200
Black Student Union (BSU), 5–7, 15, 16, 19n1, 20n8, 34, 77–9, 82–4, 122, 149
Black Studies, 2, 23–57, 59–119, 121–47, 149, 187, 229–49
Black Studies Committee, 16, 17
Black Studies: Threat or Challenge? (Ford), 96
Black Women's Studies, 18, 90, 174, 177, 179n4, 184n94
Black World Foundation, 128, 129, 138, 139, 146n69
Board of Trustees, 6, 7, 19n7
Bowdoin College, 17, 28
BPP. *See* Black Panther Party (BPP)
Brown decision, 43, 47, 187, 188, 190, 194
BSU. *See* Black Student Union (BSU)

C
California State University at Dominguez Hill, 103, 112
CAP. *See* Congress of African People (CAP)
Casa de las Americas, 133
CBC. *See* Congressional Black Caucus (CBC)
CBS. *See* Center for Black Studies (CBS)
CCC. *See* Civilian Conservation Corp (CCC)
Center for Black Studies (CBS), 16, 18, 21n21, 62, 84–6
CEP. *See* Committee on Educational Policy (CEP)
Chicago Eight/Seven trial, 12
Chicano Studies, 64, 70, 79
The Chit'lin Controversy (Morris and Henry), 24, 142n25n 248n35
City for Inner-City Studies, 13
City University of New York (CUNY), 34, 96
Civilian Conservation Corp (CCC), 193
Civil Rights Act of 1964, 205, 206
clash of civilizations, 213, 215, 220, 226n89, 247n23
The Closing of the American Mind (Bloom), 55n62, 212, 226n85
color-blindness, 133, 220, 224n61, 241, 245, 248n27
Colored People (Gates), 219
Columbia University, 86, 179n9
Combahee River Collective, 172
Committee of Inquiry, 84
Committee on African and Black American Humanities, 8
Committee on Educational Policy (CEP), 67, 231, 232
Common Differences (Joseph and Lewis), 173
Communiversity, 13
Congressional Black Caucus (CBC), 14, 15
Congress of African People (CAP), 139, 164
Cornell University, 39, 56n79, 57n86, 101, 172, 222n32, 248n29
CPUSA. *See* American Communist Party (CPUSA)

The Crisis, 42, 45, 56n83, 73, 125–7, 142n19, 162, 182n48, 182n51
The Crisis of the Negro Intellectual (Cruse), 56n83, 73, 126, 127, 142n24, 182n48, 182n51
critical community, 32, 45, 50, 53n31, 219
Crossing Danger Water (Mullane), 106
Cuban Academy of Science, 130
Cuban American, 239, 240
Cuban Institute for Friendship with People (ICAP), 130
Cultural Literacy (Hirsch), 211
cultural pluralism, 40, 44, 207, 230, 231, 233, 235, 242–4
culture wars, 139, 167, 207–10
Culture Wars (Hunter), 210, 224n64
CUNY. *See* City University of New York (CUNY)
curriculum, 8, 10, 13, 17, 24, 25, 27–31, 34, 35, 45, 48, 66, 70, 73, 74, 76, 79, 82, 83, 95, 102, 104, 107–10, 113–15, 117n22, 118n29, 118n34, 118n36, 119n40, 139, 160, 173, 177, 181n43, 191, 204, 208, 210–12, 215, 216, 221n27, 230, 236, 238

D

DCA. *See* Denison Christian Association (DCA)
democracy, 56n77, 157, 158, 177, 210, 212, 214–16, 238, 244, 245, 247n20
democratic cultural pluralism, 242–4
Denison Christian Association (DCA), 2, 3
Denison Experimental College, 5
Denison University, 1, 149
Descent of Man (Darwin), 46
discipline(s), 9, 17, 21n19, 30, 37, 45, 47–50, 57n94, 60, 62, 63, 80, 81, 84, 88, 89, 91n11, 96, 98, 99, 106–8, 111, 115, 116n1, 124, 125, 149–85, 217, 218, 236
The Disuniting of America (Schlesinger), 211, 225n81
DuSable Museum, 13

E

Ebony, 125
economics, 5, 30, 44, 48, 80, 106, 115, 128, 152, 153, 155, 156, 160, 166, 178, 218, 235
Educational Testing Service (ETS), 96, 97, 104
empiricism, 160
Encyclopedia of the Negro, 161
epistemology, 170, 174, 175, 178
equal educational opportunity, 193, 197, 198, 204–6, 216
Ethnic Heritage Studies Program Act of 1972, 211
ethnic studies, 16, 17, 22, 48, 59, 60, 63, 64, 70, 71, 73–6, 79, 82, 85, 88, 92n43, 113, 194, 208, 215, 229–36, 246n4, 246n7
ETS. *See* Educational Testing Service (ETS)
Eurocentric, 13, 25, 113, 162, 165, 173, 175
European American, 218, 233, 240

F

Federal Bureau of Investigation (FBI), 78, 133
FESTAC. *See* Second World Black Arts Festival (FESTAC)
Fisk University, 10, 98, 105

Ford Foundation, 10, 12, 14, 20n14, 36, 45, 60–2, 74, 75, 82, 86, 90, 107, 109, 110, 115, 118n33, 118n34, 124, 138, 146n69, 172, 197, 221n10
Franklin college, 8, 10, 13, 28, 42, 66, 102
Free African societies, 27
Freedman's Bureau, 28, 52n17, 191
From Black Power to Black Studies (Rojas), 20n9, 60, 91n5, 118n26
From Slavery to Freedom (Franklin), 52n16

G
General Education Board, 29, 192
Georgia State University, 101, 103, 104, 106
GI bill, 32, 194, 215
GLCA. *See* Great Lakes Colleges Association (GLCA)
Gone with the Wind, 42
Gong Lum v. Rice, 190
Great Lakes Colleges Association (GLCA), 18

H
Haitian American, 240
Harlem Renaissance, 31
Harper's, 125
Harvard Educational Review, 201
HBCUs. *See* historically Black colleges and universities (HBCUs)
Higher Education Act of 1965, 34
historically Black colleges and universities (HBCUs), 24, 98, 117n15, 123
history, 3, 5, 7, 8, 10, 13, 15, 20n8, 20n10, 24–6, 29, 30, 36, 40, 41, 43, 48, 50, 51n9, 51n10, 52n17, 54n52, 56n77, 60, 63, 65, 66, 68–70, 80, 91n13, 92n39, 93n46, 96, 99, 105, 106, 109, 112, 113, 115, 122, 126, 127, 130, 133, 134, 140, 140n6, 149, 153, 155, 156, 158, 160, 162–6, 168, 177, 178, 180n14, 182n59, 185n104, 190, 201, 206, 207, 209–12, 216, 221n20, 230, 231, 235, 241, 242, 244, 245
Howard University, 13, 14, 21n19, 25, 28, 35, 51n10, 54n58, 102, 116n5, 121, 140n6, 159, 180n26, 180n29, 222n28, 248n35
humanities, 8, 18, 86, 98, 106, 115, 123, 154, 159, 160, 165, 180n14, 207, 209, 212, 217, 234
human rights, 53n37, 170, 236–43, 247n20

I
IBW. *See* Institute for the Black World (IBW)
IDPs. *See* interdisciplinary degree programs (IDPs)
If They Come in the Morning (Davis and Aptheker), 135
Inclusive Scholarship, 20n14, 86, 91n9
Indiana University, 17, 96, 97, 99, 101, 103, 111, 116n6, 223n55, 233
Institute for the Black World (IBW), 61, 86, 87, 91n7, 107, 110, 138, 146n69
integration, 23, 24, 32, 40, 43, 48, 61, 63, 69, 89, 90, 107, 108, 112, 127, 131, 163, 187–9, 191, 197, 198, 204, 205, 218, 242
integrationist model, 90

intelligence testing (IQ), 192, 193, 198, 201–3, 223n47
interdisciplinarity, 160
interdisciplinary degree programs (IDPs), 80
International Journal of Africana Studies, 114
In the Vineyard (Hall), 57n84, 110
Introduction to Afro-American Studies (McWorter and Bailey), 105
Introduction to Black Studies (Karenga), 106
Invisible Man (Ellison), 126
Irish American, 239, 240

J
Japanese American, 239, 240
Jewish American, 239
Journal of Black Studies, 50, 141n18
Journal of Haitian Studies, 85
Journal of Negro Education, 26, 50n4, 140n6
Journal of Negro History, 26, 140n6
Journal of Political Repression, 124

K
Kawaida theory, 106, 163
Kent State University, 18, 100, 116n12
Key Issues in the Afro-American Experience (Huggins), 105
King Center, 61, 86, 133

L
League of Revolutionary Black Workers, 39
legitimation, 32, 218, 220
liberal arts education, 29–31, 192
Licking County Inter-Cultural Center, 18
Lincoln University, 15, 25
Long Time Gone (Brent), 133

M
Malcolm X City College, 12, 13, 150
Mark of Oppression (Kardiner and Ovesey), 156
Merritt College, 37
Middlebury College, 28
Milliken v. Bradley, 28
The Miseducation of the Negro (Woodson), 102
modernization, 159, 196, 218
The Moon and the Ghetto (Nelson), 216, 226n104
Moynihan report, 67, 200, 203
MPLA. *See* Popular Movement for the Liberation of Angola (MPLA)
Ms., 137, 138, 144n47
multiculturalism, 48, 75, 139, 140, 160, 177, 179n10, 207, 208, 211–15, 225n71, 229–49

N
NAACP. *See* National Association for the Advancement of Colored People (NAACP)
NAS. *See* National Association of Scholars (NAS)
National Association for the Advancement of Colored People (NAACP), 26, 32, 40, 127, 161, 170, 187–9, 195, 198, 238
National Association of Scholars (NAS), 208, 236
National Black Feminist Organization (NBFO), 172, 184n87
National Black Political Assembly, 12, 150, 176
National Black United Fund, 138

National Capitol Area Political Science Association, 15
National Commission on Excellence in Education (NCEE), 204
National Conference of Black Political Scientists (NCOBPS), 17, 100, 124
National Council for Black Studies (NCBS), 17, 18, 49, 75, 95–119
National Educators Association (NEA), 192
National Endowment for the Humanities (NEH), 18, 86, 207–9, 225n70, 225n71
National Institutes of Mental Health, 12
National Negro Congress (NNC), 26, 31, 32
National Political Science Review (NPSR), 124, 140n8
National Student Association, 2
National Youth Administration (NYA), 193
Nation of Islam, 74, 76, 150
Native American Studies, 60, 70
Nature of Prejudice (Allport), 47
NBFO. *See* National Black Feminist Organization (NBFO)
NCBS. *See* National Council for Black Studies (NCBS)
NCEE. *See* National Commission on Excellence in Education (NCEE)
NCOBPS. *See* National Conference of Black Political Scientists (NCOBPS)
NEA. *See* National Educators Association (NEA)
Negritude, 17, 18, 46, 182n53
Negro Digest, 33, 53n35–7, 140n2
Negro World, 137
NEH. *See* National Endowment for the Humanities (NEH)
The New Negro (Locke), 41
New York Review of Books, 125
NNC. *See* National Negro Congress (NNC)
North Carolina A & T Univeristy, 32
Northwestern University, 39
Notes of a Native Son (Baldwin), 126
Not Out of Africa (Lefkowitz), 167
NPSR. *See* National Political Science Review (NPSR)
NYA. *See* National Youth Administration (NYA)

O
Oberlin college, 2, 28, 29
objectivism, 159
OCBS. *See* Ohio Consortium of Black Studies (OCBS)
Ohio Consortium of Black Studies (OCBS), 18, 100, 116n12
Ohio State University, 17, 21n20, 97, 100, 101, 104, 111, 116n9
Operation Breadbasket, 12, 150
Organization of American Historians, 9
Organized Research Unit (ORU), 79–81, 84, 85
Origin of the Species (Darwin), 46
ORU. *See* Organized Research Unit (ORU)

P
paradigm, 26, 43–5, 47, 106, 117n25, 150–2, 154, 155, 161, 162, 164, 165, 174, 178, 182n59, 194, 195, 202
Peace & Conflict Studies (PACS), 238
The Peculiar Institution (Hofstader), 157
Phelps-Stokes Fund, 29
The Philadelphia Negro (Du Bois), 161
Plessy v. Ferguson, 188, 191

pluralism, 36, 40, 41, 44, 150, 151, 179n5, 207, 210, 220, 230, 231, 233, 235, 242–4
political science, 3, 8, 9, 11, 13–16, 18, 20n15, 21n19, 21n21, 22n21, 25, 51n9, 62, 76, 80, 91n12, 106, 115, 123, 124, 140n8, 149–51, 153, 155–7, 159, 160, 179n5, 179n8, 180n29, 181n30, 181n31, 216, 218, 227n111
Political Science Quarterly, 123
Popular Movement for the Liberation of Angola (MPLA), 132, 144n46
positivism, 152, 153, 212
postmodernism, 140, 168, 217, 229–49
psychology, 38, 42, 48, 62, 74, 80, 106, 115, 129, 165, 185n104, 218, 223n46, 231
Pursuit of Excellence, 194

R

Race Matters (West), 106
Reflections of an Affirmative Action Baby (Carter), 219
Renaissance Noir, 125
Republic of New Africa, 39
Rodriquez v. San Antonio, 191, 206
Roots (Haley), 200
Rosenwald Fund, 29
Rutland College, 28

S

San Diego State University, 101, 104, 172
San Francisco State University (SFSU), 2, 18, 19n7, 34, 37, 40, 68, 102, 121, 122, 164
science, 3, 8, 9, 11, 13–16, 18, 20n15, 21n19, 21n21, 22n21, 25, 29, 34, 46, 50, 51n9, 51n10, 57n88, 62, 64, 66–8, 71, 73, 74, 76, 80, 83, 86, 91n12, 98, 105, 106, 109, 115, 123, 124, 130, 140n8, 144n53, 149–62, 165, 178, 179n5, 179n8, 179n10, 180n14, 180n18, 180n29, 181n30, 181n31, 181n44, 182n55, 188, 192, 194, 195, 199, 201, 203, 204, 212, 215–18, 227n111, 231, 233, 234, 247n26
Second World Black Arts Festival (FESTAC), 18
segregation, 25, 32, 46, 47, 187–9, 191, 193, 248n38
SFSU. *See* San Francisco State University (SFSU)
Shrine of the Black Madonna, 39
SNCC. *See* Student Non-violent Coordinating Committee (SNCC)
Social Darwinism, 158, 159, 201
Social Identities, 75
social sciences, 29, 80, 86, 106, 109, 115, 123, 154–6, 159–61, 165, 178, 180n14, 212, 231, 233, 247n26
sociology, 29, 41, 47, 55n70, 62, 72, 73, 80, 83, 115, 121, 129, 153, 155–8, 160, 161, 167, 178, 182n55, 218, 222n40, 235
The Souls of Black Folk (Du Bois), 30, 52n17, 106, 160, 192
standpoint theory, 174, 175
The Structure of Scientific Revolutions (Kuhn), 152, 179n10
Student Non-violent Coordinating Committee (SNCC), 3, 37, 40, 54n60, 170, 171

T
Temple University, 59, 81, 181n30
Tennessee State University, 101, 102
Third World College, 64, 65, 69, 70, 73
Third World Liberation Front (TWLF), 59, 63, 68, 69, 71, 73
This Bridge Called My Back (Moraga and Anzaldua), 173
Toward a Democratic Science (Brown), 180n15, 217, 226n105
The Truly Disadvantaged (Wilson), 203
Tuskegee Institute, 157
TWLF. *See* Third World Liberation Front (TWLF)

U
UCB. *See* University of California at Berkeley (UCB)
UCLA. *See* University of California, Los Angeles (UCLA)
UFT. *See* United Federation of Teachers (UFT)
Uncle Tom's Cabin (Stowe), 46
underclass, 202, 203, 223n51
United Federation of Teachers (UFT), 197
universalism, 30, 168, 241, 244
University of California at Berkeley (UCB), 1, 18, 22, 50, 65, 88, 91n15, 92n42, 101, 117n22, 211
University of California at Davis, 206
University of California at Santa Barbara, 91n19
University of California, Los Angeles (UCLA), 37, 38, 49, 62, 76–9, 81, 82, 84, 86–8, 93n46, 93n52, 182n53
University of Chicago, 8, 10, 12, 13, 20n15, 51n6, 54n59, 142n27, 149, 157, 179n10
University of Cincinnati, 101, 103
University of Ghana at Legon, 101, 111
University of Guyana, 101, 112
University of Havana, 130, 133
University of Massachusetts, 101, 103, 106
University of North Carolina at Charlotte, 95, 101, 104
University of Virginia, 50n5, 62, 86, 211, 212
Up From Slavery (Washington), 22, 30
US, 38, 44, 48, 76–8, 93n47, 155, 182n53, 195, 197, 198, 224n63, 231, 233, 235, 238–41, 247n22

V
Vietnam war, 1, 10, 13, 53n38
vocational education, 30, 31, 192

W
Watts, 38, 39, 45, 56n83, 76, 77, 93n45, 163, 182n51
Western civilization, 89, 156, 168, 208, 215, 217, 226n89
West Virginia State University, 112, 113
Where the Island Sleeps Like a Wing (Morejon), 132
White Money/Black Power (Rooks), 53n40, 60, 91n4
Who Are We? (Huntington), 213, 226n90

Wilberforce University, 28
Woman, Race, and Class (Davis), 173
Women's Studies, 16–18, 90, 111, 172–4, 177, 179n4, 184n80, 184n90, 184n92, 184n94–6, 208, 230, 232, 235

Y

Yale University, 54n48, 117n21, 180n15